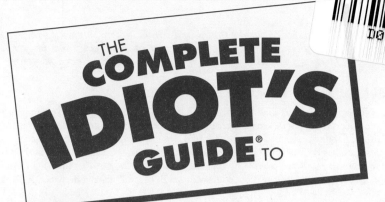

THE
COMPLETE
IDIOT'S
GUIDE® TO

The Talmud

by Rabbi Aaron Parry

ALPHA

A member of Penguin Group (USA) Inc.

In gratitude to my beloved parents, Arnold Stanley and Elinor Parry, whose lifelong devotion to each other and to raising their children as upright decent human beings should give them comfort in the Heavenly Abode. This book is dedicated in their blessed memory.

International Standard Book Number: 1-59257-202-2
Library of Congress Catalog Card Number: 2004103224

06 04   8 7 6 5 4 3 2 1

Interpretation of the printing code: The rightmost number of the first series of numbers is the year of the book's printing; the rightmost number of the second series of numbers is the number of the book's printing. For example, a printing code of 04-1 shows that the first printing occurred in 2004.

Printed in the United States of America

Note: This publication contains the opinions and ideas of its author. It is intended to provide helpful and informative material on the subject matter covered. It is sold with the understanding that the author and publisher are not engaged in rendering professional services in the book. If the reader requires personal assistance or advice, a competent professional should be consulted.

The author and publisher specifically disclaim any responsibility for any liability, loss, or risk, personal or otherwise, which is incurred as a consequence, directly or indirectly, of the use and application of any of the contents of this book.

Most Alpha books are available at special quantity discounts for bulk purchases for sales promotions, premiums, fund-raising, or educational use. Special books, or book excerpts, can also be created to fit specific needs.

For details, write: Special Markets, Alpha Books, 375 Hudson Street, New York, NY 10014.

Publisher: *Marie Butler-Knight*
Product Manager: *Phil Kitchel*
Senior Managing Editor: *Jennifer Chisholm*
Acquisitions Editors: *Gary Goldstein, Randy Ladenheim-Gil*
Development Editor: *Nancy D. Lewis*
Production Editor: *Janette Lynn*
Copy Editor: *Cari Luna*
Illustrator: *Richard King*
Cover/Book Designer: *Trina Wurst*
Indexer: *Tonya Heard*
Layout/Proofreading: *Ayanna Lacey, Mary Hunt*

Contents at a Glance

Contents

Foreword

Imagine coming across the following ad in your favorite magazine. AMAZING SPECIAL OFFER! STORE ALL OF AMERICAN CULTURE ON A SINGLE SHELF IN YOUR LIVING ROOM! What would your reaction be? You would probably say to yourself, "That's really going too far even for Madison Avenue!"

You can get some idea of what an incredible work the Talmud is when you realize that this is precisely what the Jewish sages managed to accomplish for Jewish culture! They managed to condense all that a Jew needs to know to be fully oriented in all aspects of his culture into the 20 Tomes of the Babylonian Talmud that fit very nicely on most living room shelves.

Not only does the Talmud contain the entirety of Jewish law, from ritual law, to family laws to torts; it is also a work of ethics, philosophy, biography, literature, history, and folktales. But that is not all. To fully appreciate its genius you also have to realize that the Sages compiled a work that contains all this information and is still suited to all age groups and all levels of scholarship.

Jewish children through the ages have begun to swim in its waters from the age of nine or ten. Amateur scholars, and all ordinary Jews are commanded to be such, have studied it in their spare time and found it interesting and stimulating. And yet the most brilliant Jewish minds have spent their entire lives immersed in its depths without running out of new ideas to explore.

If you run all these facts through your mind you will readily see why the Jewish people regard it with the reverence due to a work that is divinely inspired. There is no way human beings could have come up with a literary work that manages to accomplish all this without Divine assistance. It is easy to comprehend why the Jewish people consider the Talmud as holy as the Five Books of Moses.

The ability of the Jewish people to survive two thousand years of exile and persecution and still emerge vibrant and intact is one of the great mysteries of human history. It does not diminish the immensity of the feat to point out that it was the Talmud that made this possible. Observant Jews have always been one hundred percent literate. Their most sacred commandment is the one that orders them to study the Torah. In practice they have carried out this obligation by studying the Talmud. They have always carried their entire culture around with them stored on their living room shelves.

It is difficult to write a book about the Talmud that manages to describe it accurately without reducing the majesty of the work. Rabbi Parry has managed to do precisely this. No doubt this is thanks to his many years of experience at introducing the Talmud to highly intelligent and educated people who become interested in Jewish studies only later in life. His background and his book both merit our sincere admiration. The intelligent reader will be rewarded with an appreciation of the Talmud's intellectual immensity and with a taste of what it is like to swim in its deep waters even if he lacks any prior familiarity with its methods and its ways.

I feel honored to have been chosen to introduce his book and recommend it highly.

—Rabbi Noson Weisz

While studying at the famed yeshivas of Chaim Berlin, Lakewood and the Mir in Jerusalem, Rabbi Noson Weisz also received a degree in Microbiology from the University of Toronto, an M.A. in Political Science at the New School for Social Research, and his L.L.B. from the University of Toronto. Rabbi Weisz is currently a senior lecturer at Yeshiva Aish HaTorah in Jerusalem.

Introduction

As one of the world's great books of wisdom, the Talmud ranks right at the top. Yet, very few people have actually read the Talmud. It remains a mystery to most, both Jews and non-Jews, many of whom view it as an obscure collection of mental exercises, logic, and deduction written by a group of rabbis who seem to delight in debating and challenging everything said.

The Talmud is arguably one of the most enigmatic texts known to humankind. Part religious laws, part wise sayings, and part stories, it presents the beliefs and views of learned Jewish sages of antiquity, which would lead anyone unfamiliar with its contents to believe that whatever it had to say would be out-of-date and hardly relevant today. But quite the opposite is true. Contained in this ancient text is guidance for living a wholesome life that resonates as well today as it did centuries ago. Studying it requires honing one's way of thinking and reasoning, and is invaluable for learning how to organize thoughts and prioritize many facets of life.

What the Talmud has to say has challenged and delighted scholars throughout the centuries, and it continues to do so today. No less a personality than Albert Einstein, when asked near his death in 1955 what he would do differently if he were to start his life all over again, responded without hesitation, "I would study the Talmud."

When people talk about studying the Talmud, they don't say they're reading it, as the Talmud isn't meant to be read. Instead, it's meant to be learned. Traditionally, learning the Talmud took place with the help of a teacher, almost always with a rabbi. If, indeed, this work serves as a stepping-stone to actual in-depth Talmud study for some of you, our efforts will have truly been blessed.

How to Use This Book

Mastery of the actual Talmud text is not the goal here. Merely reading a book about the Talmud, no matter how complete, can't accomplish this. For this reason, the purpose of the pages ahead isn't to turn you into a Talmud scholar (or, in Hebrew, a Talmid Chacham). However, you can expect to gain a greater appreciation for the Talmud's unique rhythm and cadence; how the sages took a concept and moved it from the hypothetical into the concrete, their original system of logic, and the wise proclamations about ethics and morality that illuminate the paths of many today.

Part 1, "Introducing the Talmud," sets the stage for what the Talmud is all about, and how it came to be.

Part 2, "Inside the Talmud," deals with the actual structure of the Talmud, and the contents of each Talmudic order.

Part 3, "The Spirit of the Talmud," delves into specific qualities or themes that are expressed throughout the Talmud.

Part 4, "The World According to the Talmud," discusses Talmudic wisdom on such important subjects as science and medicine, the environment, and death and afterlife.

Part 5, "Living the Talmud Way," offers insight and assistance on how the precepts of the Talmud apply, and can be applied, to modern living.

Extras

To help you get the most out of this book, I've sprinkled it with the following helpful information boxes:

Talmud Tutor

Definitions of words and phrases that you might find in the Talmud.

Talmud Trivia

A treasury of Talmudic pearls of wisdom and other important information.

Let's Get Talmudic

Excerpts from the Talmud that you might find interesting.

Talmud Tidbits

More historical facts and interesting tidbits about the Talmud and the Jewish people.

Acknowledgments

A production of this magnitude could not be created without an outstanding "supporting cast" of stellar proportions. Foremost, I would like to acknowledge one heck of a gifted person, Sonia Weiss, whose patience, wit, literary savvy, and magnificent editorial creativity and organization helped bring this project to fruition. Communicating ancient wisdom to a contemporary audience was an awesome challenge; Sonia's keen skills were simply brilliant and helped me accomplish just that. May she be blessed manifold for her sublime work.

All of those kindred souls in CIG production, acquisitions editors: Gary Goldstein and Randy Ladenheim-Gil, development editor: Nancy Lewis, production editor: Janette Lynn, copy editor: Cari Luna, may abundant blessing be showered upon you for your unique expertise, wisdom, and patience in teaming with me on this project. King Solomon, in his wisdom said, "Better are two than one, for if the one falls, the other will pick him up." (Ecclesiastes 4:9) In that spirit, a dear colleague, Rabbi Yosef Furman, rabbi and teacher at the Yeshiva University of Los Angeles High School and Daf Yomi instructor par excellence, assiduously reviewed the manuscript in its entirety. His sagacious comments and keen eye for detail were invaluable in minimizing citation error. Additionally, another colleague and friend, Dr. Tamar Frankiel, lecturer in religious studies at a number of University of California campuses and author of a number of books related to Jewish spirituality and dreams, is acknowledged for contributing her expertise and suggestions to the chapters on dreams and mysticism.

Thanks also go to Nate Wycoff, Ph.D., for his scientific acumen and review of the chapter on Talmud and science; and Rabbi Yisrael Blumenthal, of Lakewood, New Jersey, a Talmud scholar of repute, for his general comments and input as the manuscript was taking shape. Kudos to Rabbi Benzion Kravitz, founder, Shoshana Zakar, webmaster of Jews for Judaism International, Gavriel Aryeh Sanders, and my brother Moshe, for their warm encouragement and input. It is always a good idea to recognize one's origins. With that in mind, I would like to warmly thank one of the finest Talmudic institutions in the world. It caters to college students with little or no Judaic background—Ohr Somayach (www.ohr.org.il) in Jerusalem. Rabbi Mendel Weinbach, dean and founder, has been like a father and mentor for thousands of students over the past four decades. I am deeply indebted to Ohr Somayach's entire rabbinic staff for giving me my first delectable taste of Talmud study more than 25 years ago. In the immortal words of Rabbi Akiva who, while addressing his cadre of 24 thousand students amassed over 24 years in the presence of his wife Rachel commented, "Yours and mine is because of her"—so, too, my dear wife, Mindy, whose encouragement, literary comments, undaunting patience and perseverance with her chronically absentee husband and father of our children for almost a half year—deserves most of the credit and reward for allowing this project to become a reality—"… far beyond pearls is her value."

Above all praise and thanks is The Holy One Blessed Be He for whom I owe an infinite amount of gratitude for exposing me to the brilliant illumination that He imparted to the Sages of Israel—this rich incomparable treasure called—the Talmud.

Trademarks

All terms mentioned in this book that are known to be or are suspected of being trademarks or service marks have been appropriately capitalized. Alpha Books and Penguin Group (USA) Inc. cannot attest to the accuracy of this information. Use of a term in this book should not be regarded as affecting the validity of any trademark or service mark.

Part 1

Introducing the Talmud

The Talmud truly stands apart as one of the most unique and fascinating written works known to humankind. Part religious laws, part wise sayings, and part stories, it presents ancient teachings and beliefs that are as fresh and inspiring today as they were centuries ago.

Our journey into the wisdom of the Talmud begins by exploring the history of this intriguing work, how the Jewish people received the divine instructions through Moses at the revelation at Mt. Sinai 3,300 years ago, how this information was transmitted intact through the centuries, and who the most important players were in the process.

What Is the Talmud?

In This Chapter

- ◆ Not one book but many
- ◆ How the Talmud came to be
- ◆ How the Talmud relates to today's world
- ◆ Who studies the Talmud

The Talmud is beyond a doubt one of the most unusual written works ever created. Compiled centuries ago by a group of wise men—sages—as a way to preserve the oral traditions and laws of the Jewish faith, its complex, disjointed, and nonlinear approach to exploring ideas and subjects from virtually all possible angles has challenged and thrilled some of the world's greatest minds, and continues to do so today.

What is so compelling about this ancient tome that has intrigued such diverse audiences from the founding fathers (Thomas Jefferson was known to have had a rare set of the Talmud as part of his voluminous library) to Barbra Streisand? The answer, like the Talmud itself, isn't simple.

All About the Talmud

Not one book, but instead a number of volumes, the Talmud is considered the most influential document in the history of Judaism. Of course, the 24 books of Hebrew scriptures—and especially the first five books of Moses that comprise what is known in the Jewish faith as the *Torah* or the *Pentateuch*—are vitally essential. But without the Talmud, we have no way of knowing how to interpret and apply the laws of the Torah.

Talmud Tutor

The **Torah** or the **Pentateuch** are the first five books of Hebrew scripture—Genesis, Exodus, Leviticus, Numbers, and Deuteronomy. The literal meaning of Pentateuch is "five cases," which refers to the sheaths or boxes in which the separate rolls or volumes of the ancient Bible are believed to have been originally stored.

To Jews, there is no Old Testament and New Testament, as the Christian New Testament is not part of Jewish scripture. To Jews, the Old Testament is the Bible. It consists of 24 books of Hebrew scripture, divided into three categories—the 5 books of the Torah, 8 books of Navi (Prophets), and 11 books of Ketuvim (Writings).

Jewish tradition holds that the Talmud is the "oral Torah," or a verbal explanation of the laws that God gave to Moses on Mt. Sinai, and that Moses taught to others. Just about everyone is familiar with the story of how Moses received the Ten Commandments from God, but what is lesser known about this story is that Moses and God had a good chat on that mountain that ranged far beyond what could be inscribed on the tablets that he brought with him when he climbed back down. It is this information, transmitted orally from God to Moses, and then from Moses to the generations that followed him, that is the basis for the Talmud.

According to the Talmudic sages, mention of God's oral instructions to Moses is made in the Bible. In the book of Exodus, God tells Moses to "Come up to Me on the mountain, and I will give thee the tablets of stone, and the law and the commandment, which I have written that thou may teach them." (Exodus 24:12)

Talmud Trivia

The Ten Commandments that Moses brought down from Mt. Sinai were only the tip of the iceberg. In fact, there were 603 more commandments where those came from, covering subjects ranging from dietary laws to animal husbandry. All 613 commandments are considered to be of equal importance, and are the sacred and binding word of God. Of them, 248 are positive commandments, or suggest how one should act or behave, and 365 are negative, and warn against various acts or behaviors.

Why was this extra detail or explanation important? In many instances the directives given in the Torah allude to details that the Torah doesn't contain. A good example is Deuteronomy 12:21, where God speaks to Moses and says, "You shall slaughter your cattle … as I have commanded you." Now, in every edition of the Five Books of Moses ever written, the story seems to end there. No further details are given. But unless you had been on Mt. Sinai with Moses, there was no way you would know what mode of killing is implied by the word "slaughter." Does it mean to bludgeon the poor beast to death? Or maybe just run a sword through his heart?

Only through the oral tradition that began with Moses at Mt. Sinai do we know that "you shall slaughter" means that a trained ritual slaughterer should use an extremely sharp knife without even a miniscule nick to quickly sever the jugular and carotid arteries at the animal's neck.

Another good example is the commandment that speaks to keeping the Sabbath. It is mentioned numerous times in the scriptures, so we can safely say that it's a biggie. Yet, no details are ever given as to how it should be kept. In fact, the only hint is that one is to refrain from certain labors, found in Exodus 31:17—"Between Me and the Children of Israel it is a sign forever that in a six-day period God made heaven and earth, and on the seventh day He rested and was refreshed."

Only through an unwritten tradition are we able to know what constitutes the Torah's definition of work. God even alludes to this oral tradition in his words to the prophet Jeremiah—"You shall keep the Sabbath holy, as I have commanded your fathers." The oral tradition concerning the Sabbath is preserved for all time in the Talmud. One hefty treatise even bears the same name and goes into great detail about what one can and cannot do on the Jewish holy day. Additionally, the oral tradition allows questions to be posed to a teacher for clarification. In other words, if all that we had was a written Torah, the system of learning from those with greater knowledge and clarity would never have developed.

Words into Print

As you'll read more about in Chapter 2, the oral laws that God gave to Moses were preserved in their original form for quite some time. However, after a number of centuries of being kept in this form, concerns arose over the continuing ability to maintain them in this manner. For this reason, the oral laws began to be recorded during the Roman era, ending as the fifth century C.E. drew to a close.

But the development of the Talmud didn't stop there. Throughout the centuries that followed, up through medieval times and into the nineteenth century, the sages continued to comment on the Talmud, and their thoughts were inserted throughout the text. Today, each page of the Talmud contains their running commentary, oftentimes combining thoughts from learned men who lived centuries apart.

Various Viewpoints

It is this commentary, coming from a variety of different viewpoints and spanning centuries, that makes the Talmud so complex to understand and so challenging to study. On any given page of the Talmud, you'll find comments and conversations that:

◆ Cross-reference other comments made on other pages

◆ Seem to assume knowledge of a prior discussion

◆ Explore meanings and different interpretations

◆ Seemingly diverge from the subject at hand, but which eventually reconcile and become essential to the conclusion

◆ Raise questions that are tangentially connected to the text

What's more, it's all interspersed between excerpts from the Bible, stories and legends, and bits of history.

Sounds like quite a mishmash, doesn't it? If you've never seen a page of the Talmud (don't worry, you'll be treated to some in later chapters), it can be hard to imagine what this looks like, and how anyone could make any sense of it at all. For now, a good way to visualize this running commentary is to think of it like a written debate where the viewpoints of the debaters all come together on one page. You'll even see places when a debate ends with the Hebrew word "taiku," which literally translates as "let it stand' or "tie." In these cases, neither side was able to provide a definitive argument, and it's up to the reader to decide on a conclusion or appropriate course of action.

Mysteries and Mental Exercises?

Sadly, many people—Jewish and not—have not been exposed to the wisdom of the Talmud. To some, it seems like a mysterious and closed book. Those who are not members of the Jewish faith might feel that plumbing the depths of the Talmud is inappropriate, or that they won't find anything of relevance there. Others are disinclined to dig into the Talmud because they view it as a collection of mental exercises, logic, and deduction that can be manipulated by the reader any which way he or she desires, as illustrated by the following story.

A young man comes to visit a noted rabbi, and expresses his desire to study Talmud. "Do you know Aramaic?" the rabbi asks. "No," the young man answers. "Hebrew?" "No." "Have you studied the Torah?" No, Rabbi, but don't worry. I graduated Columbia summa cum laude in philosophy and just finished my doctoral dissertation at Harvard on Socratic logic. So now I would just like to round out my education with a little study of the Talmud."

The rabbi tells the young man that he doesn't think he's ready to study Talmud. "If you wish, however, I am willing to examine you in logic. If you pass the test, I will teach you Talmud." The young man readily agrees.

The rabbi holds up two fingers. "Two burglars break into a house through the chimney. One lands inside with a clean face, the other with a dirty face. Which one washes his face?"

"The one with the dirty face," the young man answers.

"Wrong," the rabbi says. "The one with the clean face washes his face. Examine the simple logic: the one with the dirty face looks at the one with the clean face and thinks his own face is clean. The one with the clean face looks at the one with the dirty face and thinks his own face is dirty. So, the one with the clean face washes."

"Very clever," the young man says. "Give me another test."

The rabbi asks the same question, to which the eager would-be pupil responds, "We've already established that the one with the clean face washes his face."

"Wrong again," the rabbi says. "Each one washes his face. Examine the simple logic. The one with the dirty face looks at the one with the clean face and thinks his own is clean. The one with the clean face looks at the one with the dirty face and thinks his own is dirty. So the one with the clean face washes his face. When the man with the dirty face sees the clean-faced man washing, he also washes his face."

"I didn't think of that," the young man says. "Test me again."

The rabbi again repeats the question of the two men and the chimney, to which the young man replies, "Each one washes his face."

"Wrong again," the rabbi says. "Neither washes his face. Look at it logically. The one with the dirty face looks at the one with the clean face and thinks his own face is clean. The one with the clean face sees the dirty face of his companion and thinks his own face is dirty. But when the one with the clean face sees the one with the dirty face doesn't wash, he also doesn't wash his face. So neither one washes."

The young man is desperate. "I am qualified to study Talmud," he says. "Please give me one more test." Again, the rabbi asks the same question. And the young man gives the obvious answer. "Neither one washes his face."

"Wrong," says the rabbi. "Do you see now why Socratic logic is an insufficient basis for studying Talmud? Tell me how it is possible for two men to come down the same chimney, and for one to come out with a clean face and the other with a dirty face."

The young many is totally exasperated and challenges the rabbi. "Now, wait a minute. Haven't you just given me three mutually contradictory answers to the same question? That's impossible!"

"No, my son," the rabbi says. "That's the Talmud."

Agreeing to Disagree

The story you've just read is typical of the impression most people have of the Talmud, and about studying it. And yes, it also illustrates what it is about the Talmud that can admittedly be somewhat frustrating.

The sages always seem to be arguing. One says one thing, another says something completely different. Then a third voice chimes in with another viewpoint. It's enough to make you throw up your hands and wonder if the Talmudic sages can agree on anything.

> **Talmud Tidbits**
>
> The hairsplitting arguments made by the rabbis that are documented in the Talmud are called pilpul, which has come to describe the lively dispute, investigation and drawing of conclusions that is uniquely the Talmud's. Pilpul also describes a method of Talmudic study that calls for the careful study of each sentence or saying, determining the various concepts that it includes, and investigating all the possible consequences that can be deduced from it.

> **Talmud Trivia**
>
> In 1885, Rabbi Israel Rabinowitz translated a page of Talmud for the great French doctor Louis Pasteur, which dealt with a victim of an attack from a rabid dog. The words inspired Pasteur in his work to discover the key to artificial immunization.

Details, Details

Dig into things enough, though, and you'll find that Talmudic arguments are always about the most hairsplitting details possible. They might be arguing over seemingly trivial matters, but you won't find any dispute on major issues. When studying the Talmud, the challenge is trying to understand why these minute details were so important to those who argued them that they were recorded for posterity and are still debated.

This search for understanding is what keeps people engrossed in Talmud studies, and why many who pick up the Talmud as a lark end up being lifelong students. Along the way, they even find that relatively new discoveries or advances in medicine and technology have their origins in obscure passages of the Talmud.

The Importance of the Oral Tradition

As mentioned, the Talmud is the "oral Torah," or a verbal explanation of the laws that God gave to Moses on Mt. Sinai, and that Moses taught to others. For Jews, belief in the oral tradition that is the Talmud is an essential cornerstone of faith. This point, in fact, cannot be overstated.

Jews believe that virtually nothing of the Torah can be properly understood without the Talmud, a point made clear in the following story from the Talmud:

> A prospective convert goes first to the great sage Shammai and asks the venerable leader how many "Torahs" do the Jews have. He answers two—the Written Law and the Oral Law. The man states that he wishes to convert even though he doesn't believe in the Oral Code. Shammai, indignant over such unheard of conditions, summarily dismisses the fellow and shows him the door.
>
> Undaunted, the potential convert pays a visit to the sage Hillel, who welcomes him and begins to teach him the Hebrew alphabet: "Aleph, bet, gimel, dalet …" When he comes back the second day, Hillel tests him on what he has learned. He repeats the alphabet perfectly. But Hillel says, "No, it's daled, gimel, bet, aleph." Very upset, the proselyte says, "It's just the alphabet. I know the alphabet!"
>
> Hillel responds, "When you came to see me, you didn't know anything. I could have taught you the alphabet incorrectly, and you would not have known the difference. So let's study together, and at the end of our studies, you'll decide whether you believe in the Oral Code or not. Right now, you don't know very much, but when you gain some knowledge, you'll be able to make an intelligent decision."

What this passage tells us, beyond the benefits of persistence (the convert) and patience (Hillel), is that belief in the oral Torah as well as the written laws is essential to traditional Jewish practice. Denying the origins of the oral Torah constitutes denying the origins of the written text as well.

How do we know that the oral laws have not been corrupted over time? The Talmud, as previously mentioned, is full of disagreements. Is this not proof that the information is inaccurate?

> **Talmud Tidbits** _____
>
> The great nineteenth-century German Jewish scholar Rabbi Samson Rafael Hirsch compared the written law to crib notes of a university lecture. For the student in attendance, after taking accurate notes, he merely needs to glance over them in order to recall the actual live lecture. However, to the person not in attendance, these notes are unintelligible. He can't make heads or tails of them. So, too, is it with the Scriptures. But the Talmud is not only a record of the discussions and debates concerning the revelation of God's Torah at Mt. Sinai, it is the lecture itself.

When it comes to the Talmud, it's important to understand that for Moses, who heard God's revelations, there was no "doubt." Therefore, traditional Jewish practice also holds that the Talmud represents God's divine will and instruction. We trust in the power of the sages of each generation, and their followers, to accurately transmit it. This "chain of transmission" includes 120 generations of scholars and leaders dating from Moses' time forward to the completion of the Talmud in 500 C.E. For a complete list, turn to Appendix C.

In making the case for an orally conveyed tradition, the Talmudic sages assert that the Torah is like a "blueprint" for creation. As such, it covers an infinite number of situations that could arise over time. Since it would be impossible to address each situation specifically as they arose in written form, God, in his infinite wisdom, gave Moses a set of rules by which the Torah could be applied to every conceivable case.

Why Study the Talmud?

The fact that the Talmud presents not just one viewpoint but many—and at times some very conflicting viewpoints that seem to raise more questions than provide answers—is what makes it valuable for truth seekers. Not only does the Talmud provide guidance on living a wholesome life, and drawing closer to God, but it can also hone thinking and reasoning skills.

As an example, let's take a look at a chapter from a Talmudic tract called Bava Kamma (there are many tracts, all with different names, and you'll learn more about them in the chapters ahead). This particular chapter deals with torts, or personal damage laws. It spends a great deal of time discussing the hypothetical case of an ox owned by one man that gores a cow owned by another. The cow dies. When the owners of the two animals arrive at the site, they notice a dead newborn calf lying next to the cow.

The owner of the cow claims that it was gored after it had given birth, and he is therefore entitled to payment for two animals. The owner of the ox asserts that the cow died while the fetus was still inside, but spontaneously aborted at death. Therefore, he is liable for only one entity. There are no witnesses. What, then, should be done?

The Talmud presents several possible answers. One sage suggests dividing the value of the calf between the owner of the cow and the owner of the ox. Another says that the owner of the cow has to prove that the calf was stillborn as a result of the damage from the ox. Probing the wisdom of the sages requires looking at the issues critically and logically, and coming to an understanding of the underlying principle being discussed—in this case, what fair compensation would be for an unforeseen act that was perhaps caused due to negligence on the part of one of the owners.

This kind of study isn't easy. In fact, looking at all the twists and turns and asking yourself the questions necessary for understanding the full meaning of the passage could give you a good headache. But it helps develop logic and reasoning skills that are invaluable, especially in today's world.

The very structure of a page of Talmud is an excellent template for organizing thoughts and prioritizing many facets of our lives. Yes, the Talmud is the *corpus juris*, or body of law, that defines how Jews are to live, but as a teaching tool it is not restricted to religious observance. It can, and has, taught and enhanced the critical thinking skills of many people, Jewish and not.

Talmud Tidbits _____

If you're planning to visit your local Jewish bookstore and purchase an English translation or English-Hebrew version of the Talmud, beware that not all translations were created equal. Unfortunately, some versions only attempt to translate the literal text with very little notation or commentary. This can be very misleading, as the Talmud cannot be understood simply by translating the Aramaic or Hebrew words.

Becoming a Talmid Chacham (Talmud Scholar)

Study—and especially Talmud study—is a cornerstone of the Jewish faith, as it is the way that we best understand how God wants us to accomplish and act. Since the Talmud contains laws that must be applied and enforced, coming to an understanding of these laws is essential. But studying the Talmud is also essential for ensuring that the wisdom it contains continues to be passed down through the generations.

Talmud study is the traditional training ground for rabbis. Hundreds of years ago, a young Jewish man would go to a yeshiva, or rabbinical academy, to study and master all the tracts of the Talmud. It was considered a great honor for a family to house these young scholars, many of whom had left home at the tender age of 13 or 14 to study under the greatest masters.

A Guy Thing?

While Talmud study wasn't restricted to an intellectual elite, not everyone was allowed equal access to Talmudic wisdom. Women didn't study the Talmud per se, as such study was strongly discouraged, while not Biblically prohibited. Instead, they learned what they needed to know from their parents, as the Talmud directed—"Ask your father and he shall tell you."

This is a hot topic of debate among the Talmudic authorities. One point of view held that women could learn the Talmud, but not be taught it. Another held that women who learned Torah were not commanded to do so, and therefore would gain less heavenly reward for it. Still another sage wrote that women could teach each other without restriction, and could listen to men learning among themselves.

But the basic belief was that allowing women to study the Talmud threatened the Talmud's oral tradition as women in general were not trained to think intellectually or oriented to do so properly, and therefore, might make changes to it without knowing that they did so, or, in the words of one sage, "transform Torah discussions into trivia." Another belief was that their emotions might interfere with their intellectual process.

Over time as the role of women evolved throughout the world and more women were able to access secular education, Jewish women were allowed to study certain sections that pertained to everyday living. As time evolved, even great rabbis encouraged exemplary women to strive for greater involvement in the learning process. Many were able—and are able—to study virtually the entire Talmud. All said and done, in certain religious circles the restriction still holds.

> ### Talmud Trivia
>
> Rabbi Petachiah of Regensberg, who visited Baghdad in the late twelfth century, wrote about the distinguished daughter of Rabbi Shmuel ben Eli. Ben Eli had no sons, but his only daughter was an expert in Talmud. She lectured publicly through a lattice, while her students listened attentively outside. In a similar story, in the sixteenth century Rabbanit Mizrahi, the daughter of R'Shmuel of Kurdistan, listened in on the Talmudic instruction given to the boys who attended her father's academy. She became renowned for her outstanding Talmudic mastery, and eventually was put in charge of all academic duties of her father's yeshiva while he devoted himself to the needs of his followers. The Jews of that region honored her with the title "Woman Talmudist."

Talmud Studies Today

People wishing to access the wisdom of the Talmud today find no such bars to their thirst for knowledge. In fact, thanks to the information age, it is now easier than ever before to become familiar with the Talmud. Do a search on such keywords as "Talmud," "Torah," and "study" and you'll find a host of online courses, newsgroups, and mailing lists devoted to the subject. Entire websites have been developed to make this knowledge literally an Internet connection away. Thanks to modern technology, the global village has also become the virtual yeshiva.

> ### Let's Get Talmudic
>
> Once a wise man dreamt of Paradise and saw sages and righteous people studying the Talmud. "Is this, then, all there is to paradise?" he asked. He was answered; "Rabbi, you believe the sages are in Paradise, but you are wrong. Paradise is in the sages."
> —*Tales of the Hasidim*

Today, Talmud study is enjoying a renaissance that is reaching virtually every sector of society. More men and women are attending schools where they can pursue Torah study, including the Talmud, than in any time since the destruction of the second temple in Jerusalem and the exile of the Jewish people in 70 C.E. A group of engineers and scientists at the Jet Propulsion Laboratory in Pasadena, California, regularly invites guest Torah scholars to talk to them about the science and technology of the Talmud. Air Force officers at Vandenberg Air Force Base once attended bi-weekly Talmud classes.

Busy executives in Manhattan and other cities hire a rabbi on a weekly or daily basis to help them study the Talmud. Entire firms and major companies have clubs solely devoted to Torah study. Such Hollywood stars as Kirk Douglas and Barbra Streisand have studied the Talmud.

Talmud Tidbits

While it is true that a great deal of the Talmud teachings are open to non-Jews, not all are. Studying laws that pertain to ritual observances is reserved for members of the faith and to those who are either anticipating conversion or going through this process.

What compels these diverse groups to study an ancient text that was designed to teach Jews how God wants them to live? Quite simply, the "wisdom" of the Talmud transcends all boundaries as we know them. It is not limited to time or place, nor is it entirely limited to followers of Judaism. It is as relevant now as it was when it was first put down in written form, and it will always continue to be so. Because it is God's revelation to His people, it speaks to people of all walks of life and religious persuasions. When you study Talmud, you're as close to hearing God speak as you could possibly be.

The Least You Need to Know

- The Talmud was compiled centuries ago by a group of Jewish wise men, or sages, in order to preserve the oral traditions of their faith.

- For Jews, belief in the oral tradition that is the Talmud is an essential cornerstone of faith.

- The Talmud is full of hairsplitting arguments that often seem trivial or contradictory. However, the sages always agree on the important points.

- Talmud study was once restricted to men as it was feared that women might somehow corrupt the knowledge contained in the Talmud. Today, however, in most circles, no such restrictions are in place.

Chapter 2

In the Beginning

In This Chapter

- A prophet named Moses
- Revelations on a mountain
- Passing the torch
- Persecutions and preservation

Like all religions, Judaism has a set of core values, or beliefs, that lie at its heart. They form the belief system that was adopted by its founders and that has been handed down from generation to generation.

Judaism's entire belief system is based on two pieces of information. First, God is an absolute unity. In other words, he is one and there is no other force beside him. Second, Moses is the prophet of God.

Jewish history, of course, starts way before Moses, who lived in the thirteenth and early part of the twelfth centuries B.C.E. However, it is with Moses that the history of the Talmud begins. In this chapter, you'll learn more about how Moses received God's divine instructions, and how the Talmud developed from the oral tradition that began on Mt. Sinai.

A Man Named Moses

Moses, the great lawgiver and sage, was born during an uneasy period in ancient history. The Hebrews were living under Egyptian rule, and tensions were high due to concerns over what appeared to Pharaoh and his people as a nation within a nation that practiced different customs. The Egyptians became increasingly nervous over the fact that, unlike all other nationalities that emmigrated to Egypt, the Jews refused to assimilate.

This paranoia led to the erroneous belief that the Sons of Jacob would become too numerous and powerful and join enemy forces that would eventually take over the country. (See Exodus 1:9-10) So the Pharaoh issued an edict stating that all male Hebrew babies should be drowned at birth.

Moses was the third child and second son born to Amram and Jochebed, who were both members of the tribe of *Levi*. Amram and Jochebed kept the fact that they had a new son secret for a while, but soon realized that hiding baby Moses would only work for so long. Hoping that whoever found him would take pity on a foundling, they placed Moses in a waterproof basket and sent him floating down the river Nile. In an ironic twist of fate, none other than one of Pharaoh's daughters discovered the infant and rescued him. Moses was raised by Pharaoh's daughter as a royal prince, and was even tended by his own mother, who served as his wet nurse. Having a family member close at hand assured that Moses wouldn't lose his connection to his people.

Talmud Tutor

The tribe of **Levi** is one of the twelve tribes of Israel that are descended from the twelve sons of Jacob, who was Abraham's grandson. The traditional role of the Levites was as assistants to the priests of the Temple.

As he matured, Moses remained sensitive to the persecution of the Hebrews, and interceded on their behalf several times. Most notably, he killed an Egyptian guard who was beating a Jew, an act that forced him to flee for his life. He took refuge in nearby Midian and married Zipporah, the daughter of a Midianite priest. They had two sons, and Moses became a shepherd, tending to his father-in-law's flocks.

It is when Moses is tending his sheep that he first encounters God, who speaks to him from a burning bush. He identifies himself as the God of Moses' forefathers— Abraham, Isaac, and Jacob—with whom He had made an eternal covenant, and asks Moses to help lead the Hebrews out of Egypt to the Promised Land.

At first Moses tries to resist God as he feels he wouldn't be able to convince the people that he had heard God's voice. But God then gives Moses special powers that help assure him that he is indeed capable of swaying the masses. So empowered, Moses returns to Egypt to demand freedom for the Hebrews.

Let My People Go

Back in Egypt, Moses and his brother Aaron plead with Pharaoh to release the Hebrews, but Pharaoh refuses. To help convince him, God unleashes ten plagues, each worse than the one that preceded it.

Pharaoh stands his ground after each plague—as the Bible put it, his "heart grew hard"—with the exception of the tenth—the slaughter of the firstborn. The horror of losing their oldest children convinces Pharaoh and his people to let the Hebrews leave.

> **Talmud Trivia**
>
> The ten plagues that were set upon the Egyptians were: water becoming blood; infestations of frogs, lice, and flies; a disease that killed all the livestock that belonged to the Egyptians but spared those belonging to the Hebrews; boils; hail; locusts; darkness; and the death of the firstborn.

Although Pharaoh changes his mind and sends an army after the departing Hebrews, they are able to escape through the Red Sea, which God helps Moses part and then close to destroy Pharaoh's army.

Revelations at Mt. Sinai

After traveling through the desert for nearly two months, Moses and his people camp at Mount Sinai. At Sinai, Moses continues to be an intermediary between God and his people. He goes up on the mountain, where God appears to him and tells him that if the Hebrews agree to listen to God and obey his laws, God will consider them to be his own people and will give them special favor. Moses trudges down the mountain to present God's offer to the people, which they wholeheartedly accept. Moses then climbs back up the mountain to give God the people's answer. God and Moses then embark on a 40-day conversation, during which time God gives him the 613 commandments of the Torah that comprise the Oral Law.

The Ten Commandments, which were written on stone tablets by either Moses or God (the Bible presents two different sets of tablets), are an encapsulation of the Oral Law and are part of the Written Law—the Torah and the other parts of the Hebrew Bible. This information was written during the remaining 39 years that the Jews wandered the desert and God was dictating to Moses. During this time, Moses taught the Jews the law that God had revealed to them.

Moses recorded the core of his teachings in what are commonly referred to as the five books of Moses—Genesis, Exodus, Leviticus, Numbers, and Deuteronomy. These books, as well as other parts of the Hebrew Bible, are also part of the Christian scriptures. However, the Oral Law, which tells Jews how to live as Jews, has always been, and will forever be, the sole property of the Jewish people.

The Israelites finally reach Canaan, the land that God had promised them would be their own. But, for a variety of reasons, Moses isn't allowed to enter it with them. Before he parts from his people, Moses delivers a number of farewell addresses, during which he again instructs them on matters of law and on living a righteous life. He commissions Joshua as his successor and makes provisions for the safekeeping of the laws. Then, he climbs up on a nearby mountain, looks at the Promised Land, and dies.

The Talmud teaches that Moses wrote 13 letter-perfect Torah scrolls, one for each of the 12 tribes of Israel, and an additional one that was to be placed in the Ark of the Covenant, a chest that was crafted as a symbol of God's presence and that resided in the tabernacle, the portable sanctuary that the children of Israel built in approximately 1450 B.C.E. under Moses' supervision. The scroll that was placed in the Ark served as the standard for all subsequent Torah scrolls that would be written later.

When Moses died, he left behind a complete body of law. Nothing could be added to the teaching of Moses, nor could anything be subtracted from it.

Let's Get Talmudic

Two Talmudic sages—Rabbi Levi and Rabbi Shimon—were analyzing the meaning of the Biblical verse addressed to Moses, "Come up to Me on the mountain, and I will give thee the tablets of stone, and the law and the commandment, which I have written that thou may teach them." (Exodus 24:12) "Tablets of stone," these are the Ten Commandments; "The Law," this is the Pentateuch (five books of Moses), "the commandment," this is the Mishna, "which I have written," these are the Prophets and Writings (hagiographa), "That they may teach them," this is the Talmud. It teaches us that all these things were given to Moses at Mount Sinai." (Brachot 5a in the Talmud)

Passing the Baton: The Early Prophets and Scribes

After Moses, the Israelites had many prophets and teachers. You'll be introduced to a number of these leaders in the pages that follow, and particularly in Chapter 4. The Talmud suggests that there were at least one million prophets among the Jewish people from the time of Moses to the fall of the second temple in 70 C.E. For a list of the main personalities, turn to Appendix C.

These individuals did not come to introduce new laws to the people. Instead, they were appointed by God to reprove the nation when they strayed from the law of Moses, and to guide the people in bringing their lives back in line with the law.

The prophets took the basic themes that Moses had presented, such as the suffering of the Jewish nation and its ultimate redemption, and how to live in peace and harmony in the land, and gave vivid illustrations of how these concepts could be played out. But they never added or detracted from the law that Moses had given. Instead, they guided the people in the practical application of the law of Moses. Using logic arguments that Moses himself had established, they drew from the law precise instructions that made the laws applicable to every situation.

Talmud Tidbits

Regardless of how many sages and prophets came after him, or how wise and knowledgeable they were, Moses remained the only man authorized by God to deliver his holy law to the people. The prophets and teachers who came after him were recognized as authoritative only because the law of Moses delineates the roles of prophets and teachers, and Moses taught that these men should be given this respect.

Nor did these men write down the Oral Law. Instead, it was transmitted from teacher to student. Any legal opinion pronounced by a sage was assumed to have come from his teacher, unless explicitly indicated to the contrary. In fact, one would repeat a lesson or tradition in the name of the originator and imagine that the latter was standing before him, based on the scriptural passage, "But in their shadow—a man should walk." (Psalms 39:7)

This system worked well as long as the Jewish people and their leaders could dwell securely in their own land. However, the Jews were not destined to live in peace and tranquility for long. Almost as soon as they settled in the Promised Land, another tribe called the Philistines settled in southern Canaan and eventually took it over. For a while, the Israelites were again a captive group, but David, the second king of Israel, successfully defeated the Philistines and stopped their expansion.

The Rule of the Romans

Nor were the Philistines the only outsiders that the Israelites had to deal with. It seemed like almost every ancient civilization in the Middle East wanted to have a go at them, and many of them did. Of these various groups, the Romans, who first occupied Canaan in 63 B.C.E., were particularly onerous.

Threatened with execution or exile if caught teaching the Torah, many of the sages laid low or fled into hiding. Yet, they were able to reconvene twice, once in 122 C.E. in a city called Usha, and again in 158 C.E. in Yavneh. At these events, the sages enacted certain decrees and decided on legislation that called for preserving the integrity of Torah study and dissemination.

As persecutions at the hands of the Romans increased, it became clear that drastic steps had to be taken to preserve the Oral Laws. Many of the leading scholars of the previous generation had perished at the hands of the Romans, and much of the traditions had either perished with them or were on the verge of being lost. As reluctant as they were to do so, the sages had no choice but to permit the recording of the Oral Tradition.

Compiling the Oral Law

Sometime between 170 and 200 C.E., Rabbi Yehudah Hanasi, also known as The Prince, or simply as Rabbi, began the arduous task of putting the Oral Law in writing. A descendant of King David, Rabbi was the leader of the Jewish people at the time. As their head, he had made the acquaintance of the Roman emperor Marcus Aurelius, and the two eventually became good friends. This friendship resulted in a period of improved relationships between the Roman Empire and the Israelites, and gave Rabbi the chance to convene a conference and to tap the memory banks of all the sages of Israel and record their mostly memorized teachings.

Talmud Tidbits

Although it is generally a given that the Oral Tradition was transmitted word for word, exactly as it was taught, there are rabbinic teachings that stated it was permissible to keep personal notes. Some sages kept notes on teachings that weren't commonly discussed. Others even added marginal notations to the Biblical scrolls that they maintained and used as study references. Most significant were the recordings of the heads of the academies, who would preserve these as "hidden scrolls," as the prohibition against publishing the Oral Tradition was still in effect.

As he worked, Rabbi systematically organized the basic principles of the Oral Law to make it more accessible. Unlike the Torah, in which one could find information on a given subject in a number of different books, Rabbi's *Mishna* was arranged topically, and divided into six sections:

◆ Zera'im (Seeds): Agricultural law and prayer service. This section became the form of worship after the destruction of the temple in 70 C.E.

◆ Mo'ed (Time or Season): Laws pertaining to the Sabbath and other religious observances.

◆ Nashim (Women): Family law, including marriage contracts, financial obligations, women's status, annulments, divorce.

◆ Nezikin (Damages): Civil law, including court procedures, torts, personal liability, penalties and punishments.

◆ Kodshim (Sacred Things): Ritual practices in the Holy Temple, including animal sacrifices

◆ Taharot (Purity): Rules of ritual purity and impurity.

From here, Rabbi further divided each section, or *seder*, into subdivisions called tractates, and split each tractate into numerous chapters. For a list of all of them, turn to Appendix C.

As he compiled the information, Rabbi indicated primary opinions by attributing them to the majority or by simply recording them anonymously. He included dissenting opinions to prevent future students from claiming that he didn't take them into account. These opinions also helped enliven what were often extremely lengthy and dry legal discussions.

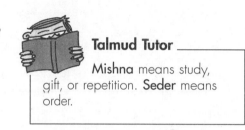

Talmud Tutor

Mishna means study, gift, or repetition. **Seder** means order.

The rabbis who contributed to the Mishna are known as Tanna'im, which is Aramaic for "teachers." As you'll soon see, another group of rabbis would add their insights on the Oral Laws sometime later.

Besides the Mishna, other teachings began to appear in written form. They include:

◆ The Tosefta (literally, addendum), which is a systematic collection of Mishnaic material that Rabbi directly taught to his chief disciples Rabbi Oshaya and Rabbi Chiya.

◆ The Mechilta, a commentary on the book of Exodus

◆ The Sifra, a legal ruling on the book of Leviticus

◆ The Sifri, which were legal rulings on the books of Numbers and Deuteronomy.

◆ The Zohar (literally, light), a book on the mystical teachings of Judaism. Many consider the study of Kabbalah, or Jewish mysticism, to be based on the writings of the Zohar. I'll go into more detail on these teachings in Chapter 12.

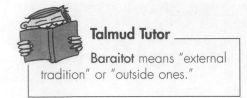

Of the works that existed outside of the Mishna, the Tosefta, which augment the Mishna information, are considered authoritative. Since Rabbi wanted to keep the Mishna as brief as possible, he had them preserved outside in a separate collection. Most editions of the Talmud include the Tosefta on the very back pages. The other works are collectively referred to as *Baraitot*. These writings came from outside Rabbi's school and may or may not augment or harmonize with the Mishna. In many cases, the Talmud will present these views and challenge them against the content of the portion of the Mishna to which they relate; if the challenge cannot be reconciled, the views of the Baraitot are generally disregarded.

Hiding the Law

The Oral Laws were recorded in an extremely cryptic fashion—somewhat like a secret code—suggesting the sages' somewhat understandable reluctance to commit them to writing. The writing lacks vowels, punctuation, and paragraph breaks, which makes it difficult to make heads or tails out of it.

To give you an idea of just how cryptic the writing is, here's an entry from MSN's Encarta encyclopedia, written Talmud style:

The Great Wall of China

Walls comprising Great Wall of China, the mountainous contours, Chinas northern frontier, stretching gulf of Bo Hai in e. to Gansu Province in w. Stretches, walls' builders watchtowers alarm signals passed in case of attack. Top of the walls, builders space soldiers march.

And here's how the actual entry reads:

The Great Wall of China

The walls comprising the Great Wall of China follow the mountainous contours of China's northern frontier, stretching from the gulf of Bo Hai in the east to Gansu Province in the west. In some stretches, the walls' builders placed watchtowers between which alarm signals could be passed in case of attack. Along the top of the walls, the builders created space for soldiers to march.

To this day, only seasoned scholars are capable of cracking the "Talmud Code."

Let's Get Talmudic

Judah, the Prince, affectionately known as simply "Rabbi," curried great favor with Rome, to the extent that he carried on conversations with and regularly hosted many of its dignitaries. One Talmud tractate relates that a query came to the Rabbi from none other than Cleopatra. She asked Rabbi the following, "I agree with the notion that those who die will eventually rise up again for resurrection. But when they do will they be fully clothed or naked?" The sage answered her, "One can deduce the logic from a simple seed. When it is put into the ground it is 'naked' so to speak. Yet, when it emerges from the ground, it is enrobed with many garments (leaves, flowers, etc.). A deceased person who is buried clothed in shrouds, does it not stand to reason that he/she should arise fully clothed?"

The Traditions Continue

After Rabbi's death circa 200 C.E., the Mishna continued to be studied and expanded upon by generations of scholars called the Amoraim, which means "explainers" or "interpreters." They helped consolidate and accurately transmit the tradition to the next generation. Some of them wrote down their discussions and commentaries. Additionally, they agreed that they were not capable of disputing any part of the Mishna, and that it was entirely authoritative.

Sometime around 400 C.E., the rabbis in Palestine gathered together their discussions of the Mishna, called the *Gemara*, and the Mishna itself into a series of books. Their work became known as the Palestinian Talmud, or in Hebrew, Talmud Yerushalmi, which means Jerusalem Talmud.

Talmud Tutor

Gemara means "to finish."

More than a century later, the rabbis in Babylon, faced with the same issues that had prompted placing the Oral Laws into writing, compiled their version of the Gemara and combined it with the Mishna to create the Babylonian Talmud, or the Talmud Bavli. As they had another century of insights and opinions to draw on, the Babylonian version of the Talmud was far more extensive than the Palestinian version had been. It quickly became the most authoritative compilation of the Oral Laws. To this day, when people say they're studying the Talmud, they are almost always referring to the Babylonian version.

By 499 C.E., the people of Israel no longer had to worry about their oral traditions being lost or corrupted. The teachings that had begun with God's revelations to Moses on Mt. Sinai had been preserved in the Talmud.

The Least You Need to Know

- The history of the Talmud begins with Moses, known as the "great lawmaker."

- At Mt. Sinai, God gave Moses the 613 commandments of the Torah that comprise the Oral Law.

- The law that God gave Moses and that Moses taught his people was considered complete. In other words, nothing could be added or taken away from it.

- Continuing persecutions and concerns over the preservation of the Oral Law led to its being committed to writing beginning around 200 C.E.

- Since it was written in haste, the Talmud has a cryptic, almost encoded style that is uniquely its own.

- The written Oral Laws were completed in 499 C.E.

Spreading the Word

In This Chapter

- ◆ Maintaining the integrity of the Oral Laws
- ◆ Early copies of the Talmud
- ◆ Printing the Talmud
- ◆ Talmud on trial

Now that the Oral Laws had been committed to writing, the Jews could breathe a little easier, but just a little. They had preserved their history and their traditions, but they were still subject to persecution—in fact, history tells us that the Jewish people are among the most persecuted people in history. In the face of unrelenting unrest and persecution, no one knew if the important documents that had taken so long to amass could be preserved without error.

If there was one thing that the Jews had learned from their years of trials and tribulations, it was the meaning of tenacity. The Jewish people, like a good Timex watch, could take a licking and keep on ticking. Their ability to persevere through all adversity would also serve them well when it came to assuring that the Talmud would survive intact and unsullied.

Protecting the Oral Laws

For many years after the Talmud was collected, the only way it could be reproduced was writing it by hand. This was a laborious task. Type had yet to be invented, and it would be centuries before moveable type made mass publishing possible. Each copy of the 2.5 million words contained in the Talmud had to be painstakingly copied, letter-by-letter, from a perfect text.

It took many scribes many hours and days to handwrite even one tractate of the Talmud. While such work might seem tedious to the nth degree, the scribes found it anything but. They were not only learned men in their own right, but they also saw themselves as artists. Writing the Talmud was an outlet for them to express their particular art form, and their artistic talents can be found in many of the handwritten Talmud tractates.

This page from the tractate Kiddushin (laws of marriage) in the Babylonian Talmud exemplifies the artistry found in handwritten Talmud tractates.

(Source: Oxford University Bodlein Library Dept. of Oriental Books, collection #Oxford 367.)

But artistry was not their main objective. Their goal was to maintain the integrity of the Talmud text, in very much the same way that the Torah scrolls had been maintained.

What made matters even more complex for the scribes was that the text they copied from combined information came from more than one source. From very early on, each Talmud page, or *daf*, contained the Mishna—the Oral Laws, committed to paper—and the Gemara, or the commentary on those laws. On any given page, other commentaries could be, and were very often, included. Given the lack of vowels, punctuation, and paragraph breaks, it could be very difficult for the scribes to be able to tell where the information from one source ended and another began.

Printed texts today also include other commentaries and study aids, many of which you'll learn more about in later chapters.

Another interesting point about how the Talmud is arranged: Each tractate begins on page 2. There are no page 1's, as it's held that there is no beginning or end in the Talmud. In the running commentary that is the Talmud, discussions are ongoing and readers can literally jump in wherever they like. All passages are constructed in a somewhat consistent manner, which facilitates this approach, and none are considered any better or any worse than the other.

Talmud Trivia

The system of writing a Torah scroll, which has remained unchanged for thousands of years, requires copying from a letter-perfect standard, not from memory. When the Torah portion is read in synagogues during worship services, the congregants pay close attention to the reader. If they hear a word read incorrectly, they immediately correct him. If while reading a Torah scroll even one error is discovered, the scroll is put away and not used again until the error is corrected.

Talmud Tutor

Daf, which is derived from the Babylonian word for tablet, scroll, or plank, refers to a page of Talmud.

From around 220 C.E. until the tenth century, the major center of Jewish learning and authority was Babylonia, which we today recognize as Iraq. As previously mentioned, it was here that the definitive Talmud, the one that is in greatest use today, was developed. By the middle of the tenth century, however, Babylonia's authority over the other Jewish communities began to diminish. Rabbis had established their own schools in such countries as Spain, Italy, North Africa, and Germany. It was in one of these new Jewish centers that the first printed Talmud was developed.

The Talmud in Type

As the site of one of the fastest-growing Jewish communities, there were a number of Jewish scholars in Spain, and therefore, great demand for copies of the Talmud. It was here that the first individually printed volumes of the Talmud were published in Toledo, sometime in the mid-1400s. Talmuds printed in Italy, Portugal, and other countries followed these copies. However, compared to other Hebrew books, generally of lesser religious importance, few books of the Talmud were published in the early days of Jewish printing. For the most part, they were still copied by hand.

Many of the publishers who printed the Talmud were Jewish, but not all. The Daniel Bomberg family, which has the distinction of being the first to publish the Talmud on a grand scale, was not. Bomberg, who had received Pope Leo X's blessing on his work, published the complete Talmud between the years 1520 and 1523.

Bomberg's formatting of the Talmud set the standard for how the pages of the Talmud look to this day:

 ◆ A section of Mishnah text, followed by its Gemara.

 ◆ The commentary of Rashi on the inner margin. You'll learn more about Rashi in Chapter 4. His commentary is a brief, precise explanation of the text, and is written in "Rashi Script," a form of Hebrew handwriting that is believed to have originated with Rashi himself.

 ◆ The commentary of the Tosaphists, mostly grandsons and great-grandsons of Rashi, on the outer margin. These commentaries are longer, more involved discussions of the legal implications of the text, as well as comments on Rashi.

The commentaries of the Tosaphists spawned other commentaries. A current edition of the Talmud could contain some two dozen major and more than 100 minor commentaries.

A number of major commentaries, namely the Rif, Rosh, Ran, Rashash, and Maharsha, are now standard inclusions and are placed in the back of each tractate, following the last daf. Other commentaries, including Ayin Mishpat, Hagose HaGra and Hagose HaBach, Gilyon HaShas, and Mesoras HaShas, and the largest, Rabbenu Chananel, are all placed on the pages they relate to, near the commentaries of Rashi and the tosaphists. These commentaries are mostly brief notes, references, or text corrections.

The first page of the Babylonian Talmud, as it appears in the standard Vilna edition.

Here is the first page of the Babylonian Talmud, as it appears in the standard Vilna edition. The standardized pagination follows that of the third Bomberg edition, Venice, 1548. Pages are numbered by folio. This page is Berachot 2a, the first tractate of the Talmud. The text of the Talmud itself is in the middle, written in square Hebrew letters. As noted in the accompanying key, commentaries and marginal notes surround this text. Rashi (Rabbi Solomon ben Isaac) is the most important commentary; he is always found on the side of the page closest to the binding. The Tosafists are found just on the other side of the Talmud.

1. Mishnah (Palestine, about 220 C.E.)

2. Gemara (Babylonia, about 500 C.E.)

3. Comments of Rashi (France, 1040–1105 C.E.)

4. Comments of the Tosafists (France and Germany, twelfth to thirteenth centuries)

5. Comments of R. Nissim ben Jacob (Tunis, eleventh century. In many tractates, the early medieval commentary of Rebbenu Chananel appears here.)

6. Notes by R. Akiva Eiger (Austria-Hungary, 1761–1837)

7. Anonymous commentary, possibly made by the printer

8. Key to scripture questions

9. Cross references to medieval codes of Jewish law

10. Cross references to other passages in Talmud

11. A textual emendation from the proofs of Joel Sirkes (Poland, 1561–1640)

The consistency that Bomberg established was a boon to Talmud scholars. It made for easy, standard reference citation, and it served as a symbol of the unity of the Jewish people. No matter where they lived, and what edition of the Talmud they picked up, they saw basically the same text as did their counterparts around the world.

> **Talmud Trivia**
>
> A complete set of the Talmud, often ranging from 11 to 20 volumes, was considered a luxury only affordable by a privileged few as recently as 200 years ago. Finding an entire set in a shtetl or village was a rarity. Today, a sharp looking leather-bound set is a common household item for many Jews around the world.

The edition of the Babylonian Talmud that is in use today was first printed in Vilna, Poland, between 1927 and 1932 by the Widow and Brothers Romm, who were widely known for their quality editions of classical Jewish texts. It is one of the last complete sets of the Talmud to be printed in Europe before the outbreak of World War II. The "Vilna Shas," as this edition is called, became a standard and continues to be photographically reproduced in the United States and abroad.

Trials of the Talmud

As much as the Jews regularly suffered at the hands of their persecutors, so too was the Talmud put to the test. The Roman emperor Justinian was the first to record the censorship of Jewish texts, doing so in 553 C.E. Motivated by a resentful anti-Jewish clergy who wrongfully accused the Talmud of blasphemies against Jesus and the church, Justinian issued an edict that strictly forbade the Hebrews to read the law in their own language, and restricted the "wretched Hebrews" to use only a Greek or Latin translation of the Torah in their synagogues.

Justinian was just one of the many authorities, both secular and not, who sought to separate the Jews from their heritage. Doing so, it was believed, would cause the Jews to perish.

Talmud Tidbits _____

Rabbi Chanina ben Tradion, arrested and condemned by the Romans for publicly teaching the Talmud, was wrapped in a Torah scroll and tied to a stake atop a pyre of green wood. As the smoke and flames rose around him, his students cried out to him in anguish, "Rabbi! Tell us what you see!"

Rabbi Chanina calmly answered, "I see the letters—the holy letters are flying away!" By this he meant that although the parchment scroll burned, the words did not, but rose toward heaven, returning to their maker.

The Talmud and the Church

The passages of the Talmud that so enraged Justinian and the early leaders of the Christian church were believed to have dealt with Jesus' life and death, and they made some statements that would be inflammatory in any context regarding the sexual proclivities of Mary, Jesus' mother, and that Jesus was "a bastard born of adultery." However, a significant number of historians and Talmudists have studied these passages and have concluded that they do not refer to Jesus. In fact, the individual that they do refer to lived an entire century before Jesus did.

Still, given the cryptic, almost coded nature of Talmudic writing, it's easy to understand how someone, perhaps a Jewish heretic, could suggest to early church leaders that there was some code word in certain Talmudic passages that referenced Jesus.

Because of the controversies that these passages incited, they were censored from every printed version of the Talmud except for Bomberg's 1520 text. Today, they are restored in several versions.

While the trials and tribulations that preceded the Dark Ages managed to close every school of philosophy and learning in the Christian world, they did nothing more than make the Talmud all the more dear to the Jews. The more they were persecuted for their faith's sake, the more desperately they clung to the immediate cause of their martyrdom.

Fires Fueled by Fanaticism

By the eleventh century, concerns over Talmudic tracts like these had let loose the passions of a fierce fanaticism against the Jewish communities in Europe. Not only was the Talmud targeted for extinction, but whole villages were often destroyed by the church's crusaders as they marched forward. In many towns, not even a single prayer book remained behind.

In later periods, the French church entered the fray. In 1240, a man named Nicholas Donin, a Jew who had renounced the faith, told authorities in northern France that the Talmud contained blasphemies against Jesus. In June of that year, Rabbi Yehiel of Paris was forced to defend the merits of Judaism, and, in particular, the merits of the Talmud. He won the battle, but lost the war. Two years later, under the authority of Pope Gregory, 24 wagons full of Jewish handwritten texts and manuscripts were taken from their owners and hauled into the center of Paris, where they were publicly burned.

Although often censored, the Talmud was not burned on a large scale until an order by Pope Julius III in 1552 led to a big bonfire in Rome, followed by many others in Italy. In Venice, it was reported that more than 1,000 copies of the Talmud and other sacred literature were burned.

The Horrors of Nazi Germany

Other desecrations of the Talmud followed, but nothing matched the atrocities faced by the Jews when they fell under the maniacal clutches of Nazi Germany. It is estimated that more irreplaceable religious books were confiscated or burned by the SS and Gestapo than in all the previous persecutions of the millennium combined. Yet, in ghettos, bunkers, and concentration camps, Jews gathered around and studied the Talmud. Sometimes they had nothing more than a single torn page, worn from use, which had somehow survived from a holy book. Sometimes they didn't even have that torn page. Still, scholars reconstructed the pages of Talmud on papers torn from things like sacks of cement, which were eagerly passed around as though they were priceless.

Today, the Talmud is no longer the target of persecution by the heads of other religions. While some misinformed individuals may still take Talmudic verses out of context to support their arguments that the Talmud is anti-Christian, no known church authority supports their actions. In fact, the greatest repository of handwritten Jewish manuscripts in the world today resides in the vaults of the Vatican in Rome.

> **Talmud Tidbits**
>
> Jewish law has a unique "recycling program" for worn out, torn, or otherwise unusable holy books, including the Talmud. Rather than simply discarding them, they are gathered together and placed in a special box or bag. The burial society of each community generally has a drop off repository at its mortuary. These items are then bound together and buried in the ground. In this way, they are treated with the same dignity afforded a human being.

The Least You Need to Know

- ◆ Talmudic wisdom was meticulously preserved and maintained orally for nearly 1,500 years.

- ◆ Handwritten copies of the Talmud began to appear in the sixth century C.E.

- ◆ Printed editions of the Talmud first appeared in Spain in 1508 C.E.

- ◆ The Talmud has endured many trials and tribulations since its inception, including censorship and burnings.

Chapter 4

People of the Talmud

In This Chapter

- ◆ Carriers of faith and tradition
- ◆ Dynamic duos
- ◆ The scholar and the gladiator
- ◆ Collectors of the Gemara

There were hundreds of great men—and a few women, too—who contributed to the development of Talmudic wisdom. Many were early Talmudists—the first generation of the carriers of the Oral Tradition. Others were commentators who continued to expand on these traditions in later centuries.

You'll read the writings of many of these people in the chapters ahead. While it's impossible to give you a complete accounting of all of them, this chapter will introduce you to some of the names you'll come across, and give you some background on their contributions and where they fit into Talmudic history. Their stories also demonstrate the remarkable resilience of the Jews during centuries of relentless persecution.

Hillel, the Great Sage

Rabbi Hillel lived in Jerusalem during the time of King Herod, about a century before the destruction of the Second Temple in 70 C.E. He is renowned for his patience and devotion to study, as well as for his kindness and concern for those around him.

During his lifetime, Hillel was elevated to the position of *nasi*, a position equal to being the king of Israel and one that honored Hillel's heritage as a direct descendent of King David. However, Rome ruled Israel during Hillel's time, so he couldn't actually be anointed king.

Talmud Tutor

Nasi means patriarch, ruler, prince or president in Hebrew.

Hillel wrote many of the teachings in the Talmud. One of the most famous is "If I am not for myself, then who will be for me? And if I am only for myself, then what am I? And if not now, when?" (Pirkei Avot 1:14)

Let's Get Talmudic

The Talmud is full of stories extolling Hillel's great teachings. Among some of his most famous sayings:

"Hillel said, be of the students of Aaron, loving peace and pursuing peace, loving people and bringing them closer to Torah." (Pirkei Avot 1:12)

"What you don't like done to you don't do unto others. This is the entire Torah; the rest is commentary. Go and learn." (Shabbos 31a)

"Do not separate yourself from the community; do not trust yourself until the day you die; do not judge your fellow until you have reached his place; do not make a statement that cannot be fully understood on the ground that it will be understood eventually …" (Pirkei Avot 2:4)

Hillel and Shammai, another great Torah scholar who you briefly met in Chapter 1, often appear together in Talmudic discussions. Although the two men were contemporaries, they led two very different schools of thought. Still, in arguments that contrast their views, they agreed with each other far more often than not. As patient and kind as Hillel was, Shammai was very much the opposite and didn't suffer fools lightly. Chapter 1 relates one story that contrasts the differences in their approaches. Another Talmud story tells of a gentile who comes to Shammai and tells the sage that he would convert to Judaism if Shammai could teach him the whole Torah while the man balanced on one foot. Shammai chases him away with a measuring stick (he was an engineer by trade).

In contrast, Hillel coverts the gentile with three simple sentences: "That which is hateful to you, do not do to your neighbor. That is the whole Torah; the rest is commentary. Go and study it."

Rabban Gamliel Hazaken

The grandson of Hillel, Rabban Gamliel Hazaken is also known as Gamliel, the Elder. As the president of the Sanhedrin, the ancient judicial system in Israel that dated back to the time of Moses, he was the first to bear the title of Rabban, which means "our master."

Talmud Tidbits

The Sanhedrin (from the Greek word syn, meaning together, and hedra, meaning seats) governed Israel's judicial system from the time of Moses—who chose the body's first 70 members—until it was disbanded sometime around 360 C.E. The Sanhedrin ruled on legal disputes and passed legislation, much of which strengthened religious observances and unified the people. All rulings and laws were tailored to meet specific situations that arose over time.

The Sanhedrin made a number of key rulings and enacted some important laws under Rabban Gamliel's reign. Among them were several that stressed the necessity for extending to all people the same courtesies shown to Jews who were poor, sick, or dead.

Shimon ben Gamliel

Another descendant of the family of Hillel, Shimon ben Gamliel was the father of Judah, the Prince, who committed the Oral Laws to writing for the first time. He lived through the Bar Kochba revolt, which was a Jewish uprising against Roman rule, and the Roman persecutions that followed it. He helped establish a new rabbinic center at Usha during this time.

Talmud Tidbits

After the destruction of Solomon's Temple in 70 C.E., the roman emperor promised to rebuild the city, but his plan was to rebuild it and rename it Aeila Capitalina, dedicating it to the roman god Jupiter. This outrageous act, along with the harsh laws forbidding the study of the Torah and observance of many of the Mitzvot, led to the Bar Kochba revolt over 60 years later, after the destruction of the temple, in the year 132 C.E.

Rabban Shimon ben Gamliel is noted for encouraging the Jews to persevere in the face of tragedy. As the Talmud notes:

> "There has never been a greater Yom Tov (holiday) for the Jewish people than the fifteenth of Av … (Taanis 26) What happened on that day? After the massacre at Beitar the Rabbis began to institute a policy of mourning. 'We must not build homes or plant vineyards,' they proclaimed, 'we must not play music or sing songs.' It was prohibited to smile or certainly to laugh. Rabbi Yishmoel Ben Alisha said, 'we can no longer marry and we can no longer have children.'

> It was the fifteenth of Av when the great Rabban Shimon ben Gamliel said, 'Stop! If we continue to mourn we will destroy whatever little bit we have left. Build houses, get married and rebuild your families. For a few years our strength was in our arms—now our strength must be in our hearts.' So, it was on that the 15th day of Av, only six days after the anniversary of the Jewish Day of National Mourning (Tish B'Av), that they found a new inner strength and learned how to go on with life. They were a crippled people, yet they started to marry and where possible built homes and planted new fields." (Baba Basra 60b)

Let's Get Talmudic

"Rabban Shimon ben Gamliel said: The world is established on three principles: truth, justice and peace, as it is said: 'You shall administer truth, justice and peace within your gates.'" (Pirkei Avot 1:18)

Rabbi Yochana ben Zakkai

Rabbi Yochanan ben Zakkai was the last of the disciples of Rabbi Hillel. A passionate advocate of pacifism, his actions during the siege of Jerusalem by the Roman general Vespasian helped ensure the continuation of Jewish scholarship.

According to Talmudic tradition, ben Zakkai had urged his people to surrender, but they would have none of it, preferring to die at the hands of the Romans than to be ruled by them. When it was apparent that Rome was going to triumph, a group of supporters, concerned about Judaism's survival following the Roman conquest, came up with a plan that they felt would save the faith. It called for smuggling ben Zakkai out of the city so he could surrender to Vespasian. They placed ben Zakkai in a coffin along with some rotten food scraps (to make an odor like a dead body) and wheeled him out of the gates. The stench convinced the guards that the Hebrew leader was dead.

The men carried the coffin to Vespasian's tent, at which time ben Zakkai emerged and exposed the ruse. He told Vespasian that he had had a vision that Vespasian would soon become emperor. Ben Zakkai then asked Vespasian to protect a nearby town called Yavneh where he and his students could continue studying Torah without worry. Vespasian agreed to grant ben Zakkai's request if his prophesy came true.

Ben Zakkai's prophecy did indeed come true, and he and the sages of Yavneh were allowed to continue their scholarship unmolested. The school prospered and was a foremost center of Jewish learning for many years.

Let's Get Talmudic

"Rabbi Yochanan ben Zakkai received the Torah from Hillel and Shammai. He used to say, 'If you have studied much Torah, do not keep the goodness for yourself, because this is what you were created to do.'

"Rabbi Yochanan ben Zakkai had five [primary] disciples .... He said to them, 'Go out and discern which is the proper way to which a person should cling.'

"Rabbi Eliezer says, 'A good eye.'

"Rabbi Yehoshua says, 'A good friend.'

"Rabbi Yose says, 'A good neighbor.'

"Rabbi Shimon says, 'One who considers the outcome of a deed.'

"Rabbi Elazar says, 'A good heart'." (Pirkei Avot, Chapter 2, Mishnah 9, 10, 13)

"He said to them: I prefer the words of Elazar ben Arach to your words, for in his words yours are included." (Pirkei Avot, Chapter 2, Mishnah 9,10,13)

Eliezer ben Hyrkanos (the Great)

Rabbi Eliezer ben Hyrkanos took over as head of the yeshiva in Yavneh after the death of Yochanan ben Zakkai. He was renowned for his great knowledge, far greater than that of his colleagues, which led to his being referred to as Rabbi Eliezer the Great, and as "Sinai," in recognition of his vast repository of Torah knowledge.

Despite his greatness, Eliezer the Great appreciated the need to recognize the accomplishments of others. He penned a treasure-trove of poetic writings called Pirkei De Rabbi Eliezer, which contains rabbinic mysticism, chapters on astronomy and the calendar, and *aggadot*, or stories that embellish some of the most important episodes in the Bible, such as the creation, the flood, the binding of Isaac, and the revelation.

Talmud Tutor

Aggadot are stories or sections in the Talmud and other rabbinic writings that deal with biblical narrative and stories, rather than religious law and regulations.

In his most famous lamentations and predictions, Eliezer the Great stressed the need to rely on God for all things, as the following excerpt from his writings shows:

> "Since the day the Temple was destroyed, the scholars became like school teachers (meaning diminution in scholarship), and the school teachers like synagogue attendants, and the synagogue attendants like common people, and the common people grew ever more feeble, and no one intercedes (intercessory prayer heard above): upon whom can we rely? Upon our Father in Heaven." (Sotah 9:15)

Akiva ben Joseph

Akiva ben Joseph may have been a poor, semi-literate shepherd, but his contributions to Talmudic study confirm the fact that he's also one of Judaism's greatest scholars. The *exegetical* method of studying the Talmud, which explains and interprets the text by linking each traditional practice to the appropriate Biblical text, began with him and continues to this day. He is also credited with systematizing the material that would later become the Mishna.

Talmud Tutor

Exegesis is an explanation or critical interpretation of a text. "Talmudic exegesis" of a biblical verse means extracting meaning from every phrase and nuance. It was the technique used by the sages to derive novel insights or support teachings from every superfluous phrase.

Akiva's brilliance in Torah study didn't prevent him from making a serious misstep that cost him his life. He believed in Bar Kochba, the man who led the rebellion against Rome that you read about earlier in this chapter, and supported Bar Kochba and his troops during the rebellion. As it turned out, however, Akiva was virtually alone in his beliefs about Bar Kochba, and when the rebellion he led failed, even a number of Akiva's own people refused to come to his aid.

When the rebellion failed, Roman authorities arrested Rabbi Akiva, for openly defying their decree banning the public study of Torah. Tradition says that after being imprisoned for three years, he was put on trial and sentenced to death. While the Romans were torturing him to death, combing his flesh with iron combs, he recited the Shema and explained to those present that all his life he was looking forward to the opportunity to fulfill what is meant by loving the Lord with all thy heart, soul, and might.

Talmud Tidbits

The Shema (pronounced "shma") is the most important of all Jewish prayers. According to a Biblical commandment, it is recited twice daily—in the morning and the evening. It is also recited at special occasions, such as the removal of the Torah scroll from the ark during Sabbath public readings, at circumcision ceremonies, and is even recited on one's deathbed.

Interestingly, the Shema is a prayer that speaks not to God, but to the Jewish people. Its verses remind Jews of the importance of following the instructions that God gave them to live by. In part, it reads: Hear, O Israel, the Eternal is our God, the Eternal is One. Blessed be God's Name and glorious kingdom forever and ever. You shall love the Lord your God with all your heart, with all your soul, and with all your might. And these words, which I [God] teach you this day, shall be upon your heart. You shall teach them diligently to your children, speaking of them when you sit in your house, when you walk by the way, when you lie down and when you rise up. And you shall bind them as a sign upon your head, and they shall be for a reminder before your eyes. And you shall write them on the doorposts of your house and upon your gates. (Deut. 6:4-9)

Shimon bar Yochai

A student of Rabbi Akiva, Shimon bar Yochai was also pursued by the Romans. With his son, Elazar ben Shimon, bar Yochai took refuge in a cave, where he remained for 13 years. The two studied Torah together, both the revealed Torah and the hidden, or secret Torah, also known as the *Kabbalah*.

Bar Yochai wrote down the secret Torah for the first time in a book called the Zohar, which means "splendor" or "radiance." Although his teachings were committed to writing, only seasoned scholars and savants preserved and studied its contents. These esoteric teachings were not intended for the masses, for reasons that will be discussed more fully in Chapter 12.

Talmud Tutor

The **Kabbalah** collects the parts of the Torah that deal with such subjects as the process of creation, the nature of divinity, and the origin and fate of the soul. The name Kabbalah is derived from a Hebrew word meaning "to receive" or "to accept."

Talmud Trivia

Any statement or saying in the Mishna that isn't attributed to some other sage is believed to be a ruling of Rabbi Meir.

Rabbi Meir and His Wife

Perhaps the most enigmatic and colorful personality of the Talmud is arguably its greatest. The second-century Torah scholar Rabbi Meir was the best of Rabbi Akiva's students, and was

> **Talmud Trivia**
>
> Although there are 53 women mentioned in the Talmud for their ethical teachings and for their exemplary piety and devotion, Bruriah is the only one who is quoted. Bruriah is also attributed with having taught 300 rulings of Jewish law to 300 students, in one day!

noted for the brilliance of his arguments. Virtually every part of the Mishna is said to bear his imprint.

Meir's wife was the brilliant Bruriah, who was the daughter of Rabbi Chanina ben Tradion, one of the great sages who met his death at the hands of the Romans. It is said that when she heard Meir praying that certain wicked people who were harassing and annoying him should die, she told him he should rather pray that they repent. He took her advice and changed his approach toward them. Eventually, they did repent and become God-fearing people.

Rabbi Judah Ha-Nasi

As more fully detailed in Chapter 2, Rabbi Yehudah Hanasi, also known as The Prince, or simply as Rabbi, was responsible for continuing Rabbi Akiva's work in organizing and compiling the Mishna.

The sages you've read about to this point are called Tanna'im. From the Aramaic word meaning "reciter" or "repeater," Tanna is the term used to designate the Jewish sages whose teachings are recorded in the Mishna and its contemporary works, from the middle of the first century until about 220 C.E. The word's origin seems to come from the individuals who were responsible for memorizing and reciting the oral traditions in the academies of later generations, and was subsequently, by extension, applied to the teachers who were actually being quoted.

The ones who follow are called the Amora (plural Amora'im). These are the rabbis of the fourth to fifth centuries. The term Amora means "speaker," and originally referred to the officials in the academies whose jobs were to project the teachings of the rabbis strongly enough so that all students could hear. It later came to denote the rabbis themselves.

Rav and Shmuel

During Rabbi Yehudah Hanasi's lifetime, seeds were being sown for the establishment of Talmud centers in other parts of the ancient world. Two of Rabbi's students, Rav and Shmuel, founded academies in Babylon. By the time the last sages of Israel had to flee the Romans, Babylon already provided a vibrant and flourishing center of Torah. Now Babylon became the spiritual center of the Jewish people, and as long as the communities of Israel still remained, there was communication between the great sages of each land.

Rav was the greatest student of Rabbi Yehudah Hanasi. He was unique in that he represented the link between the period of the Tanna'im, the scholars of the Mishnah, and the Amoraim, the scholars of the Talmudic period.

Shmuel was a multifaceted personality with expertise in many disciplines, including medicine and astronomy, and factors prominently in Talmud study. Both sages are mentioned quite frequently, and often in colorful ways, throughout the Talmud.

Yohanan and Shimon ben Lakish

One was the head of the most prominent rabbinic academy in third-century Palestine; the other has variously been described as a leader of a group of gladiators or bandits. Together, they are at the heart of Talmudic stories that exemplify the meaning of devotion and friendship.

Yohanan and ben Lakish met in an unlikely place—the Jordan River—where Yohanan was bathing. Suddenly, a wild young man—ben Lakish (also known as Resh Lakish)—plunged into the water and swam to him. Startled, Yohanan tells him, "Your strength should be devoted to the Torah!" Ben Lakish, not to be outdone, comes back with, "Your beauty should be devoted to women." (Yohanan was known as being one of the best-looking men of his time).

> **Let's Get Talmudic**
>
> Resh Lakish said: He who utters words of Torah so that they are not sweet to those who hear them would do better not to utter them at all. (Exodus Rabbah 41:15)

Ben Lakish eventually becomes Yohanan's student and marries his sister. In time, he surpasses his brother-in-law in wisdom, however, in a dispute, the law generally follows Rabbi Yohanan's opinion. Debates between the two comprise the majority of discussions found in the Talmud.

Rabbi Yohanan, who compiled the Jerusalem Talmud, is the most quoted sage in the entire Talmud, appearing on almost every page of the Babylonian version, which is the one in broadest use.

Rava and Abbaye

Rava and Abbaye were childhood friends who later became two of the great rabbis of Babylon in the fourth century C.E. The debates and discussions between the two men, who disagreed on virtually everything, are found throughout the Talmud and are held as a seminal element in the development of Talmudic analysis and discussion. In fact, the surname of the Talmud is "the discussions of Abbaye and Rava." (Talmud Baba Batra 134a)

Rav Ashi and Ravina

Another Talmudic dynamic duo, these fourth-century C.E. sages are noted for their work in editing the Babylonian Talmud. Rav Ashi was the master editor; Ravina, a colleague (some sources refer to him as a student), assisted Rav Ashi with his great work. Discussions that mention Ravina's debates over *halakhah*, or matters of Jewish law, with other colleagues appear frequently in the Talmud. Of the two, Rav Ashi generally sides with more stringent rulings; Ravina is more lenient.

> **Talmud Tutor**
>
> Halakhah, which can be defined as "the path that one walks," is derived from a Hebrew word that means "to walk," "to travel," or "to go."

At least one source suggests that Rabbi Ashi actually drafted two versions of the Talmud, one that was wordier, and the second that is more concise, the version that is in use today. In doing so, it is estimated that he spent 30 years on the first and 30 years on the second.

Up to now, you've read about sages that were directly related in some way to the development of the Talmud. The men who come next are distinguished from the others for their more contemporary contributions to Talmudic study.

Rabbi Shlomo Yitzchaki

Also known by the acronym Rashi, Rabbi Shlomo Yitzchaki was the most outstanding Biblical and Talmudic commentator of the Middle Ages, and perhaps, of all time. His writings are prized for being brief, clear, and easy to understand. Meant to be read as part of the Talmud, Rashi has become inextricably connected to formal learning of the Talmud text. While he paid great attention to words that needed elaboration or explanation, he also spent great time formulating succinct explanations that used the fewest words possible.

> **Talmud Trivia**
>
> Ironically, Rashi's students are the actual authors of many of the commentaries attributed to him. When Rashi taught, many of his students would take notes in the margins of their books. Rashi used these notes for his commentary, but it is known that he accumulated manuscripts that he edited himself.

A wine grower and manufacturer in France, Rashi used the proceeds from his business to support a Torah academy in Troyes, where he lived. He most likely also used these funds to pay for the printing of his commentaries.

Rashi had three daughters who were great scholars in their own right and who married men of greatness. Their children, who would continue the scholarly traditions of their parents, became known as the "Baalei Tosafot," or "those who extended," added important commentary to Rashi's explanations of the Talmud.

Moshe ben Maimon

Also known as Maimonides (Greek for "son of Maimon") or by the acronym Rambam, Moshe ben Maimon was a twelfth-century physician and Torah scholar who produced some of the most important commentaries on the Talmud. He was the first to develop a systematic codification of all Jewish law, which he compiled into a book called the Mishneh Torah. He also wrote what is still considered to be a leading work on religious philosophy, *The Guide to the Perplexed.* But his lifework didn't end here. In his spare time, Maimonides, who was born in Spain but spent most of his life in Egypt, also wrote numerous books on medicine and served as physician to the sultan of Egypt. He also compiled the Thirteen Principles of Faith that are part of the Jewish prayer book. Along with Rashi, Maimonides is one of the most widely studied Jewish scholars. At times, however, his commentaries on the Talmud have drawn fire, because he didn't credit his sources. Because some of his writings didn't approach theological issues strictly from a Jewish perspective, his teachings have also had a significant influence on the non-Jewish world.

Moshe ben Nachman

Also known as Nachmanides (Greek for "son of Nachman") or Ramban, Moshe ben Nachman was a thirteenth-century scholar noted for the width and depth of his Torah knowledge. Like Maimonides, Nachmanides was Spanish and a physician by trade. He was also a prolific author, and produced noted Talmudic commentaries and other works on Jewish law.

Unlike Maimonides, Ramban's commentaries had a strong mystical bent and were the first to incorporate Kabbalistic teachings. A forceful defender of the Jewish faith, he was chosen by the king of Aragon to argue against Christianity in a 1263 debate with Pablo Christiani, a converted Jew.

The Least You Need to Know

- ◆ While he wasn't permitted to actually rule over Israel as a king, Rabbi Hillel was given a position that was the equivalent of this title, and that recognized his having descended from King David.

◆ Yochanan ben Zakkai's negotiations with the Roman emperor Vespasian helped assure the survival of the yeshiva system for future generations.

◆ Under Rav Ashi, the explanations of the oral teachings were arranged by tract for the first time, becoming the Talmud that we have today.

◆ Nachmanides' writings were among the first to incorporate the mystical teachings of Kabbalah.

Part 2

Inside the Talmud

As you learned in Part 1, the Talmud is actually a series of books that compiles two different types of writings—the Mishna, or the primary body of Jewish civil and religious law, and the rabbinic discussions on the Mishna, which are known as the Gemara.

In the Mishna are found explanations on and details of the laws of the Torah—the five Books of Moses—organized topically into six general subject categories, or orders, which are further divided into tractates. Each tractate is then divided into chapters, which contain units of learning and thought.

In this part, we'll take a closer look at the individual orders and tractates of the Mishna and Gemara.

Chapter **5**

Of Seeds and Blessings

In This Chapter

- ◆ Blessings all around
- ◆ Praying daily
- ◆ Praying silently
- ◆ Laws of agriculture

The first order of the Talmud is Zeraim, which means "seeds." It contains many tracts and laws relating to agriculture, primarily in the Land of Israel. It also includes the tractate Brachot, which means blessings.

While it may seem odd to include laws about agriculture and blessings in the same Talmudic order, it actually makes quite a lot of sense that they're paired in this manner. You'll see why in the pages ahead.

Count Your Blessings

How do seeds and blessings relate? Why are laws about both contained in the same Talmudic order? Perhaps the best explanation was made by Maimonides (you met him in Chapter 4). He taught that Zeraim (Seeds) being the inaugural order of the Talmud suggests that agriculture, particularly to an agrarian people, is the basis of all sustenance. Without such physical support, it isn't possible to be of service to God, which is the central tenet of both the Oral and Written Laws. And, since no one can eat without first blessing the food and giving thanks for it, it follows that Brachot should be the first tract of this order.

With this said, most of the agricultural tracts in Zeraim are not very relevant to today's world. They cover such subjects as the portions (tithes—see Chapter 9) that must be gifted to temple officials. There are also laws governing how one should leave parts of his field open for the poor to glean, the tithes that should be separated from the harvest for the poor, the giving of first fruits to the priests in Jerusalem, prohibitions of deriving benefit from fruits of the first three years, and the like.

Talmud Tidbits

The Jerusalem Talmud, which predates the Babylonian Talmud, does contain commentary on the agricultural tracts of Zeraim. However, since it is written in Western Aramaic, which is difficult to understand, it is rarely studied.

What's more, in the Babylonian Talmud, which is the Talmud in greatest use, none of these tracts contain commentary from the sages. In other words, they are Mishna tracts, but there is no Gemara to accompany them.

In most discussions of Talmudic literature, these tracts generally wouldn't even be included. However, I've included brief descriptions of them—you'll find them near the end of the chapter—to illustrate the content of this Talmud order as completely as possible.

Brachot, as one of the most beloved tractates in the Talmud (and the longest), is decidedly still relevant to modern living, and will be the main focus of this chapter.

Blessings on Everything

It's hard to overstate the importance of brachot in Jewish prayer and daily service. A typical *siddur*, or Jewish prayer book, contains hundreds of blessings recited on virtually every occasion affecting a Jewish person, literally "from the womb to the tomb."

Talmud Tutor

Siddur, the name for the Jewish prayer book, comes from the word seder, meaning order.

What are brachot? Simply put; there are moments throughout the day when Jews step back and acknowledge the immensity and brilliance of God's creation. Brachot are these acknowledgments, given in thanks to just about every component of our existence—the beauty of our world, majesty, sadness, love, compassion, and suffering in the world.

Some brachot are quite spontaneous, like those said when viewing the Grand Canyon, or whenever one is moved to offer prayer or thanks. However, brachot can also be, and are, fixed elements of Jewish worship. Religious Jews recite certain brachot every day or at specific times, like on the Sabbath. Here, the Kiddush, or the blessing over the wine, is an example of a blessing recited in the observance of a commandment— "Remember the Sabbath to keep it holy." (Exodus 20:8)

The Talmud details many different types of brachot, including blessing said:

♦ Over food (the sages considered reciting a blessing over a food as a form of "payment," in order not to "steal" from God's world)

♦ Over pleasant scents

♦ When experiencing natural phenomena

♦ When seeing sages

♦ When visiting a place where a miracle has occurred

♦ When hearing good or bad news

♦ Over the performance of certain commandments

For Jews, these prayers, or blessings, serve as a constant reminder of God's presence in daily life. Fulfilling the laws of Brachot literally requires remaining in a prayerful state at all times, which means that even sitting down to a simple meal of bread and water, and offering a prayer over it, can have profound meaning. But the intention of brachot is not to trivialize prayer. While it's possible to simply go through the motions when praying brachot, the Talmud admonishes against such apathy.

Let's Get Talmudic

Rabbi Akiva was traveling. At the end of the day he came to a town and requested lodging at its inn. He was told that there was no place and was summarily rejected. He camped in the forest on the outskirts of town. During the night, the donkey he used for riding and the rooster that he relied upon to wake him suddenly died, and to turn injury to insult, the candle with which he learned Torah was extinguished by wind. He accepted these hardships calmly and went to sleep. Then, a band of thieves came, plundered the town and killed everyone in it. Had Rabbi Akiva been there, or had he been seen or heard due to the animals or light, he too might have been robbed and killed. Upon this Rabbi Akiva exclaimed, "All which compassionate God does is for the good." (Talmud Brachot 60b)

The tractate Brachot contains nine chapters that go into great detail on various aspects of these brachot and more. They describe when to pray, how to pray, and where to pray. They also discuss such issues as:

- ◆ Who is exempt from prayer, and who is not

- ◆ Whether laborers are allowed a break from their work to recite their prayers

- ◆ The acceptable time for prayers

- ◆ What to pray when entering or leaving a house of study

- ◆ How one should prepare for prayer

- ◆ What happens if a prayer leader makes a mistake

Specific disputes between the House of Hillel and the House of Shammai (you read about them in Chapter 4) concerning the appropriate way to break bread are also included.

Brachot Basics

Basically, all Brachot begin in the same way: "Blessed are you God, our Lord king of the world ..." They then go on to note the specific things for which one is thankful. It should also be noted that when one recites a blessing, one is not actually "blessing" God, rather acknowledging Him as the source of all blessing.

Let's Get Talmudic

In Talmudic thinking, a prayerful moment can come from simply waking up and acknowledging the good fortune of having one's soul restored to him/her. (Brachot 60a) The sages teach that sleep is like "one-sixtieth" of death. Every night we send our souls above, tired from the worries of the day, and God returns them to us reinvigorated—like new! It is an axiom of Jewish belief that just as God returns our souls and reinvigorates our bodies every morning, so, too, he will return life and rebuild the bodies of the righteous people at the Resuscitation of the Dead (Techiyat Hameitim).

Praying Daily

Brachot are said all daily, and many times a day. The concept of daily prayer and blessings dates back to the earliest of times. One of the first mentions of timely prayer comes from the stories about the patriarchs in Genesis. The Torah teaches us:

> "And Jacob left Be'er Sheva and went to Charan. He arrived at the place and stayed over night there, because the sun set .... (Genesis 28:10-11)

In the Talmud, Rashi draws special attention to two very specific elements in this story—the where and the when:

"And he arrived at the place: From here we learn that Jacob originated the custom Evening Prayer." (Rashi)

Jewish traditional practice basically states that Jewish men age 13 and older are obligated to pray three times a day: morning, afternoon, and evening.

About the Amidah

The obligation to pray three times a day was established by the prophet Ezra and codified in Brachot. It is fulfilled by reciting the *Amidah*, which can also be found in this tract, and is the central prayer in all three prayer services.

The Amidah, which is recited in silence (or very quietly, so that only the speaker can hear the words) when one is standing, is also known as Shemoneh Esrei, which means eighteen, because it originally contained 18 blessings. In the second century C.E., an additional blessing was added as protection against heretics—specifically, the Samaritans and Sadducees, two sects that threatened the Jews. (Talmud Brachot 29a) It was permanently added to the Jewish liturgy when Jews who had converted to Christianity began to turn in those who remained dedicated to the faith to the Romans.

Let's Get Talmudic

Rabbi Meir, one of the great Talmudic sages, wrote that when a person prays, his words should be few and not hastily issued in the presence of God. (based on Psalms 5) Put simply, "KISS" (keep it short and sweet). At any rate, the Talmudic sages epitomize their basic attitude toward prayer by declaring, "The Merciful One desires the heart." It is, in other words, quality over quantity.

Sometimes nonverbal communication is very powerful and speaks louder than words, as the following story illustrates:

> The Talmud relates a story about a man who was walking through his vineyard on Shabbat. He noticed a breach in the wall around his property and immediately thought to himself that he should repair it after the Sabbath ended. But then he felt that he had profaned Shabbat by using its rest to mentally plan his weekday work activity. He resolved never to repair the breach in the wall. God recognized his sincerity of heart and was very moved. God recompensed his righteous thought by causing a huge fruit tree to grow in the gap, mending the wall and providing enough fruit to sustain the man for the remainder of his life. (Talmud Shabbat 150b)

Miracles and Visions

The last chapter in the tractate Brachot deals with, among other subjects:

- Thanking God for miracles

- Blessings over witnessing natural phenomenon (like thunder and lightning)

- Petitioning God regarding the sex of a child

- Good and bad tidings

- Explanations for certain catastrophic events

- Dream interpretation

Let's Get Talmudic

The Talmud derives the concept of blessing on miracles from Jethro, the father-in-law of Moses. One such blessing is "… Who made miracles for our fathers in this place …" when seeing the place where a miracle occurred for the entire Jewish people. (Berachot 54a) The Talmud derives it from the passage in the Torah: "Jethro rejoiced over all the good that God had done for Israel, that He had rescued them from the hand of Egypt. And Jethro said 'Blessed is God, Who liberated the people from Egypt's power and from the hand of Pharoah ….'" (Exodus 18:9,10)

Several pages of this last chapter deal exclusively with dreams. There is a case in the Talmud of a rabbi in Jerusalem who had a dream. He told his dream to 24 different interpreters and ended up with 24 different interpretations for his dream. The chapter relates the story of the unscrupulous behavior of certain "professional" dream interpreters. And there are two general proclamations made by the sages in the Talmud—"No dream is without an admixture of nonsense," and "Every dream goes after its interpretation" that we'll explore in more depth in Chapter 13.

This chapter contains quite a few segments about what may seem like trivial issues, such as proper bathroom conduct, fertility advice, how many and what type of friends one should keep, and avoiding houses of worship for mundane purposes.

The Agricultural Tracts of Zeraim

As previously mentioned, most of these tracts have little relevance today and are little studied. However, they can be interesting from an historical point of view.

Peah (The Corner of the Field)

The second tract in Zeraim, Peah primarily deals with laws governing how a farmer is to harvest his field while leaving one corner unharvested for the poor to glean. These laws specifically address what to do with individual grape clusters that remain on the vine after harvest, forgotten sheaves of grain left in the field, and even tithes for the poor called *Maaser Ani*. Some laws governing distribution of charity are also found in this tractate.

Demai (Tithes in Question)

What if a person is in doubt as to whether he has tithed his harvested produce or not? That is the subject of this tractate. Specific produce that this law applies to is identified, as well as various circumstances that determine what must be done.

Kilayim (Mixtures)

Can one graft different species of plants or trees together? This tractate contains an interesting discussion on the biblical prohibition against sewing diverse seeds, such as wheat and grapes, within certain proximity of each other. Crossbreeding of animals (or yoking them) is also included, as is another unusual law, called Shatnez that prohibits a sewn or woven mixture of wool and linen.

Shevi'it (Seventh or Sabbatical Year Observance)

This tract discusses the Biblical mandate requiring farmlands in Israel to lie fallow every seventh year. There are two major prohibitions related to sowing seed and harvesting grain and fruits. The laws also cover the releasing of debts (*Shmittat Kesafim*), and a related rabbinical enactment that allows a creditor to collect his debt after the sabbatical year.

> **Talmud Trivia**
>
> Many Israeli farmers continue to practice the laws of Shevi'it to this day.

Terumot (Contributing a Portion of One's Harvest to the Priest)

Terumah, meaning to "lift up" or "gift," was a percentage or portion of one's harvest given to the Cohanim (Priests) by the Levites and Israelites. The laws contained in this tract discuss how these gifts were to be apportioned, what happened if they became ritually impure, as well as what remedy was to be followed if Terumah inadvertently becomes mixed with undedicated produce.

Ma'aserot (Tithes)

The first tithe, called Maaser Rishon, was given to the Levites. They were then required to take a tenth of this tithe and give it to the Cohain. Questions such as at what point is one obligated in Maaser and if portions are allowed to be eaten before the separation takes place are discussed in this tractate.

Maaser Sheni (The Secondary Tithe)

This tractate details the second tithe that was required from all nonpriestly harvested produce. It was to be eaten in the holiness of Jerusalem or redeemed in coins and the money spent on produce in Jerusalem. The laws of Neta Revai, or Plantings of Fourth year, are also discussed.

Challah (Flour Dough)

When one separated bread, it was required that a portion be given to the priests. How much dough should be separated, and exactly how one is to separate it is discussed in this tractate.

Orlah ("Uncircumcised" Fruits)

Eating or deriving benefit from the fruit of most trees within the first three years of their planting was prohibited in ancient Israel. This tractate discusses exactly which trees fall under this prohibition, and what to do if fruit from these trees is combined or gets mixed in with fruit from permitted trees. General principles of the Laws of Nullification, known as *bittul*, are also discussed.

Bikkurim (First Fruits)

Each landowner was required to bring of the very first ripening of certain species of fruit to the Temple in Jerusalem. There is a Biblically mandated procedure to follow that is discussed in detail in the three chapters of this tractate.

The Least You Need to Know

- Seder Zeraim (Seeds) contains many tractates without Talmudic commentary in the Talmud most often used. The mishna tracts deal mostly with agricultural laws, almost all of which are no longer applicable in today's world.

◆ Brachot (Blessings) is the longest tractate in words and repository of virtually all discussions and records of Jewish prayer and recital of blessings.

◆ The Talmud teaches that blessings should be offered at all times.

◆ Seder Zeraim contains the Amidah, which is the central prayer in Jewish prayer services.

◆ Although blessings should be offered frequently, the concept of thanking and praising God is not meant to be taken lightly, or treated in a trivial manner.

Chapter 6

All About Appointed Times

In This Chapter

- ◆ Welcome to the Sabbath
- ◆ The Day of Atonement
- ◆ The Jewish New Year

The name of the second order of the Talmud, Seder Moed, is taken directly from the Bible itself; "God spoke to Moses saying, "Speak to the Children of Israel and say to them: 'God's *appointed festivals* that you are to designate as holy gatherings …" These appointed festivals, or times, are then listed in the passages that follow. (Leviticus 23:1–44) The implication is that God is "inviting" His people to celebrate these days that commemorate special events in the calendar.

This section of the Talmud explains how to observe these special days, or "appointed times" in order to capture their spiritual qualities.

The Tractates of Seder Moed

Seder Moed is comprised of 11 tractates:

- Shabbos—Laws pertaining to observing the Sabbath

- Eruvin—Laws concerning carrying items outside of one's house on the Sabbath

- Pesachim—The laws of Passover observance

- Yoma—The laws of Yom Kippur

- Sukkot—The laws of the festival of Tabernacles (Sukkot)

- Beitza—General laws regarding festivals

> **Talmud Trivia**
>
> Jews who follow Daf Yomi and study a folio of Talmud a day also study tractate Shekalim—laws concerning the annual contribution to the Temple—which is found in order Moed in the Jerusalem Talmud, but not in the Babylonian Talmud.

- Rosh Hashana—The laws of the Jewish New Year

- Ta'anit—Laws concerning the fast days in the Jewish calendar

- Megilla—Laws regarding the festival of Purim

- Moed Katan—Laws of the intermediate days of both Sukkot and Pesach

- Chagigah—Laws concerning sacrificial offerings during Passover and Sukkot

All About the Sabbath

For the Jewish people, the Sabbath is more than a day of rest. It's a time of enjoyment and of reconnecting with God, family, and friends, of reflecting on the blessings of the week that is past and of looking forward to those that may come in the week ahead.

To derive the fullest enjoyment out of this special weekly break, there is a right way and a wrong way to go about observing it. Tractate Shabbos details the how and the why behind this most important weekly holiday.

Shabbos contains 24 chapters primarily devoted to what constitutes the Biblical definition of "labor," that is proscribed on this holy day. Very early in the Torah we learn, "Thus the heaven and earth were finished, and all their array. And on the seventh day

God completed His 'work' which He had done, and he abstained from all His work which He had done." (Genesis 2:1–2)

In the Ten Commandments, the Bible instructs, "but the seventh day is a Shabbat unto HaShem thy God, in it thou shall not do any manner of *Melachah*, thou, nor thy son, nor thy daughter, nor thy man-servant, nor thy maid-servant, nor thy cattle, nor thy stranger that is within thy gates." (Exodus 20:11)

> **Talmud Tutor**
>
> **Melachah**, which means creative work in Hebrew, refers to work that is creative or that exercises control or dominion over one's environment. The best example of melachah is the work of creating the universe, which God ceased from on the seventh day.

The Meaning of Work

As it's stated in the Bible, on the seventh day, God rested. The seventh day of every week is meant to be a day of rest for God's people as well. But rest can mean many things, and different things to different people. The ambiguities in these meanings are what the Talmud addresses in the tractate Shabbat.

The Bible doesn't prohibit work in the classic sense of the word. But it does prohibit melachah, which conventionally translates as work but which, as previously mentioned, does not mean precisely the same thing as the English word. Confused? If so, know that you're in good company. The distinction between work and melachah can be difficult to grasp, and it really isn't important to do so unless you're going to study the Talmud, or if you're an observant Jew.

> **Talmud Tidbits**
>
> The word melachah may be related to "*malach*" (angel). Jewish mysticism depicts angels as "creative beings," each with its unique role and task. The quintessential example of melachah is the work of creating the universe, which God ceased from on the seventh day. Hence God's work, per se, had nothing to do with great physical effort. He simply "spoke," and it was done. By extension, we can envision a malach, with its ethereal motion, going about its creative talents, as well.

The word melachah is rarely used in scripture outside of the context of Shabbat and holiday restrictions. The only other repeated use of the word is in the discussion of the building of the tabernacle sanctuary by the Israelites in the wilderness. As such, it's clear that God wishes the construction of this worldly sanctuary to accommodate his presence on Earth, but he also still wishes for the Sabbath to be revered. The specific labors that are mentioned in this tract as ones to be avoided are those directly related to the building of the tabernacle. The entire tractate discusses the application of these concepts, and special rabbinical "fences" that are enacted to preserve the Biblical laws.

The entire tractate contains detailed descriptions of these 39 Melachot:

Sowing	Separating two threads
Plowing	Tying
Reaping	Untying
Binding sheaves	Sewing two stitches
Threshing	Tearing
Winnowing	Trapping
Selecting	Slaughtering
Grinding	Flaying
Sifting	Salting meat
Kneading	Curing hide
Baking	Scraping hide
Shearing wool	Cutting hide up
Washing wool	Writing two letters
Beating wool	Erasing two letters
Dyeing wool	Building
Spinning	Demolishing
Weaving	Extinguishing a fire
Setting up a loom	Kindling a fire
Weaving two threads	Striking final hammer blow

Taking an object from the private domain to the public, or transporting an object in the public domain

All of these tasks are prohibited, as well as any task that operates by the same principle or has the same purpose.

In addition, the rabbis prohibited coming into contact with any implement that could be used for one of the above purposes (for example, one may not move a hammer or a pencil), traveling, buying and selling, and other weekday tasks that would interfere with the spirit of Shabbat.

Some question the applicability of these categories of "labor" to contemporary society. They have a hard time seeing the relevancy to implications of modern living that include the light bulb, microwave oven, and the automobile, for example.

Let's take the issue of the use of an automobile on Shabbat. It doesn't take much labor to drive a car, for the most part. However, the principle of creative manipulation of physical resources is universal. Most cars are powered by an internal combustion engine, which operates by burning fossil fuels, gasoline, and oil.

This constitutes a clear violation of the Biblical prohibition against kindling a fire (one of the last items on the previous list). In addition, the movement of the car would constitute transporting an object in the public domain, another violation of a prohibition. And, in all likelihood the car would be used to travel a distance greater than that permitted by rabbinical prohibitions. For these reasons, and more, the use of an automobile, or any similar mechanical contraption, on Shabbat is clearly not permitted. The light bulb, which completes an electric circuit when turned on, poses similar difficulties, although virtually no measurable exertion in needed to switch it on.

As with all of the commandments, except for three: committing adultery, worshiping idols, or committing murder, these 39 Shabbat restrictions, and their derivatives, can be violated if necessary to save or preserve life. Almost an entire chapter in this tractate is devoted to various extenuating circumstances where these restrictions are suspended.

Preparing for the Sabbath

The tractate Shabbat also describes the preparations that a Jewish household should make to welcome the Sabbath, which holds a very special place in the hearts of the Jewish people. Everything must be in order to properly greet this day, which is welcomed as one would a very honored guest.

Several pages in this tractate extol the virtue of eating three meals on Shabbat (symbolic of the manna that fell in the wilderness) as they can protect a person from many misfortunes. The

> **Talmud Trivia**
>
> In Jewish homes, the Sabbath is sometimes referred to as the Shabbat "Queen." In fact, the Talmud mentions certain sages who would exit the house of worship during a certain point in Friday evening services to symbolically greet this important "dignitary."

tractate also speaks of special healing remedies and even amulets that can be worn to protect from negative forces. For instance, women going out on the Shabbat were allowed, as the rabbis teach, to carry with them a certain stone believed to counteract spontaneous miscarriages.

Public and Private Spaces

The tractate Eruvin details one of the 39 prohibited Sabbath melachot—carrying an object from a private domain to a public domain. While the Torah permits unrestricted carrying of objects in the private domain, one can only carry objects a distance of about six to eight feet in a public domain.

> **Talmud Tidbits**
>
> The laws of the eruv are still followed in many Jewish communities. Private spaces are created based on the Talmudic principles of enclosure, using such mechanisms as fences, overhead wires, bridges, buildings, and other physical structures to indicate boundaries.

The definition of private and public spaces is essential to knowing where objects can be carried on the Sabbath. Private spaces can be as small as a small home, but can also extend to an entire community. The Talmud defines what constitutes an enclosure, and describes how to make an entire area into a private domain to allow unlimited carrying.

Free at Last, Free at Last

The festival of Passover, or *Pesach*, commemorates the exodus of the Jews from Egypt and the birth of the Jews as a nation, led by Moses, more than 3,000 years ago. It marks both the Israelites' physical liberation from bondage and the foundation of their spiritual freedom.

> **Talmud Tutor**
>
> **Pesach** means "to pass over" in Hebrew. **Matzah** are specially prepared, unleavened flatbreads eaten in observance of Passover.

The most significant observances associated with Pesach, and covered in the tractate, are the removal of all leavened, or risen, baked products from the home, and the eating of specially prepared, unleavened flatbread called matzah.

As discussed in Chapter 2, the Jews left Egypt in haste when Pharaoh finally gave his consent for them to leave. Because of this, they didn't have enough time to prepare their bread for their journey. So they took the unrisen dough and fled.

To commemorate this event, Jews annually reenact the exodus from Egypt in the seder ceremony, which is performed on the first two nights of the Passover festival (in Israel, only on the first night). As you now know, seder means order, and this ceremony is so named because of the step-by-step order of what is recited and performed throughout the evening, which includes:

- Recounting the history of the Jews leading up to the time of their bondage, starting with the forefather Abraham and his discovery of monotheism, through the initial descent of the children of Jacob to Egypt, the trials and tribulations of the resulting bondage, and the plagues and the other great miracles that God performed upon the exodus of His people.

- Giving praise to God

- Singing traditional Pesach songs

Also included is a festive meal that includes a number of symbolic foods in addition to the matzoh, again in memory of the exodus from Egypt, including:

- Bitter herbs, (often Romaine lettuce or horseradish), to symbolize the tears shed by the Jewish slaves in Egypt.

- Four cups of wine at specific points during the meal to symbolize freedom.

- The shank bone of a lamb, which is placed on the table as a reminder of the Passover offering.

- A mixture of dates, nuts, cinnamon, and wine (charoset), which symbolizes the mortar used by the Israelite slaves to build the pyramids.

- A hardboiled egg to symbolize the festival offering that was brought to the Temple in Jerusalem.

It is also traditional to recline rather than sit up straight when eating the festive meal.

Yom Kippur—The Day of Atonement

The tractate name dealing with the subject of the holiest day on the Jewish calendar is Yoma (Aramaic for "day"). It opens with information regarding the specific preparations of the High Priest for this holiday, which include:

- Special review of the services he would perform in the Temple

- Avoidance of ritual impurity

- Ablutions and clothing changes

- ◆ Actual services performed seven days before the Day of Atonement

- ◆ Participating in a lottery to determine which animals would be used for sacrificial purposes on the holiday

A description of the vessels that were constructed and utilized in the tabernacle and Temple are also covered in this tractate, as well as a discussion on the present location of the Ark of the Covenant.

Talmud Tidbits _____

The tabernacle was a portable tent that the Israelites used for worship when they fled Egypt. It contained the altar for the daily and seasonal sacrifices, an elaborate candelabra (menorah) of solid gold, and numerous other vessels used during worship services. The tabernacle had an inner chamber called the Holy of Holies that housed the magnificent Ark of the Covenant, which contained, among other sacred items, the tablets of the Ten Commandments brought down by Moses at Sinai. When the first Temple was built in Jerusalem, the Ark of the Covenant was placed inside, and the rests of the tabernacle was buried beneath in an underground vault.

Here are other details of Yom Kippur observance covered by this tractate that have relevance today:

- ◆ The length of time of observance—from dusk to dusk, or just before sunset on the first evening until three medium-sized stars can be seen in the night sky on the next.

- ◆ One is only to beg forgiveness for sins between man and God. Sins against people require the offender to ask for forgiveness from the offended party in addition to divine forgiveness.

- ◆ Eating heartily on the day before Yom Kippur. The Talmud teaches that one who feasts the day before is reckoned as fasting two days.

- ◆ Certain prohibitions, such as refraining from eating and drinking, washing (except direct cleansing of dirt), anointing with creams, lotions, etc.; wearing leather or leather-covered shoes. Marital relations are also prohibited.

- ◆ Sounding a shofar (ram's horn) after evening service, indicating the end of the fast and the end of Yom Kippur for another year.

At all times, actions considered necessary to prevent loss of life and limb overrides all Yom Kippur prohibitions. This would include such things as breaking one's fast, extinguishing a fire to save the inhabitants of a building, or driving someone who is seriously ill to the hospital.

Let's Celebrate—The Feast of Booths

The Biblical holiday that follows Yom Kippur is Succot, often translated as the Feast of Booths (Leviticus 23:42). Following the "Days of Awe" that just transpired, the Talmud views this holiday as a time of reconciliation with God, and cause for expressing joy. In this tractate is contained information on what is to be done in the succah, how should one dwell there, and who is exempted from dwelling in the succah.

There are two distinct aspects to the holiday of Succot, represented by two commandments in the Torah:

> "On the fifteenth of the seventh month, when you have gathered in the fruit of the land, you shall keep a festival for God seven days … And you shall take for yourselves on the first day the fruit of a "beautiful" tree, branches of palm trees, the boughs of thick-leaved trees, and willows of the brook, and you shall rejoice before your God seven days. You shall sit in booths [*succot*] seven days, … in order to inform all generations that in succot the Jews dwelled when I liberated them from Egypt." (Leviticus 23: 39-43)

> **Talmud Trivia**
>
> Of all the "appointed days" designated by the Bible as holy, Succot is the only one in which the phrase, "And you shall rejoice in your Festival," is mentioned.

A modern Succah.

(Source: Holly Mendel and Steve Herman Sukkot.com)

Why were the Jews commanded to dwell in booths? The Talmud records two opinions. Rabbi Eliezer likened God's protection of the Jews, described by the Biblical term "Succah," to a cloud of glory. Rabbi Akiva taught that when the Jews were liberated from Egypt they lived in actual booths that protected them from the elements.

Either way, one demonstrates ultimate trust in his creator when he takes leave of the creature comforts of home, and roughs it outdoors.

Let's Get Talmudic

The tractate basically teaches that a succah must have at least three walls covered with a material that will not blow away in a nominal wind. The succah roof must be made of material referred to as se'chach (literally, covering). To fulfill the commandment, se'chach must be something that grew from the ground and is severed from it, such as tree branches, corn stalks, bamboo reeds, sticks, or even two-by-fours. A canvas covering, either tied or nailed down, is acceptable and quite common in the United States. A succah may be any size, so long as it is large enough for one to fit most of the body and a table.

Toward the end of tractate Succot are several pages on the subject of rejoicing during the holiday. They specifically pertain to special events that took place on the Temple Mount associated with the wine and water libations on the altar.

Rosh Hoshana—The Head of the Year

Many Jews in America acknowledge two New Years, one on January 1, and one in the fall (specifically, on the first and second of Tishrei on the Hebrew calendar). Because the Hebrew calendar is based on a Lunar calendar, these dates change somewhat, but they fall in September and sometimes in October.

Rosh Hashanah literally means, "Head of the Year." Unlike its secular counterpart, it's not celebrated with a wild party. Instead, the Jewish New Year is a solemn time of introspection, evaluation, and reflection. On Rosh Hashanah, Jews look inside their souls, evaluate their actions of the past year, and reflect on where they would like to be a year from now.

The Bible specifically commands the Jewish people to proclaim this day in a very special way:

> "In the seventh month, on the first of the month, there shall be a rest day for you, a remembrance with 'Teruah' (shofar) blasts as a holy convocation." (Leviticus 23:24)

A major discussion as to why the seventh month happens to be the "Head of the Year" is taken up in the Tractate as well. One explanation is that although Nisan (the month of Passover) is acknowledged in the Torah as the first of all the months for it commemorates the Israelites leaving Egypt and being formed into a nation, Tishrei is significant because it is the month in which the Creation of man took place.

Furthermore, on this anniversary, we are taught that God, "sits in judgment" over mankind and it behooves us to recognize this event with a special observance.

Talmud Trivia

The term Rosh Hoshana is only mentioned once in Scripture (Book of Ezekiel), and is simply a description of the word implied (lit. Head of the Year). In the Talmud, "Rosh Hashanah" appears first in the Mishnah *(Rosh Hashanah* l:l), where we are told that there are actually four "Rosh Hashanahs" or "new year" days. One of these, the first of the month of Tishrei, was designated for calculating the years of foreign kings and the sabbatical and Jubilee years, and for planting trees and vegetables. We are also told (*Rosh Hashanah* 1:2) that on this day, "… all who come into the world pass before God like sheep." The Mishnah understands this metaphor to indicate that on this day, all human beings pass before God in judgment.

A Ram's Horn Coronation

The blowing of the shofar is the only specific commandment for Rosh Hashanah. Just as trumpeters announced the presence of their mortal king, the shofar is used by Jews to proclaim the coronation of the King of Kings.

The shofar has become the most well-known symbol of Rosh Hashanah, and is one of the earliest instruments used in Jewish music. Usually made from a ram's horn, a shofar can also be made from the horns of other animals, including those of a goat or sheep. It hasn't changed much in over 5,000 years. Many Jewish educators around the month of September can be found instructing their young charges in the actual making of a shofar, fit for blowing on Rosh Hoshanah, according to Talmudic instructions.

In Biblical times the shofar was blown to announce an important event, such as the alarm of war. At the revelation on Mt. Sinai, the Torah states that there were to be long shofar blasts. Rashi comments that the shofar blown at Mt. Sinai was the same shofar that came from the head of the ram that was offered in Isaac's place. Additionally, it was blown on Yom Kippur of the Jubilee (fiftieth) Year to proclaim freedom for all servants and the return of ancestral lands to their rightful tribal owners. The coming of the End of Days will be signaled by a loud, long shofar blast. (Isaiah 27:13)

Let's Get Talmudic

Rabbi Abahu asked, "Why do we only blow on the *Shofar* of a ram?" Answered The Holy One Blessed Be He, "Blow for Me on a ram's *Shofar*, and on account of it I will remember the binding of Issac (and the ram that was sacrificed in his place). I furthermore will consider it as if you bound yourselves up before me like Isaac." (Tractate Rosh Hashanah 16a)

Finally, this tract discusses the nature of the shofar blast. Is it a series of three short sounds, or is it instead a broken staccato sound, or is it perhaps both? The Talmud equates these sounds with types of crying. Is the "cry" of the shofar to be a series of short sighs or a staccato of wails? As a unifying reconciliation of these opinions, the Talmud concludes that both approaches should be used. And that is what traditional Jews do today. The tractate contains a number of other discussions, including:

- The way in which the Jewish months and the holidays that depend upon them were determined.

- How God views the world

- The concept of an afterlife, or world to come

Also presented are the sage's thoughts on the appropriate steps toward repentance, and how God judges the world on this day.

Let's Get Talmudic

The Bible only mentions one day of Rosh Hoshanah. However, Jews celebrate two days. Here's why: Before the exile from Israel, the Jewish people did not have a fixed calendar as they do today. Instead, lawmakers in Jerusalem determined the calendar on a month-to-month basis. They did this on the first day of every month, based on witnesses testifying that they had seen the new moon. Because of this, people living outside of Israel (and even some who lived in Israel) often didn't have enough time to find out the exact date in time for the festivals. The "two-day festival" was established in Yavneh to correct this situation.

One interesting concept found in the Zohar teaches a deeper reason behind the two-day observance of Rosh Hoshanah. The first day is referred to as "the elevated judgment," and the second day is called "the reduced judgment." This is explained as follows; At one time it was sufficient for people to endure one "trip to court," so to speak. Once the Temple was destroyed, however, our merits were diminished. Now, the individual is judged on the first day based on his/her merits, as he/she stands alone. It is tougher to be so exposed and go it alone. However, God in His infinite wisdom allows us a "second chance," and judges us based on how we are interrelated to others and how others need and rely on us. It's easier to be seen in that light and for this reason the sages proclaimed "Do not separate yourself from the congregation." (Chapter 1 of Pirkei Avot, or Ethics of the Fathers)

Remaining Tractates

Several smaller tractates round out the Order of Moed and cover issues related to other "Appointed Times," of significance, including rabbinical fast days and mourning.

Shekalim

Shekalim contains laws concerning every Jew's annual contribution to the temple, including the annual half-shekel head tax paid to the Holy Temple in Jerusalem.

Beitza

This tractate deals with general laws of festivals. It also contains in-depth discussions concerning the ramifications of observing two days instead of one day of the festival as holy.

Ta'anit

This tractate contains laws concerning the days of fasting ordained by the prophets in the Jewish calendar, the procedures to follow when there isn't any rain, and special services that are conducted to encourage priests and supplicate God to accept the public offerings.

Megilla

Megilla, the final tractate in Appointed Days, discusses various laws surrounding the festival of Purim.

Moed Katan

This name of this tractate translates to "minor days of festival." It discusses how the intermediate days of the holidays of Succot and Passover should be celebrated (there is a distinction between the observances and restrictions of the first and last days of these holidays, and the intermediate five days). Also here is a chapter devoted to the laws of mourning, as well as several anecdotes about souls "crossing over" and communicating with the living.

Chagigah

Tractate Chagigah focuses on the festival pilgrimages, when Jews traveled to celebrate Pesach (Passover), Shavuoth, and Succot in Jerusalem and brought sacrificial offerings. One main theme of tractate Chagigah covers Jews visiting the Holy Temple "to see, and to be seen." Not only would they observe the physical structure of the Building, but became inspired by gaining deeper insights through the services.

The Least You Need to Know

♦ The tractate Shabbat contains detailed discussions of the laws pertaining to the observance of the Sabbath.

♦ Observance of the Sabbath is more than simple dos and don'ts. It's a day of enjoyment and reconnecting with God, family, and friends.

♦ Unlike the secular New Year, Rosh Hashanah, the Jewish New Year, is a time for reflecting on one's relationship with God.

♦ The tractate Pesachim is devoted to Passover, the most observed Jewish holiday, which commemorates the exodus of the Jewish people from bondage in Egypt and their becoming a nation.

♦ Minor tractates in Seder Moed discuss other important appointed times such as Succot, public fast days, Purim, and the laws of mourning.

All About the Women

In This Chapter

- Ensuring women's rights
- Biblical prenuptial agreements
- The Jewish bill of divorce
- The adultery test

Before the Jewish people received the Torah on Mt. Sinai, there was no known legislation that protected a woman's rights. The Israelites, through divine guidance, were among the first people to delineate what rights a woman had, and to commit such legislation to writing.

Nashim (Women), the third order of the Talmud, contains these laws as well as many others having to do with oaths and agreements. It has been, and continues to be, one of the most studied sections of the Talmud.

The Rights of Ancient Women

Ancient societies were based on patriarchal rule, which mean that men, for the most part, called the shots (there were some notable exceptions, especially in ancient Egypt). In many cultures, women were treated as little more than property—tradable for cattle, money, even bodily pleasures, if one were so inclined. What's more, if there were laws or regulations pertaining to women, they were rarely codified. Local customs and mores, rather than the law of the land, governed what a woman's rights were, and how she would be treated.

As mentioned, things were somewhat different for Jewish women. Traditionally, women and men were seen as equals, but with different responsibilities and obligations. Thanks to God's revelations to Moses at Mt. Sinai, the Jews even had laws in place that governed the intricacies of marriage and divorce, as well as laws that specify what is to happen to a woman suspected of adultery.

Seder Nashim contains seven tractates:

♦ Yevamoth, or the laws of Levirate marriage. These regulations pertain to the practice that called for a childless widow to marry her deceased husband's brother to ensure that her husband's name would not die out.

♦ Kethubboth, which specifies the rights and duties of husband and wife, as well as how property is divided in the event of death or divorce

♦ Nedarim, or the making and annulment of vows

♦ Nazir, which details the vow requirements of a Nazirite

♦ Sotah, which details what happens to a woman suspected of adultery

♦ Gittin, which are the laws of divorce and the annulment of marriage

♦ Kiddushin, or the laws of marital status

Of the tracts in Nashim, Kethubboth, Nedarim, Gittin, and Kiddushin are the ones that garner the most attention. As you'll soon see, the wisdom and laws they contain are still relevant in today's world.

Talmud Tidbits

There is an interesting logic to how the tracts in Nashim are arranged. They begin with one that contains compulsory laws pertaining to a specific type of marriage, then move to betrothals, two tracts on vows, and then two tracts that deal with how marriages break up. Kiddushin, which also pertains to marital laws, comes last in reflection of the scriptural passage to which it pertains—"And he shall write her a bill of divorcement and give it in her hand and send her out of his house, And when she is departed out of his house, she may go and become another man's wife." (Deuteronomy 24:1-2)

Kethubboth—Spelling Things Out Before the Wedding

In the tract Kethubboth can be found one of the Talmud's most progressive legislations—the ketubah, or pre-nuptial contract. It is also considered to be one of the most important. Judaism regards the family as the cornerstone of the Jewish people. For this reason, marriage tops the list of priorities in the lives of both Jewish men and women. It is considered a natural state for Jewish people, and necessary for personal fulfillment.

The Importance of Marriage

According to Jewish thought, marriage is considered one of life's greatest treasures. What's more, it's believed that the relationship that most closely parallels the relationship between man and God is the marital union between a man and a woman. The Talmud teaches that if the Divine Presence resides in a home, its most likely location is the bedroom.

Let's Get Talmudic

Being single is greatly discouraged and, in fact, shunned in Talmudic tradition, as illustrated by the following Talmudic excerpts:

"A wifeless man exists without joy, without blessing or boon." (Yevamoth 62b)

"It is better to live one's life with a spouse than alone." (Yevamoth 118b)

"Whoever finds a wife finds great good and finds favor with G-d." (Yevamoth 63b)

"If a man and wife are worthy, the Divine Presence is with them." (Sotah 17a)

"A man cannot live without a woman, a woman cannot live without a man, and the two of them cannot live without the presence of God." (Berachot 9:1)

How central is the institution of marriage as part of the divine plan? It isn't necessary to search long for the answer. The first time God speaks to Adam in the Bible, he says, "It is not good that Man should be alone; I will make a helpmate for him." (Genesis 2:18)

Talmud Trivia

In the Jewish tradition, the use of the expression "helpmate" in describing a woman has been taken to mean that the purpose of a husband and wife is to help each other reach a positive physical and spiritual state, and not that a woman is subordinate to her husband within a marital union. In fact, a husband is commanded to love his wife as himself and honor her more than himself. (Sota 47a) Furthermore, a husband who fulfills this obligation will merit a household of peace. (Yevamoth 62b)

Defining Marital Responsibilities

The ketubah ensures that a husband does all that he is supposed to do in his marriage. In fact, it is very one sided, as it mainly outlines the responsibilities of a man toward his wife and not vice versa. Typically written in Aramaic, it protects the wife financially, emotionally, physically, and socially should her husband abandon her. It is divided into two sections:

◆ The first section outlines the obligations that a husband must fulfill in marriage—to honor his wife, to provide the necessities in life, such as food, clothing, adornments, and shelter, and to fulfill his wife's sexual needs, as specified in the Bible.

◆ The second section specifies that the husband will pay his wife a particular sum of money in the event of death or divorce. In most cases it even specifies from which properties this can be appropriated.

The ketubah also makes divorce more difficult in that it requires the payment of a "divorce penalty" that involves costly monetary obligations. This penalty consists of an amount determined at the time that the ketubah was signed, as well as whatever capital and personal possessions the wife brings to her husband at the time of marriage, and the amount of money that her family spends for the dowry and trousseau.

The ketubah is considered to be so important that a husband and wife are forbidden to live together without the wife (or her agent) having it in her possession.

The following is an example of a ketubah:

On the ____ day of the week on the ____ day of the (Hebrew) month of ____ in the year ____ according to the counting from the Creation of the World, the counting that we are keeping in (name of place). (We testify) How the groom ____ the son of ____ from the family of ____ said to this virgin (or woman) ____ the daughter of ____ of the family of ____, "Be my wife according to the laws of Moses and Israel, and I will cherish, honor, support and maintain you in accordance with the custom of Jewish husbands who cherish, honor, support and maintain their wives faithfully. And I here present you with the marriage gift of wives, two hundred silver zuzim, which belongs to you, according to the Law of Moses and Israel, and I will also give you your food, clothing and necessities, and live with you as husband and wife according to the universal custom." And the virgin (woman) ____ the daughter of ____ consented and became his wife. The trousseau that she brought to him from her father's house, in silver, gold, valuables, clothing, furniture and bedclothes, all this ____ the son of ____, said bridegroom, accepted in the sum of one hundred silver zuzim, and ____ the son of _____, the bridegroom, agreed to increase this amount from his own property with the sum of one hundred silver zuzim, making in all two hundred silver zuzim.

And thus said, the bridegroom, _____ the son of _____ : "The responsibility of this marriage contract, of this trousseau, and of this additional sum, I take upon myself and my heirs after me, so that they shall be paid from the best part of my property and possessions that I have beneath the whole heaven, that which I now possess or that which I may hereafter acquire. All my property, real and personal, even the shirt from my back, shall be mortgaged to secure the payment of this marriage contract, of this trousseau and the addition made to it, during my lifetime and after my death, from the present day and forever." _____ the son of _____, the bridegroom, has taken upon himself the responsibility of this marriage contract, of the trousseau and of the addition made to it, according to the restrictive usages of all marriage contracts and the adjoins to them made for the daughters of Israel, according to the institutions of our sages of blessed memory. It is not to be regarded as a mere forfeiture without consideration or as a mere formula of a document.

We have followed the legal formality of delivery and acceptance (kinyan) between _____ the son of _____, the bridegroom, and _____ the daughter of _____, the woman, and we have used a garment legally fit for the purpose, to strengthen everything that is said above,

AND ALL IS VALID AND BINDING.
Attested to: _____—Witness
Attested to: _____—Witness

Get Going!

What happens if a marriage should sour? Of course, all channels should be explored, including marriage counseling, to see if the relationship can be salvaged and even flourish. But as much as Judaism encourages the institution of marriage, it also accepts the fact that being mired in a bad marriage can be worse than being alone. If the union is lost and can't be saved, it's probably time to get a *get*.

The tractate of Gittin contains the details on how and why a divorce is to be granted, including information on the legal document—the get—that makes it very clear that the marriage is over.

Talmud Tutor

The word **get**, according to the Vilna Gaon, is formed from the Hebrew letters gimmel and tet, which don't appear together in any other Hebrew word. It is thought that the uniting of these letters connotes separation. **Beit Din** means a duly qualified "religious court" of three rabbis who are specifically trained to rule on matters pertaining to divorce, conversion, monetary disputes and the like.

Generally, a man is to initiate the process when it is obvious that this marriage cannot endure. However, a woman can also approach the Jewish court—called the *Beit Din*—to pressure a recalcitrant husband who refuses a legitimate request for a divorce.

A get can be granted for the following reasons:

♦ If either side has demonstrated gross violation of their marital vows

♦ If the husband is abusive or refuses to honor the marital commitments generally spelled out in the ketubah

♦ There are irreconcilable differences

In these instances, the Torah not only allows the complete separation of the marriage by giving a get, but considers such an act a mitzvah.

The following is a basic translation of the Talmudic get:

"On the _____ day of the week, the _____ day of the month of _____ in the year _____ from the creation of the world according to the calendar reckoning we are accustomed to count here, in the city _____, which is located on the river _____, and situated near wells of water, I, _____, the son of _____, who today am present in the city _____, which is located on the river _____, and situated near wells of water, do willingly consent, being under no restraint, to release, to set free and put aside thee, my wife _____, daughter of _____, who art today in the city of _____, which is located on the river _____, and situated near wells of water, who has been my wife from before. Thus do I set free, release thee, and put thee aside, in order that thou may have permission and the authority over thy self to go and marry any man thou may desire. No person may hinder thee from this day onward, and thou are permitted to every man. This shall be for thee from me a bill of dismissal, a letter of release, and a document of freedom, in accordance with the law of Moses and Israel."

According to the Talmud, any lasting material can be used to write a get—ink, paint, tar, etc. A get can also be written on virtually anything, as long is it's not a living thing. Leaves, paper, even pottery shards are all grist for the get mill. Modern scribes typically stick to paper (sometimes parchment) and pen. A get can also be written in any language. Like the ketubah, two people must witness it. The get takes effect when the wife or her agent accepts it from her husband in the presence of these two witnesses.

Even today, in Jewish law a marriage is not considered dissolved until a get is written and accepted by both husband and wife. In fact, most rabbis in the United States, and all rabbis in Israel won't conduct wedding ceremonies for Jews wishing to remarry unless gets were issued to end the previous unions. The get does not replace the civil proceedings that are also necessary to legally end a marriage. Instead, it is considered a religious divorce, done in accordance with Jewish law.

> **Talmud Trivia**
>
> Those who write gets must first go through a strict course of study, and must have a firm understanding of the underlying laws. Making errors in a get can render it invalid, and could prevent the parties involved from remarrying. Rabbis typically draw up these documents, but not all ordained rabbis know how to do it.

Gets are also important when it comes to having children. Technically, if a woman does not have her previous marriage terminated with a get, and then has children with her new husband, these children may be considered illegitimate.

Kiddushin

Traditionally, Jewish marriages had two stages—kiddushin, or betrothal, and nisu'in, the marriage itself. The tractate of Kiddushin discusses this first stage, and details what must happen before moving to the second.

The tractate details three ways in which a man may "take" a wife in marriage, as it states in the Torah; "If a man takes a wife and comes to her ..." (Deuteronomy 22:13) They are:

- ◆ Giving something of value
- ◆ Offering a contract where the groom writes "Behold you are betrothed to me with this ring." (not done today)
- ◆ Having intercourse

In ancient times, only one of these conditions was necessary to create a binding marriage. Then, as now, when a woman accepted them, it indicated her willingness to marry and to be faithful to her husband.

In ancient times, kiddushin and nisu'in were accomplished in two separate stages, often separated by as much as a year as both parties prepared themselves for marriage. Today, however, rituals signifying both are part of the wedding ceremony. In modern weddings, placing a ring on the bride's finger symbolizes kiddushin. Her acceptance of the gift assumes her acceptance of the other two conditions. The ketubah is also presented during the ceremony. (Any expression of intimacy, of course, waits until afterward.)

Let's Get Talmudic

For centuries the marriage ritual has been performed under what is called a "chuppah," or marital canopy. This word appears twice in scripture (Isaiah 4:5 and Joel 2:16) Its root is the word "chofeh," meaning to cover. It implies that the chuppah is an act of intimacy symbolizing the husband's intention to shield and protect her. According to Maimonides and others, this act is completed later, when the bride and groom enter a "heder yichud," or private room, where the husband secludes his bride from everyone else. This essentially accomplishes what consummating the relationship through intercourse would.

The nisu'in is then held under a chuppah, or wedding canopy, which signifies the couple's new home and the husband bringing his wife into it. During this part of the ceremony, the groom recites seven blessings, and he joins his wife in drinking wine from a common glass. The groom then smashes the glass in remembrance of the destruction of the Temple in Jerusalem.

Levirate Marriages, Nazirite Vows, and Adultery

The remaining four tracts in Nashim largely pertain to ancient traditions. For this reason, they're interesting to read but not relevant to today's world. Two—Nazir and Sotah—also offer interesting insights on the nature of evil and temptation.

The Laws of Levirate Marriage

The book of Leviticus in the Torah forbids marriage with a brother's widow as a general rule. However, Deuteronomy 25:5 states that such a marriage is required: "When brothers live together and one of them dies without a son, the widow of the deceased shall not marry anyone outside the family; but her husband's brother shall go to her and perform the duty of a brother-in-law by marrying her. The first-born son she bears shall continue the line of the deceased brother; that his name may not be blotted out from Israel."

According to Talmudic teachings, however, the Torah did not compel a woman to accept her brother-in-law in Levirate marriage unless she freely wanted. The tractate on Levirate marriage in Nashim addresses issues related to these unions.

Nazirite Vows

In ancient times, Nazirites were people who chose to live apart from others in order to obtain greater closeness to God. In the Bible, the institution is introduced in Numbers 6:2. In order to become a Nazirite, one had to agree to certain conditions, including not drinking wine or eating anything made from grapes, not cutting his or her hair, and not coming in contact with the dead, which would render the individual unclean.

While the tract Nazir contains laws that pertain to both men and women, as both genders could become Nazirites, it is included in Nashim as Nazirite oaths are also included among the laws of vows. Plus, if a woman should make a Nazirite vow, her husband could void it, as it would affect her relationship with him and any previous agreements she had entered into.

> **Talmud Trivia**
>
> By Talmudic times, Levirate marriage was considered objectionable. The main reason was lack of pure intent on behalf of the surviving brother, coupled with the general prohibition of marrying one's sister-in-law. (Yeb 39b and Bechorot 13a) Therefore men were encouraged to perform what was called "Chalitzah" and sever any connection. This is the practice today.

> **Talmud Trivia**
>
> Samson was a Nazirite. The uniqueness of his "oath," according to scripture, is that it was prophetically conveyed to his parents and thus he became a Nazirite upon birth

> **Let's Get Talmudic**
>
> The High Priest Shimon Hatzaddik once said, "I never ate of the offering of a Nazir except that of one man. He was handsome with beautiful eyes and hair locks. I asked him, why have you become a Nazir and destined to cut your nice hair? He said to me, 'I was a shepherd for my father in my hometown, and I once went to draw water from the spring. As I looked at my reflection, my evil inclination welled up in an effort to distract me and undermine my existence (one of the commentaries explains that he contemplated becoming a male prostitute). At that moment I was motivated to become a Nazir, and remove this object of temptation." Immediately, I (Shimon Hatzaddik) stood up and kissed him on his forehead and said to him "My son, there should be many more Jews like you who commit to a nazir period. It is those like you to whom the Torah refers in the verse 'A man who will make a nazir oath, for the sake of God.'" (Talmud Nedarim 9b)

Information contained in Nazir pertains to compulsory Naziriteship and being a Nazirite for life, and the differences between the two. The tract also goes into detail on whether vows in general that are expressed incorrectly can be considered binding, and what happens to a Nazirite who breaks his or her vows.

Standing the Test of Adultery

The tract Sotah, meaning "one who has strayed," defines the rules of procedure in determining whether a wife has been unfaithful or not. After her alleged transgressions are discovered, she is warned by her husband. If she doesn't heed her husband's warnings, or denies them, she is brought before a temple priest. Women who denied allegations of adultery were given the chance to take an "adultery test." This involved drinking a vile concoction of consecrated water flavored with dirt from the open area of the Temple and a root that gives it a bitter taste. A parchment with holy writings, including the ineffable Name of God is pulverized and added to the mixture. If she is innocent, when she drinks the water God will shower her and her family with fertility blessings. If she's guilty, the drink will rupture her stomach and kill her as well as her paramour. This procedure was only effective if the husband was innocent of any sexual improprieties.

The Least You Need to Know

- The Order of Nashim (Women) is one of the most studied sections of Talmud today.

- The ketubah, which specified the responsibilities of a husband to his wife, was the ancient equivalent of a prenuptial agreement.

- The tractate Kiddushin details how a man "takes" a woman in marriage.

- While marriage is preferable to being single, Judaism recognizes that being stuck in a bad marriage is worse than living alone, and allows the dissolution of a marriage through issuing a get.

Chapter 8

The Law of the Land

In This Chapter

- ◆ About oxen and holes
- ◆ The Three Gates
- ◆ The role of the Sanhedrin
- ◆ Ethics of the fathers

Property law, estate law, and laws that pertain to dealings between individuals are all grist for the mill in Seder Nezikin, the fourth of the six orders of the Talmud.

The basis for Seder Nezikin can be found in the last three of the Ten Commandments, which states that people shouldn't steal or kidnap, bear false witness against others, nor covet another's belongings.

While on the face of it these might seem like straightforward edicts, when you look a little closer it's clear that they're full of nuance and can be fairly open to interpretation. Seder Nezikin explains what these commandments mean and shows us how they apply to real life, both in antiquity and today.

Seder Nezikin is the largest of the Talmud's orders, which reflects the importance of the information it contains.

Living Under the Law

Nezikin deals with laws that have to do in some way with judgment or the carrying out of judgment. These laws are called *mishpotim*, the plural of the Hebrew word mishpot.

The same term, mishpotim, is used to describe the section of the Bible where most of these civil laws come from.

Nezikin is comprised of 10 tractates, and covers the following areas of law:

- Baba Kama (First Gate)—direct and indirect damages

- Baba Metzia (Middle Gate)—losses, loans, work, and wage contract

- Baba Batra (Final Gate)—real estate and property law, laws of inheritance

- Sanhedrin—various types of courts, criminal law, principles of faith

- Makot—Noncapital punishment, such as whippings

- Shevuot—oaths and their annulments

- Eduyot—a collection of testimonies on various legal issues

- Avoda Zarah—laws pertaining to idol worship

- Avot—Ethics and proper conduct. This is the famous "Pirkei Avot"—Ethics of the Fathers

- Horayot—Erroneous court rulings and their rectification

Talmud Tutor

In Hebrew, **mishpot** means judgment or justice.

Talmud Trivia

The information contained in The Three Gates originally was contained in one tractate that contained 30 chapters. Because it was so long, it was necessary to divide it into three separate tracts. No one knows for sure how these "gate" tractates got their names. One theory is that they allude to a Biblical passage where God commands Moses to establish "judges and offices in all your gates ..."

The main part of Nezikin is called The Three Gates, and is divided into three tractates. Each focuses on a different aspect or category of civil law. Although the names of the tractates don't tell us anything more about the information they contain, each opens with a few lines that describe the types of issues they deal with.

Baba Kamma—The First Gate

Baba Kamma, the first gate, contains the principles of Jewish civil law and discusses four basic causes of damage:

♦ Something that one owns, such as an ox that kicks or gores another

♦ Hazards placed on public property, such as a pit placed in the way of others

♦ People harming others

♦ Creating or failing to prevent potentially dangerous situations, such as starting a fire on one's own property that then spreads to another's

Now, some of this may not seem very relevant to this day and age. Most teachers today would answer that we learn principles and a form of logic even though the actual case law is somewhat archaic. But is it?

Some time ago, the *Australian Jewish News* reported that former Prime Minister Malcolm Fraser and his family were required to pay more than $400,000 in damages to a South Australian couple trampled by a Simmental bull during a cattle sale at the prime minister's property. On the day of the sale, the bull was brought into a fenced area and displayed before about 100 people. But when it sighted other bulls in a nearby corral, it made a beeline for them, scaling the fence and charging between two temporary grandstands nearby. In the process, it trampled the Tippets, breaking Mr. Tippet's leg and fracturing Mrs. Tippet's arm and ribs.

"In my view," said the judge who awarded the damages, "there was a risk of injury here which was plainly foreseeable. Such a risk was not far-fetched or fanciful."

Perhaps Fraser would have been better off had he studied Talmud. He would no doubt have discovered that the propensity of oxen to cause damage brings about requirements for care in their handling. He would have also known the requirements for proper fencing that would provide greater fortification when dealing with an ox capable of goring, which is one of the major principles discussed in Baba Kamma.

Problems with Pits

Just as the rabbis established the rules and regulations that came from the ox that gores, they developed a whole system of responsibilities and consequences related to open pits, which addresses hazards placed or created on public property. "When a man opens a pit, or digs a pit, and does not cover it, and an ox or an ass falls into it, the one responsible for the pit must make restitution; he shall pay the price to the owner, but he shall keep the carcass. (Exodus 21:33)

Damages Inflicted by Individuals

On page 26a in Baba Kamma, we learn another fascinating detail of just how far-reaching liability can be for damages inflicted by an individual. Let's say you're staying at a Motel Six, and you've just had a great night's sleep. Not only did they "leave the light on" for you, they placed the lamp right there on your nightstand. Much to your horror, you notice that it is now lying on the floor, shattered to smithereens. The only reasonable suspect: you! You must have knocked it over while you were snoring the night away, oblivious to the fact that your rather substantial forearm swept it right off the stand! According to the Talmud, you are responsible, for you should have considered the possibility that your nocturnal habits could lead to such an occurrence.

Damages Related to Direct Bodily Injury

In a later chapter, Baba Kamma discusses the specific five types of damages a person is liable for in the event he caused direct bodily injury to his fellow. These are based on a Biblical passage (Exodus 21:18–19), which reads, "If men shall quarrel and one strikes his fellow with a stone or a fist, and he does not die but becomes bedridden. If he then gets up and goes outside under his own strength, the one who struck is absolved. Only for his lost wages should he pay and he shall provide healing."

The damages detailed in this part of Baba Kamma include:

- Suffering permanent damage affecting one's vocation
- Pain and suffering
- Embarrassment (either for the act or later consequences)
- Healing
- Job loss compensation

Talmud Tutor

A **mitzvah** is a duty, obligation, or act of kindness carried out in keeping with the commandments of Jewish religious law.

Stolen Items

The second half of Baba Kamma continues with cases involving stolen items. There are rulings about things like what happens when there is a change in the name to the item that alters its identity, or if it becomes useless for its original purpose. Also considered are the cases of skilled craftsmen who err in the work entrusted to them, and whether a *mitzvah* can be fulfilled when returning a stolen object by merely placing it on the victim's property.

Let's Get Talmudic

Baba Kamma also contains the famous line, "But if there shall be a fatality, then you should award a life for a life, an eye for an eye, a tooth for a tooth, a hand for a hand." The Talmud engages in a lively debate to prove conclusively that the intention of the Torah, as promulgated from Moses at Mt. Sinai, was that the responsible party should pay the monetary value for an eye. (Baba Kamma 83b–84a) Critics, ignorant of this oral tradition, revel at mocking Biblical teachings by pointing out its archaic and barbaric laws. The Torah uses the expression "eye for an eye" because in divine reckoning the perpetrator deserves to lose his eye for his negligence. According to Maimonides, he cannot find restitution for his crime merely by paying the requisite fine; he must beg the victim's forgiveness as well.

Regulations regarding articles that remain after the death of the thief, if one recognizes his stolen article in someone else's possession, and laws determining what to do in the event real property was confiscated and requisitioned by the government are fully debated and deliberated as well.

Baba Metzia–The Middle Gate

The tractate Baba Metzia continues with civil law. Among the topics discussed are:

♦ Found and loaned articles

♦ Real estate

♦ Loans and titles

♦ What constitutes usury and fraud

♦ Labor law

There are a few scattered legends about the life and death of the principle authors of the Talmud, and some very notable passages, including one concerning a heated dispute between two great sages, a heavenly proclamation, and reconciliation.

One of the most significant issues dealt with in this tract is based on a passage in Exodus (22:6–14) that describes four types of watchmen, or bondsmen, and the different laws that apply to them:

1. A free watchman—someone who watches an item without demanding compensation from the owner. He is liable for damages only in cases of negligence, but

not in cases of theft or loss, and certainly not in the case of an unavoidable accident.

2. The borrower, one who borrows an item in order to use it and becomes obligated to take care of it. He is liable for damages in cases of negligence, theft, or loss, and unavoidable accidents. He is exempt from damages only in a case of when the item was damaged in the normal manner of usage, or if the item was damaged while its owner was working for the borrower.

3. The bearer or receiver of reward or compensation is one who is paid to watch an item but is not permitted to use it. He is liable for damages in cases of negligence, theft or loss, but is not liable in a case of unavoidable accident.

4. The renter, who pays money to rent an item. He is liable for damages in cases of negligence, theft, or loss, but is not liable in a case of unavoidable accident, according to some sages. Others assert that a renter is liable for damages only in cases of negligence, but not in cases of theft or loss, and certainly not in the case of unavoidable accidents.

Very detailed instructions are also presented concerning how watched items should be treated. On page 38a, for example, there is a dispute over what a watchman who is guarding someone's produce should do once he realizes that the produce is rotting. Should he sell it? May he eat it and give their value to the owner. Or does he simply watch it spoil?

According to one opinion, he shouldn't touch the food since as "A person favors a Kav (about a bushel) of his own produce over nine Kavim of his friend's," he is disinclined to have his produce sold even if 9/10 of it will be lost. Rabban Shimon ben Gamliel, who you met in Chapter 4, suggests the watchman sell the produce for it is like returning a lost object to its owner. The final ruling? The sages struck a compromise, and instruct that if the produce is spoiling more than a nominal amount it should be sold. If spoilage is nominal, then the farmer should be happy with even a fraction of the fruits of his hard labor.

Let's Get Talmudic

Ethical business practices frown upon the practice of price gouging. Restrictions are placed on the amount one may charge for moveable property. Tractate Baba Metzia discusses the restriction of not charging more than a sixth of the market value of an item. This is based on the verse in Leviticus (25:14) "When you make a sale to your fellow or make a purchase from his hand, do not aggrieve one another."

Baba Batra, the Final Gate

The third part of the "Gate" sequence of tracts deals with issues of civil law regarding property, including real estate, moveable possessions, and inheritance.

Squeezed in these wordy legal discussions is one of the most fascination sections of *aggadata*, or legends, found in the Talmud. The end of Chapter 5 consists of some very metaphorical (tall) tales about fish, alligators and nautical activities of Talmudic figures. The first chapter also contains a fair amount of *apocryphal* material about the lives of Abraham and Job, as well as identifying the authors of the various books of Scripture.

Talmud Tutor

Aggadata are sections of the Talmud and other rabbinic literature that deal with biblical narrative, stories and legends on biblical themes rather than with religious laws and regulations. *Apocryphal* refers to information or stories that are widely believed to be true, but may be meant to be understood metaphorically.

Baba Batra also contains teachings on a variety of moral issues. Regarding robbery, for example, it notes the following:

♦ The sin of robbery caused the great flood

♦ The first question that God will ask us is whether our business dealings were conducted honestly

♦ Robbery is "more difficult" than adultery

♦ That God abhors social sins but can tolerate idolatry

Other moral teachings include the necessity of following the civil code of the country in which one resides, and that idolatry is a far lesser evil than social sins in God's eyes.

The Ethics of the Fathers

Perhaps the most endearing of all Talmudic literature is called Pirkei Avot (literally, Chapters of the Fathers). Although it's possible to find important ethical advice and instruction interspersed throughout the Talmud, these six chapters concentrate the most significant teachings into one convenient list. It represents 1,500 years—50 generations—of continuous reflection on how to live a wholesome life.

Talmud Trivia

There are an estimated 500 commentaries that have been published on Pirkei Avot.

The first chapter of Pirkei Avot contains a timeline of sorts, as it opens with a chronology of who received the Oral Traditions and transmitted them to whom; e.g. Moses received instructions—Torah—from Sinai, and passed them on to Joshua; Joshua passed them on to the elders; the elders passed them on to the prophets; the prophets passed them on to the men of the Great Assembly.

While this may seem like relatively insignificant information, it contains a vital message—that tradition is a vitally important source of wisdom. Each group of sages made decisions about what was worthy to preserve from the previous generations.

As a book of ethical principles rather than specific legal rulings, Pirkei Avot continues to be revered by all branches of Judaism, and by many non-Jews who also revel in its straightforward, to-the-point wisdom. Some of the great sayings that can be found in Pirkei Avot include:

Shammai said:

> Say little and do much, and receive all men with a cheerful face.

Shimon the son of Gamliel said:

> All my days have I grown up among the wise and I have not found anything better for a man than silence.

Rabbi Judah, the Prince said:

> Which is the proper course that a man should choose for himself. That which is an honor to him and elicits honor from his fellow man. Be as scrupulous about a light precept as of a weighty one, for you do not know the reward allotted for each precept. Balance the loss incurred by the fulfillment of a precept against the gain and the accruing from a transgression against the loss it involves. Reflect on three things and you will never come to sin: Know what is above you—a seeing eye, a hearing ear, and all your deeds recorded in a book.

Talmud Tidbits

As with the more legal sections of the order of Nezikin, Pirkei Avot is preferably studied with an experienced teacher. Some of the chapters it contains are very succinct and come with little or no explanation. Literally following some of them, or taking them out of context, might lead to unrealistic outlooks on life.

Hillel said:

> Do not separate yourself from the community; and do not trust in yourself until the day of your death. Do not judge your fellow until you are in his place. Do not say something that cannot be understood but will be understood in the end. Say not: When I have time I will study because you may never have the time. He was also wont to say: A brutish man cannot fear sin; an ignorant man cannot be pious, nor can the

shy man learn, or the impatient man teach. He who engages excessively in business cannot become wise. In a place where there are no men strive to be a man.

Other Nezikim Tractates

The remaining Nezikim tractates—*Sanhedrin*, Shavuoth, Eduyot, Makkoth, Avodah Zara, and Horayoth—are also about various aspects of crime and punishment. Of them, the tractate Sanhedrin discusses the role, makeup, and location of this august group, which served as the Jewish Supreme Court in ancient times.

Consisting of 71 great sages, the Sanhedrin debated the fundamental principles of the Torah, and made rulings based on majority vote. This august council, which met in chambers adjacent to the temple in Jerusalem, decided cases that were the most difficult or the most critical for the Jewish people.

Talmud Tutor

The **Sanhedrin** was the Jewish Supreme Court. Its name is based on the Greek word sunedrion, or council, or from sunedros, which means sitting in council.

Sanhedrin branches far and wide, dispensing wisdom on such topics as the location of the lost tribes, what the windows on Noah's ark were made of, when the Messiah is due to arrive and what his qualifications would be. There is also a lengthy discussion regarding the concept of the world to come (though it is not explicitly identified as such) and the biblical verses that support it.

Much play is also granted to discussion about the role, responsibilities, and restrictions concerning a coronated Jewish king.

Let's Get Talmudic

One of the most notable discussions in the tractate Sanhedrin is that of the stubborn and rebellious son, which appears in Chapter 8. In it, the rabbis openly express skepticism that a son, who wantonly rebels against his parents in the way described by the Torah, can be put to death. Out of this emerges a key principle of Talmudic jurisprudence found throughout the tractate: that the execution of divine law must be tempered by human mercy.

Other subjects discussed in these tractates include:

♦ The concept of a universal code of living called the Seven Noahide Laws, which will be discussed in Chapter 19.

- The administering of corporal punishment for the willful transgression of some of the Bible's 365 prohibitions

- Oaths—what constitutes an oath, false oaths, and when and if they can be annulled

- What constituted idolatrous practices

- Erroneous court decisions and their rectification

One of these tracts—Avodah Zara—is also the source of many contemporary Jewish dietary laws.

The Least You Need to Know

- Nezikin is the repository of most of the Talmud's civil laws.

- The Three Gates contain legal discussions that have direct application to modern observance and even contain principles of secular law.

- The Sanhedrin was the Supreme Court for ancient Israel.

- Pirkei Avot's wisdom and guidance has inspired Jews and non-Jews for centuries.

9

Holiness

In This Chapter

- ◆ Defining holiness
- ◆ All about God's plan and purpose
- ◆ The holiness of garments
- ◆ The holiness of "firsts"
- ◆ Kosher laws

Kodashim (Holy Laws), the next to the last Talmudic order, primarily deals with issues related to the construction of the temple in Jerusalem, the service of priests, and sacrificial offerings. With minor exceptions, most of this order is not relevant today, as the temple in Jerusalem does not exist. So, why study it?

The simple answer is that learning about these matters brings purity of mind. This order deals with two of the most profound concepts known to humankind—holiness and sanctity. The search to define the concept of "holiness" is the underlying theme to all content found in the Order of Kodashim.

Understanding God's Plan and Purpose

Kodashim contains the following Talmud tractates:

- ◆ Zevachim—Laws concerning animal offerings in the Temple
- ◆ Menachos—Laws about meal offerings in the Temple
- ◆ Chulin—Laws of ritual slaughter and kosher laws
- ◆ Bechorot—Laws of the firstborn male child, both human and animal mainly deals with kosher laws
- ◆ Arachin—Estimating appropriate pledges to the Temple
- ◆ Temurah—Illegally substituting holiness from one consecrated animal to another
- ◆ Keritos—Bringing sin offerings or other offerings for more serious sins
- ◆ Me'ila—The unlawful use of consecrated things
- ◆ Tamid—Laws regarding daily services in the Temple
- ◆ Midot—Laws dealing with measurements of the Temple structure and service
- ◆ Kinim—Laws regarding details of bird offerings

At first glance, it's easy to understand why these tractates could seem irrelevant today. After all, it's been thousands of years since the Temple in Jerusalem was destroyed, so why bother learning about rites and rituals related to it? And, why would you even care about them if you weren't directly involved in these services anyway?

When children begin their Torah studies, one of the first lessons they learn is that there is a purpose and a plan to everything that God has created. As such, no physical entity is intrinsically good or evil; one's ultimate free will determines how it will be treated.

In addition, there is often a fine line as to what is considered holy and what is not. For instance, wanton slaughter of an animal for sport, e.g. hunting, is wrong, but the humane ritual killing of the animal for kosher consumption is a mitzvah.

Studying Kodashim explains these fine lines. Those who delve into its teachings are also better able to understand God's infinite plan. In a way, studying these teachings allow one to experience what it's actually like to perform these commands. Finally, many Jews fervently believe that the Holy Temple will be rebuilt in Jerusalem. Becoming familiar with these teachings readies them for that time.

Let's Get Talmudic

There is some debate in the schools of later rabbinic thought concerning which order of the Mishna or Talmud an aspiring Torah scholar should start off with. One opinion suggests the very placement of tractate Brachot (blessings and prayer) as the opening tractate of the Talmud makes this tract the strongest candidate, as prayer forms such a central theme in Judaism. Others believe that beginning with Nezikin (Damages) makes sense as it constantly reminds one of one's responsibilities with another's property. In this way, a student will develop the correct attitude toward learning and Jewish practice.

There is yet a third option that is practiced in certain circles today. It comes directly from the "horse's mouth," so to speak:

Rabbi Ashi asked, "Why do the children start learning Torah with Torah Cohanim (Leviticus) and not from Bereishis (Genesis)? This is because the children are pure and the worship in the Book of Leviticus is also pure; let the pure come and busy themselves with purity." (Midrash, Vayikrah Rabbah, Chapter 4).

Now that we've put the content of Kodashim into context, let's take a closer look at its teachings.

The Holiness of Garments

In the Bible, God directs the Hebrews to "… make sacred garments for Aaron your brother, for honor and for beauty. And you shall speak to all who are wise hearted, whom I have filled with the spirit of wisdom, that they may make Aaron's garments to consecrate him, that he may minister to me in the priest's office. And these are the garments which they shall make: a breastplate, and an ephod, and a robe, and a quilted undercoat, a mitre, and a girdle; and they shall make holy garments for Aaron your brother, and his sons, that he may minister to me in the priest's service … And you shall place the *Urim V'tummim* in the breastplate of judgment, and they shall be over Aaron's heart when he comes before God." (Exodus 28:1–4,30)

Clearly, wearing specific and sacred garments was a requirement for serving in the Temple, and no priest was fit for duty unless he wore them. Zevachim, the first tractate in Kodashim, affirms this by stating, "While they are clothed in the priestly garments, they are clothed in the priesthood; but when they are not wearing the garments, the priesthood does not rest upon them." (Zevachim 17b) In other words, conducting the service without these garments would render the priests the same as those who are not descendants of Aaron—all of whom are unfit for service in the Temple.

Why does the Torah attribute so much significance to these garments? Ever hear the expression "the clothes make the man?" Well here is the source. The Talmud tells us that the quality of these garments is such that they elevate the wearers, Aaron and all his descendants, to the highest levels of sanctity required from those who come to serve before God in the holy place. The garments themselves were imbued with certain holiness; powerful enough to sanctify all those who merely came in contact with them.

Talmud Tidbits

The *Urim V'Tummim* (literally the light and the perfection) was the oracle-like aspect of the breastplate that delivered heavenly answers to earthly questions. According to the Talmud, the expression *Urim v'Tummim* actually refers not to the breastplate itself, but to the mystical and divine name of God that was written on a piece of parchment and inserted into a pouch of the garment. The name facilitated the reception of divine guidance through the illumination of specific letters on the stones. The priest would then interpret the message that appeared through these stones.

The garments themselves show that their wearers are standing in divine service. This is one of the deeper aspects of wearing these garments, and something for the priest to ponder while he wears them. In this way, a priest's daily actions in the Temple went beyond his own personal expression and allowed him to affect atonement and spiritual growth for all mankind.

The vestments worn by the High Priest.

(Copyright 2003 by Torahtots, Inc.)

Each garment worn by the priests helped atoned for specific wrongs:

◆ The tunic, which covered most of the priest's body, atoned for the community's collective transgressions of murder.

◆ The pants atoned for sexual indiscretions of the community.

◆ The turban atoned for haughtiness.

◆ The belt, wound around the body and worn over the heart, atoned for sins of the heart (specifically idolatry, or improper thoughts).

◆ The breastplate atoned for errors in judgment, primarily for court judges.

◆ The ephod (an embroidered overgarment, similar to an apron) atoned for idol worship.

◆ The robe atoned for evil speech.

◆ Finally, the High Priest's crown or headplate atoned for brazenness.

All About Sacrifices

In our world, animal sacrifices are a touchy subject. At their best, they're politically incorrect. At their worst ... well, let's just say that it's a subject that many people feel is better left alone. Regardless, some Jews still believe strongly that they will be reinstated when the Holy Temple is rebuilt. According to certain Talmudic authorities, only flour or produce offerings will be brought.

In the ancient world, however, animal sacrifices were commonplace. Zevachim, the first tractate of Kodashim, addresses all the fine points of the sacrificial system and discusses the various sacrifices that could be brought to the Temple, as well as the sanctuary that was used before the Temple was built.

Basically, sacrifices were offered for the following reasons:

◆ To atone for breaking the law in some way

◆ To observe the festival of Passover

◆ As a tithe offering

Talmud Tidbits

On a daily basis, pious Jews recite and study from the prayer book various passages from scripture and the Talmud in place of the daily offerings, including the sin offering. The last practice is alluded to by the prophet Hoshea "Take words with you and return to the Lord; say to Him: "Forgive all guilt and accept what is good. Instead of bulls we shall pay [the offering] with our lips." (Hosea 14:3)

◆ As a thanksgiving offering

◆ As voluntary peace offerings

◆ As communal daily and additional Shabbat or holiday offerings

Today, without the Temple in Jerusalem, none of these offerings can be brought. However, certain symbolic observances throughout the year remind Jewish people of these occasions. On Passover, for instance, Jews place the shank bone of a lamb on the Seder table to remind them of the sacrifices that were once done in observation of this festival.

Atoning for Unintentional Transgressions

About a fifth of the 207 Biblical violations for which an offering was required were acts committed out of neglect or error. In other words, all sin offerings came for unintentional transgressions.

Accordingly, the remedy ultimately had to come with greater awareness of what God's laws are all about. How was this accomplished more than 2,000 years ago?

The most efficient way was for the transgressor to travel to Jerusalem; where he (it was almost always a "he") would purchase an offering, have it properly prepared, hand it to the priests on the Temple Mount, and talk with these teachers.

Those who traveled to Jerusalem to make sin offerings would be out quite a few gold coins for their ordeals. This could range from a week's wages for an average laborer for a she-goat or ewe, a bit less for a couple of turtle-doves or pigeons, or if he was really poor, a few coins for some flour and oil. Even the richest man does not want to see his resources depleted through negligence in observing the law.

Talmud Tidbits

Even non-Jews could bring a sacrifice to the Holy Temple. Leviticus 1:2 teaches, "A man from amongst you offers a free-will offering …" The fact of that it says "a man," and not necessarily an Israelite, implies that making sacrifices was not restricted to followers of the faith.

Fiscal penalty coupled with proximity to holy people constituted a great formula for greater sanctity and self-improvement, which were essentially the goals of the sacrifices in the first place. In fact, korban, the Hebrew word for sacrifice, is from the root word karev, which means to draw close.

Nachmanides, commenting on Leviticus 1:9 explains the concept of sacrificing animals for atonement in the following way:

A person should realize that he has sinned, albeit unintentionally, against God with his body and soul and that "his" blood should really be spilt and his body burnt. It is only that God in His loving kindness accepts a substitute and a ransom, namely this offering. Its blood is in place of the sinner's blood, its life is in place of his life, and the chief limbs of the offering are in place of the chief limbs of his body. The simple message is: the sinner, who contemplates this, should be inspired to sincerely repent.

The Passover Sacrifice

Many other offerings had nothing to do with sin and atonement. Let's take a look at one of them.

When the Temple stood in Jerusalem, every Jewish household (or combination of smaller households) would bring a lamb or goat to the Temple on the fourteenth of Nissan, the day preceding the festival of Passover, in accordance with scripture. "They shall eat the flesh [of the Passover offering] on that night, roasted on the fire, with matzot and bitter herbs." (Exodus 12:8)

The animal would be ritually slaughtered in the Temple courtyard, its blood would be sprinkled on the altar, and certain portions of it would be burned atop the altar. It would then be roasted on a spit over a fire and consumed at night as part of the Seder.

Often called the Passover offering, it had nothing to do with sin or atonement. In fact, the Passover offering was unique in many ways, for it was governed by a set of laws that applied to no other offering—in other words, this offering could only be roasted over fire, no bones could be broken, etc.

The Tradition of the Tithe

Another offering not related to sin has to do with *tithing*. The Torah commands the Jew to bring the firstborn of his cattle, goat, or sheep as an offering to God. One could bring portions of the meat to any priest he wished, but any meat of the offering was eaten only by the priests and their families.

Also to be offered is a tithe of the animals born in the herd or flock. This was done once a year. The year's yield was herded into a pen and let out one at a time; every tenth animal to emerge was specially marked and pronounced holy to God, and brought as an offering.

> **Talmud Tutor**
>
> **Tithing** is the payment of one tenth of one's income or produce, either voluntarily or as a tax, to support a religious house and its officials.

Giving Thanks

Finally, the Talmud discusses details of the thanksgiving offering based on Leviticus (7:11–17), which was generally offered when someone survived a life-threatening event.

A passage in Psalms (Chapter 107) defines four categories of individuals who are required to bring this offering:

♦ Those who have traversed a desert, wilderness, or potentially hazardous journey

♦ Those who have survived a dangerous incarceration

♦ Survivors of serious illness

♦ Survivors of sea voyages

> **Talmud Tutor**
>
> **Kiddush** means sanctified or unique. It is a special blessing, usually over wine, said to consecrate a Sabbath or holiday meal. It also refers to a reception for congregants of a synagogue, at which drinks and snacks are served after the kiddush blessing is said.

In the time of the Holy Temple, a person saved from peril recited a special public prayer in the synagogue and offered a festive meal for having been saved from one of these four dangers. The meal would consist of a large bull, sheep, or goat, and 40 loaves of bread. Since he couldn't eat it himself, he would invite all of his friends to feast with him. Today, one might say a special blessing—a *kiddush*—in the synagogue, and/or prepare a feast at home to celebrate.

Holiness of the Firsts

Among the Israelites, as well as among other nations, the firstborn enjoyed special privileges. Besides having a greater share in the paternal affection, he occupied the first place after his father (see Genesis 43:33), and had a kind of directive authority over his younger brothers (see Genesis 37: 21–22, 30, etc.). Not only this, a special blessing was reserved to him at his father's death, and he succeeded him as the head of the family, receiving a double portion among his brothers (Deuteronomy 21:17). Moreover, the first-birthright, up to the time when Moses received the laws on Mount Sinai, included a right to the priesthood. There is a Talmudic tradition that the firstborn will be restored to this service when the Temple is rebuilt.

One of the twenty-four gifts that a Jew was required to give to a priest is the male firstborn of domesticated animals, such as cattle, sheep and goats. A source of this law is Exodus 13:2 "Sanctify unto Me all firstborn, whatsoever opened the womb among the Children of Israel, both of man and beast; it is Mine." And what was done with it?

"… the firstborn of a cow or the firstborn of a sheep or the firstborn of a goat, you shall not redeem; they are holy; you shall throw their blood upon the Altar and their fat, you shall cause to go up in smoke, a fire-offering … their meat shall be yours." (Numbers 18:17,18)

Let's Get Talmudic

The tractate Bechorot in the order Kodashim deals with other offerings related to "firsts." The consecration to God "of every firstborn in Israel, man and beast" is a recurring theme in the Bible, dating back to the time of the tenth plague in Egypt when God killed all the firstborns in Egypt and saved the firstborn of the Israelites. The reasoning is straightforward: As God is the creator of all living things, vegetable, animal, and human, they belong primarily to him, and therefore, are considered holy. When human beings offered the first of these, it was done in exchange for the right of the use of the animals in general. Another connection between first fruits is found in a passage that offers a long list of the durations of pregnancy of various animals with parallels to the fruition span of certain species in the vegetable kingdom.

Bechorot is the address for many interesting facts about animals, birds, and insects. In fact, one very important kosher issue having to do with bee honey (bees are not considered to be kosher, but honey is) is raised near the beginning of the tractate:

> "That which comes from something which is non-kosher is non-kosher, and that which comes out of that which is kosher is kosher." (Bechorot 5b)

In other words, the product of a non-kosher animal is not Kosher. So, how can honey be kosher?

The Talmud then quotes a *Beraita*, or a legal teaching by one of the sages from the Mishnaic age, which says:

> "Why did they say that bee-honey is permitted? Because even though they bring it into their bodies, it is not a product of their bodies [it is stored there but not produced there]." (Bechorot 7b)

Surprisingly, all the sages of the Mishna agree with this ruling. However, one of them, Rabbi Yaakov, disagrees with the reckoning. He claims that bee-honey is kosher based on his original

Talmud Tutor

A **Beraita** (pl. beraitot) is a legal teaching or saying by one of the sages of the Mishnaic age. They were not included in Rabbi Judah the Prince's Mishna for any of a number of reasons, but many of them were later recorded in the Talmud. The literal meaning of beraita is "outside."

explanation of Leviticus 11:21; "Only this may you eat from among all flying teeming creatures …".

According to Rabbi Yaakov, the verse prohibits one to eat the actual flying creature, but not that which is excreted from it. Bottom line, bee honey, pollen, and royal jelly are all kosher consumables.

Another part of this tract discusses the consecration of the first born of animals and people to God. Interestingly, it also touches on the subtle conflict between the scholarly and priestly classes. According to Deuteronomy 15:19–23, the firstborn offered for sacrifice must have no blemish on it. If there is a blemish on it, the animal may be eaten by the priest rather than sacrificed.

The rabbis determined that the priest could eat the beast only if the blemish came about naturally or by accident. If, however, the blemish was inflicted intentionally so that the priest might eat it or sell it, then it may neither be sacrificed nor eaten nor sold. A non-priestly Jew would never be able to keep his or her firstborn animals, so it made no difference to him or her who received it: the Temple cult or a priest. However, priests would be tempted to inflict injuries on their animals so that they might eat them or sell them instead of sacrificing them to the Temple cult.

Kosher Laws (Tractate Chulin)

The tractate Chulin, one of the longest tracts of the Talmud, is the repository for virtually all subjects related to the dietary laws of *kashrut*.

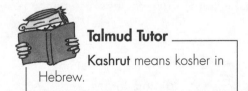

Talmud Tutor

Kashrut means kosher in Hebrew.

The laws of kashrut, commanded by the Torah (primarily in Leviticus 11 and Deuteronomy 14) and interpreted and expounded on in the Talmud, establish which foods Jews can and cannot eat. If something is to be considered kosher for Jewish consumption, it probably needs to pass the scrutiny of the principles and details of this tractate.

The Hebrew word "kosher" simply means fit. The laws of kashrut, therefore, involve the fitness of food for the Jewish table. Before an animal can be eaten, three conditions must be met:

◆ It must be determined to be kosher

◆ It must undergo a ritual slaughter as dictated by Torah and Talmudic law

◆ It must pass a very strict post-mortem inspection.

Let's take a brief look at some of these laws.

Classes of Foods

According to kosher dietary laws, animal food cannot be consumed at the same time as dairy food. All unprocessed vegetables, fruits, grains, and minerals, however, are inherently kosher and *pareve*, or neutral, neither dairy nor meat. They can be combined or eaten with either meat or dairy.

Talmud Tutor

There is no literal English translation for **pareve**, or **parve**, but it comes close to "neutral." The term describes food made without animal or dairy ingredients.

Clean or Unclean

Eating animals, however, is much more restricted. Chapter 11 in the book of Leviticus designates which mammals may or may not be consumed. Animals are either spiritually "clean" or "unclean." Only ruminants—animals that chew their cud—with completely cloven hooves are considered spiritually clean.

Although the Torah lists 20 species of unacceptable fowl, all birds of prey are strictly forbidden. Sea creatures must possess fins and scales to be deemed kosher.

Talmud Trivia

The identification of kosher birds is handed down from generation to generation. Since the exact identities of some non-kosher birds have become obscure, the Code of Jewish Law rules that only birds with a well-established tradition can be eaten. For this reason, certain Sephardic, or Oriental Jews, of the Middle East do not eat turkey, a bird indigenous to North America, as their traditions prohibit it.

Laws Regarding Slaughter

In order for even a "clean" animal or fowl to be kosher, it must be ritually slaughtered following very precise guidelines. For example, the slaughterer, or shochet, had to draw the slaughtering knife *across* the animal's vital passages. Any deviations from the required to-and-fro movement would render the animal non-kosher, or *nevailah*.

In addition, certain parts of ruminants—the sciatic nerve and certain fats—must be removed.

Talmud Tutor

Nevailah technically means "corpse." It refers to any animal that was improperly slaughtered or died by natural cause, rendering its meat non-kosher.

Fish are treated differently than cattle and fowl, and therefore, the various laws of slaughter do not apply. The Talmud basically equates them with vegetation.

Let's Get Talmudic

Land animals, which were created from the "earth," are rendered fit to eat by the severing of both vital passages (the windpipe and the gullet). Fish, which were created from water, do not require any slaughter to render them fit to eat. Birds, which were "created" from a mixture of earth and water, are rendered fit to eat with the severing of either one of the two vital passages. (Talmud Chulin 27b)

Laws of Preparation and Inspection

The Bible also strictly forbids consuming the blood of animals and birds. Therefore, the blood must be removed—koshered—usually by soaking and salting, a subject meticulously covered in this tract. But, in some cases, and with some foods, other means of preparation must be applied, such as:

- ◆ Liver can only be koshered by broiling.

- ◆ Hearts of animals and birds can only be made fit through special cutting and broiling (in general, however, the sages discouraged their consumption).

- ◆ Fish did not have to be koshered, but one could not collect the blood of a fish in a glass and gulp it down.

If a period of three days passed following slaughter without washing and salting the meat, it was assumed that the blood in the capillaries had congealed and could only be removed by broiling. However, to avoid mistakes, meat that was not salted or rinsed within a 72-hour period was not considered kosher.

Let's Get Talmudic

The Torah proclaims, "meat from an animal that has been torn in the field you shall not eat." (Exodus 22:30) The Talmudic sages interpreted this verse to mean that even if that animal was ritually slaughtered before death, to be kosher an animal must be free of any mortal injury. According to the Talmud (Chulin 43a), eight types of life-threatening injuries were revealed to Moses: mauling by a wild beast or bird of prey, perforation of any of 11 major organs, a birth-deficiency of one of the lobes of the lung, any missing or additional organs, severing of the membrane covering the spinal cord, an internal organ punctured by a fall, tearing of most of the flesh of the rumen, and broken rib bones. In Chulin 3:1 can be found 10 more types of injuries or blemishes that would also render an animal unfit to eat.

What About Cheeseburgers?

This tractate also contains detailed explanations on one of the better-known Kosher prohibitions, eating a cheeseburger. As the Bible states several times, "You shall not boil a kid in its mother's milk." (Exodus 23:19; Exodus 34:26, and once in Deuteronomy) The Talmud points out that this restriction teaches that one is not allowed to actually cook such a combination, eat it, or derive any type of benefit from meat and milk that was cooked together. (Chulin 115b)

According to Nachmanides, (you met him in Chapter 4), the act of mixing meat and milk is a cruel act. However, it is not a despicable act. Instead, this law is primarily teaching a sensitivity lesson. Milk was created to sustain life, while flesh represents the cessation of life. While there is a Biblical concession to consume meat, one is warned not to flaunt this privilege by wantonly "seething a kid in its mother's milk."

The remaining sections of Chulin tractate deal with other dietary, agricultural and priestly laws, the precept to send the mother bird away before taking the eggs or chicks, and the like.

Many fascinating passages addressing animal science and identification of obscure species are also found in these pages. You'll learn more about some of them in Chapter 16.

Temple Maintenance, Misappropriations, and Losing a Favorite Animal

The balance of the tractates in Kodashim cover a variety of topics that relate to temple service. Arachin, or values, discusses fundraising and the appropriate pledge amounts for individuals. Temurah (a substitute) deals with the procedure that should be followed should someone lose a dedicated animal (replace it, then find the original animal before offering the second). Keritot covers general laws concerning the 34 negative and two positive commandments for which a transgressor could have one's soul cut off from his people and God. Me'ilah discusses which acts of misappropriation of consecrated items would make a person guilty of the Torah prohibition covered by these laws. It also discusses the rectification for such indiscretions. Tamid primarily speaks about the continual or daily offering brought to the Temple.

The Least You Need to Know

◆ The tractates of the Order Kodashim (Holiness) primarily deal with the consecration and sanctity of the environment, animals, clothing, and vessels used for
service in the Holy Temple.

◆ Though most of these laws are obsolete, many still study them, as they provide
a template for understanding how to appreciate holiness and they are thought to
purify the mind of those who study them.

◆ According to the Talmud, the vestments worn by priests not only reminded
them of their divine duties, they also signified specific acts that could be
atoned for.

◆ While animal sacrifices are a touchy subject today, they were very much a part
of ancient religious practices for the Jewish people.

◆ Prohibitions against eating meat and milk at the same time, and other aspects of
Jewish kosher law are found in Kodashim.

Chapter 10

Pure or Impure?

In This Chapter

♦ Purifying waters

♦ Talmudic contraception

♦ The Talmud on childbirth

♦ Rites and preparations

♦ Courtesies and converts

Taharot, the last Talmud order, deals with a group of topics related to rituals and right living. For example, there are laws pertaining to how one should deal with certain people, such as lepers and Samaritans, and the proper way to mourn or wear ritual garments.

Also in Taharot are discussions of laws related to what is generally referred to euphemistically as "family purity." Behind this euphemism lie a number of laws that pertain to very private matters—specifically, sexual relations between a husband and a wife—and what one must do to preserve the purity of those relations.

As is the case with Zera'im, the first Talmud order, not everything that Taharot contains is presented with Talmudic discussion, or gemara. In this chapter, we'll primarily focus on Niddah, the one tract that does have it.

Being Separate

The tractate Niddah, which means separate, primarily deals with one topic—the menstruating woman and her ritual purification. Much of the discussion is based on passages from the book of Leviticus, "When a woman has her regular flow of blood, the impurity of her monthly period will last seven days …" When [the woman] is rid of her discharge, she must count seven days for herself, and only then can she undergo purification (by immersing her body in a mikvah) …" (Leviticus 15:19,32)

Talmud Tidbits

The concept of "taboo" associated with the menstruating woman is not unique to Judaism. Among certain Native American tribes, a menstruating woman would remain in a "Red Tent" until her menses ended. While there, she could not prepare food or touch or look for medicine as it was believed that doing so would be harmful to anyone who ingested them. Japanese Shinto custom called for a menstruating woman to sequester herself in a hut called a Gekkei-goya. Religious Muslim women also avoid intercourse with their husbands during their periods.

To put this biblical reference into modern terms, women are considered spiritually impure when they are menstruating and for a certain period of time afterward. During this time, husband and wife are not to engage in sexual relations, and, in fact, they're not to indulge in any sort of contact that might lead to it. In other words, they remain physically separate.

Why was a menstruating woman considered spiritually impure, or tameh, in Hebrew? Many commentaries on the Talmud link all forms of impurity with death or, at least, the loss of potential for life. Since a woman's anatomy allows the possibility of fertilization every month, menstrual flow, which indicates the lack of conception, is the sign of thwarted life potential, and therefore, impurity. However, neither the Torah nor the sages ever view the woman as actually being "impure," as often the word tameh is erroneously translated.

Waters of Purification

Biblically speaking, with the cessation of her period, and the passage of seven days from onset of her flow, the woman becomes ritually purified and able to resume sexual relations with her husband, but only after she immerses herself in the "living waters" of a *mikvah*.

In context, a mikvah is a collection of water that comes directly from natural sources. In a typical mikvah, rainwater flows directly into two pits, which are hidden from view. Waters from those pits are mixed with waters in the main pool of a modern structure in accordance with Jewish law. A Jewish community cannot exist without a proper mikvah, which must be constructed even before a synagogue is. A mikvah must contain a minimum of 40 *seahs*, or between 70 to 80 gallons of water, to be valid.

Talmud Tutor

The word **mikvah** literally means "gathering."

Primordial Waters

As a mikvah contains natural rainwater, it is considered to be part of the primordial waters that flowed from the Garden of Eden. In the times of the Temple, the mikvah was used to purify oneself from many forms of impurity, and was biblically mandated for both men and women. It was essential for the High Priest's service in the Temple on Yom Kippur, the Day of Atonement.

In this context, what better place to remove the taint of "thwarted life-potential," than to go back to the source where it began? Is that not where Adam and Eve faced their mortality for the first time? This impurity is not "dirt," but rather a state a person enters after having come in contact with death, in any of its forms. If life brings sanctity and holiness, then the absence of life leaves in its wake impurity. The gist of the concept is by connecting to the waters of creation, one is reconnecting to life, and re-establishing holiness.

Keeping Marriage Alive

The Talmud makes clear that the purification process of the mikvah is a *chok*, which means a law that doesn't seem logical, or though it has a logical meaning behind it, we are not privy to it.

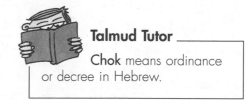

Talmud Tutor

Chok means ordinance or decree in Hebrew.

However, its proper use can bring happiness, freshness, and fulfillment to a marriage. Niddah 31b tells us that, "Rabbi Meir used to say, 'Why did the Torah ordain that the uncleanness of menstruation should continue for seven days? Because being in constant contact with his wife [a husband might] develop a loathing toward her. The Torah, therefore, ordained: Let her be ritually unclean for seven days in order that she shall be beloved by her husband as at the time of her first entry into the bridal chamber.'"

Becoming New and Pure

The institution of the mikvah has even been called the secret of the Jewish survival. To explain why, it's necessary to look at things from a more mystical level. Ritual immersion is done in a minimum of 40 *seahs* (a unit of volume) of water. The Hebrew letter "mem" begins both the words mikvah and mayim (water). Each Hebrew letter has a numerical value (called gematria). The numerical value of "mem" is 40.

> **Talmud Trivia**
>
> According to one opinion in Niddah, since a fetus takes 40 days from conception to develop into human form; it is at that point it receives a divine soul.

When God wanted to rebirth the world, it rained for 40 days causing a flood. The flood eradicated all trace of the appalling spiritual state that existed up to that point and created a new mankind. In a sense, the entire world was immersed in a mikvah! The Jewish people were born during 40 years in the desert. Similarly, by receiving the Torah conveyed to Moses over 40 days, the Jews were born as a new nation.

The number 40 clearly has great meaning in Judaism. According to at least one source, it always means cataclysmic change and new creation.

In Judaism, one who is impure immerses in the mikvah and emerges as a new person who is pure. And a convert to Judaism goes through this process, for indeed upon emerging from the waters is as if he/she were born anew.

This mikvah, found in the excavation of Solomon's Temple in Jerusalem, conforms perfectly to the dimensions specified in the tractate Mikvaot in the seder Taharot. The institution of mikvah is alive and well today, with very modern, clean, sanitary, and heated structures to make the experience a pleasant one.

(Photo credit: BiblePlaces.com)

Ancient Birth Control

Throughout history women have used various substances to prevent pregnancy. For instance, vegetable seedpods were used in South Africa, and various corks of grass and crushed roots were used in other parts of Africa.

Sponges, which blocked and absorbed semen, were perhaps the most commonly and universally used contraceptive devices substances. The oldest known reference to using sponges for contraception is found—you guessed it!—in the Talmud.

According to Rabbi Meir, Niddah 45a recommends, and sometimes requires, that a sponge (called a moch) be soaked in vinegar and be used in the following situations:

- If a girl was too physically immature to bear a child and survive pregnancy.

- When a woman was already pregnant, yet there was a concern for a rare situation (called superfetation) where another ovum might become fertilized.

- If woman was nursing, and becoming pregnant would force her to wean her child prematurely.

Superfetation is the development of a second fetus when one is already present in the uterus and is a phenomenon that has been observed in some animals. The Talmud in Niddah 27a tells us that a woman cannot become pregnant and then become pregnant again. In other words, superfetation is basically an impossibility in humans. However, a contradictory statement can be found in Yevamot 12b. The Talmud says that a pregnant woman may (or must) use contraception lest her fetus become compressed and destroyed. So how do we reconcile this strange anomaly?

The commentators resolve the contradiction between Talmudic texts in different ways. Rashi explained that superfetation is possible, but the resulting fetus will not survive. A woman can become pregnant more than once at a time, but cannot deliver viable babies from these pregnancies. Rabbi Shlomo ben Tzemach Duran, a sixteenth-century commentator, explained differently. He said that the passage in Niddah is speaking in general terms. Most of the time, women cannot become pregnant more than once at a time. The passage in Yevamot is speaking of the remote possibility of superfetation. It can happen, but it is indeed rare.

A fourth reason to permit contraceptive devices is indirectly alluded to in a passage found both in Yebamoth (65b) and Niddah (27a). In the former, the sages of the Mishna discuss whether both men and women are commanded to procreate, or "Be fruitful and multiply." The first unattributed opinion holds that only males are required, while Rabbi Yochanon ben Berokah opines that both are enjoined to procreate. The sages of the Talmud, in typical fashion, argue this point back and forth. Some even cite scriptural passages in support. In the end, the conclusion is that they are not both commanded as such.

Talmud Tidbits

In November 2001, the British Broadcasting Corporation reported that Flavia D'Angelo, a 20-year-old Italian woman, who had not used any fertility drugs, claimed that she was ready to give birth that week and then again three months later. Superfetation as discussed in the Talmud, was presented to experts, who admitted that this phenomenon is possible. Even though D'Angelo's claim was later proven to be false, the doctors who evaluated it concluded that it was possible. The Talmud's assertion is not nonsense.

Later codifiers, such as Rabbi Nisim Gaon, offer a logical explanation for the difference in commands. Childbirth is both hazardous (particularly then) and taxing on the strength and general well being of the mother. God, in his infinite wisdom, does not command in the Torah performance of a mitzvah that clearly presents a danger. In other words, it's a woman's prerogative not to bear children if it would endanger her health. (There are exceptions, but this is the guiding principle.)

Biblical support is brought as well, for it says, "… That a person shall do them and live by them …" (Leviticus 18:5) The Talmudic sages comment on these last words, "and not die by them." King Solomon alluded to this concept in his proverb, "Its ways are ways of pleasantness and all its paths are peace." (Proverbs 3:18)

Coupling two of these reasons together, the Talmud brings a fascinating dialogue between husband and wife, where she wishes to close the spigot, so to speak, while he wishes to continue having more children. On page 27a of Niddah we are taught that Rabbi Chiya (chief disciple of Judah the Price) had twin children who were evidently the product of superfetation (the phenomenon mentioned previously). They are identified as Judah and Hezekiah. One had been born at the end of nine months of his mother's pregnancy and the other after only seven.

Judith, the mother of the twins, suffered excruciating labor pains because of this strange twin birth, and wanted to stop having children. She disguised herself, and came before her rabbi-husband, R. Chiya, and posed the question, "Is a woman obligated to procreate?" He answered, "No." She went and drank a sterilizing potion. After awhile he caught on to the fact that she was avoiding pregnancy. Rabbi Chiya lamented to her, "If only you had given birth to one more bellyful."

Notwithstanding her clever subterfuge, Rabbi Chiya ruled in his wife's favor, exempting her from the obligation to procreate, consistent with the Talmud's own conclusion. Ironically, his decision undermined his own cause; for had he felt women were obligated to procreate, his wife would have had no choice, even after this unusually difficult birth, but to continue to have more children, which would have been very much to his liking. Nonetheless, he could not deny the reality of his petitioner's situation and ruled appropriately.

Let's Get Talmudic

The most lenient view in regard to contraception, when one of the health issues is a factor, is that held by Rabbi Solomon Luria, the Maharshal(1510–74), a great legal authority in Poland. According to Rabbi Luria, as long as normal intercourse takes place, and "… one body derives natural gratification from the other," birth control is permissible. Based on the precedent set by Judith in Talmudic times, women are allowed to take oral contraceptives, under restricted situations with rabbinic guidance, but men are not. According to Jewish law, neither gender is allowed to have themselves permanently sterilized, hence, hysterectomies, tubal ligation, and vasectomies are forbidden.

The Talmud on Childbirth

Not only is the oldest mention of a contraceptive device found in the Talmud, so too, is the oldest obstetrical calendar. "The regular pregnancy from the day of fertilization until the delivery has a duration of 270 days or 9 months, each month counted as 30 days." The Talmud finds an allusion to the period of time for a full-term pregnancy in the Hebrew word for pregnancy, "harayon" (heh, raish, yud, vav, nun). The numerical value (Gematria) of "harayon" is equal to 271 (5+200+10+6+50), which is equal to nine full months with the count starting one day after intercourse. (Niddah 38)

Let's Get Talmudic

The Talmud attributes different parts of the baby's existence and anatomy to a partnership between God, the husband, and the wife, with each partner contributing unique components. As the Rabbis taught: "There are three partners in the creation of a person: The Holy One, Blessed is He, the father, and the mother. The white seed (allusion to sperm) results in the bones, tendons, nails, brain, and the white of the eye. The red seed (perhaps the ovum) results in the skin, flesh, blood, hair, and the black of the eye. The Holy One, Blessed is He, provides the Ruach (spirit) and Neshamah (soul), countenance or facial appearance, eyesight, hearing, speech, ability to walk, understanding and common sense. When it comes time to leave this world, God takes His part back and leaves behind the father's and the mother's." (Niddah 31a)

Here are a few more statements made by the sages concerning childbirth:

◆ During the first three months of its prenatal life, the baby lives low down in the mother's womb, for the next three months, in the middle section, and for the last three months, at the top.

◆ According to the Talmud, the girl turns round as it is being born, whereas a boy does not, and it is that which causes the excessive pain at childbirth.

◆ A girl turns around, because she needs to face upward and during the pregnancy she is facing downward like a boy.

◆ If a man "sews" his seed (i.e. ejaculates before wife climaxes during intercourse) and there is conception, the child will be female. If the woman climaxes first the child will be a male.

◆ During the second three months of pregnancy intercourse is bad for the mother (probably because they feared for superfetation), but good for the baby; and during the last three months, it is good for both the mother and the baby.

At first glance, some of these concepts may sound strange to the modern ear. Most likely, the sages were merely reflecting what was considered common knowledge or folk medicine in their time. In Chapter 17, we will discover that many proclamations made by the sages in these matters were actually right on the mark.

More Ritual Laws

Most of the remaining subject matter in Taharot deals with issues pertaining to ritual purity and impurity as it was practiced while the Holy Temple stood in Jerusalem.

Talmud Tidbits

An organization comprised of Jews with Cohanic (priestly) lineage have a center of learning in Jerusalem where they have even fashioned specific clothing and vessels that conform to the descriptions of the material here and in Seder Kodshim.

Talmudic authorities believe that the details of these laws will again become applicable upon the rebuilding of the Temple in Jerusalem. For this reason, many students of the Talmud take it upon themselves to regularly review them.

◆ Kelim (Vessels): Discusses the various forms of ritual impurity that can affect vessels primarily of wood, metal, and earthenware. Issues such as their rectification or purification, at what stage do they contract and convey ritual impurity, and what parts of the vessel is liable to become impure. This is the single longest tract of Mishna chapters in the Oral Law.

◆ Ohalot (Tents): An enclosure that contains a corpse or even part of one causes all items in that tent to become ritually impure. Specific laws concerning impurity of corpses in general are discussed.

◆ Nega'im (Leprosy): A couple of chapters in Leviticus mention the laws pertaining to a person afflicted with a spiritual punishment that manifested itself in a skin disease. This was called Tzra'at. It could also affect one's clothing and one's home. This section of the Mishna elaborates in length on "Biblical leprosy."

◆ Parah (Red Heifer): A red heifer was a necessary component for the purification of a person who came in contact with a dead body. There was a special ritual entailing the sprinkling of its ashes.

◆ Teharot (Purifications): The very name of this order is also the name of a tract dealing with various laws of ritual impurity. Both Biblical and rabbinical decrees are mentioned here.

◆ Mikvaot (Ritual Baths): The how, what, and where of building a mikvah for ritual immersions of all sorts is discussed in this tract. Many of the details found within are applicable today.

◆ Makhshirin (Preparations): Discussions of how foods and beverages can become ritually impure when coming in contact with any of 7 liquids are found here.

◆ Zavim (Secretions): Generally recognized as someone afflicted with a sort of venereal disease, or having a gonorrheal emission, a Zav required a special process for purification.

◆ Tevul Yom (Immersion during the day): Most regaining of the state of purity occurs at night. There is unique dispensation for certain types of individuals and impurities that immerse during the day, yet must wait until sunset to complete the process of purification.

◆ Yadayin (Hands): One handling certain consecrated food items, for example, Terumah, was required to maintain a purity of the hands. Most issues discussed deal with rabbinical regulations, a fraction of which is practiced today.

◆ Uktzin (Stems): As mentioned, foodstuffs can become ritually impure. Whether and how this applies to the stems of these fruits is discussed in these chapters.

The 14 "Minor" Tractates

These tractates are not part of Seder Taharot, but are part of Talmudic literature. They are generally referred to as Mesechtot (Tractates) Ketanot (Minor) or Chitzoniyot (External). That is somewhat of a misnomer, as some are quite lengthy.

Some suggest the information contained in them suggested an expanded collection of the Mishna. They do not contain Talmudic discussions in the conventional sense in that the language and approach is more straightforward statements of fact, rather than the traditional give and take arguments, counter-proofs and reconciliation techniques of the Talmud.

These tractates are of very diverse subject matter. However, they do have one thing in common: They are somewhat "oddballs" and don't seem to have a well-defined place within the other tractates. Still, the material they contain can be fascinating and often forms the basis of contemporary observance.

1. Avot of Rabbi Natan—Clearly a supplement to Pirkei Avot, it expands on the ideas and teachings that were promulgated by the original authors. It contains a whopping 41 chapters.

> **Talmud Tutor**
>
> **Tefillin** are the small leather boxes containing Hebrew texts ritually worn by orthodox Jewish men. **Mezzuzot** (plural of mezzuzah) are scrolls with biblical passages on one side and a name of God on the other, inserted in a small case attached by religious Jews to doorposts in the home.

2. Sofrim (Scribes)—A very methodical layout of the detailed laws of the scribe and how they are to form the letters of Torah scrolls, *tefillin* parchments, and *mezzuzot*. Collected here are many laws governing the public reading of the Torah and *Haftarah* (additional readings from the Prophet on Shabbat and special occasions).

3. Semachot (Joyous Occasions)—This is actually a euphemism given to the tractate that hides its true contents, which are laws of mourning. Laws of burial, eulogies, and the like are laid out in this tractate.

4. Kallah (Bride)—The laws of a bride and groom and sexual relations are covered in a single chapter.

5. Kallah Rabbati (the Greater Tractate on Brides)—Most of the discussion here concerns proper manners and behavior of a scholar in regard to modesty, sexual relations and marriage in general. This tract was given its name to indicate its expansion on the limited content of the tractate Kallah.

6. Derech Eretz Rabbah (Longer Tract of Proper Conduct)—Derech Eretz is an oft-used idiom for just about every mundane part of one's life, including livelihood. It also means proper behavior and personal ethics.

7. Derech Eretz Zuta (Short Collection on Courtesy)—Mostly dealing with conduct befitting of a talmid chacham, or torah scholar. There is one appended chapter called Perek Hashalom, which means Chapter of Peace.

8. Gerim (Converts)—This tractate serves as a guide for rabbis involved with conversion of non-Jews. What constitutes renouncing of idolatry and repudiation of incompatible religious beliefs is discussed here. The identification of a Ger Toshav (resident alien) who accepts the Seven Noahide Laws (you read about them in Chapter 19) in the Land of Israel is also covered.

9. Kutim (Samaritans)—The Good Samaritan expression is quite an oxymoron. These people, also referred to as Shomronim, exist even today as a sect identifying with some tenets of Judaism and non-Judaism. Today's descendents live on Mount Eval and are somewhat hostile to the Jewish state. This tractate discusses how to deal with their unusual status.

10. Avadim (Slaves)—These are a collection of detailed laws concerning the phenomenon of Jewish slaves as described in Exodus 21:2–6.

11. Sefer Torah (Torah Scroll)—Certain words of the Torah had to be written in a special way. Also the general laws overlapping some of Tractate Soferim is covered here.

12. Tefillin (Phylacteries) —The Torah commands both head and arm phylacteries containing certain sections of the Torah to be written. Their basic laws are gathered here in one chapter.

13. Tzitzit—The laws governing the special fringed garment are covered here.

14. Mezuzah—A Jew is required to have special scrolls written on parchment placed on all his doorposts. The placement and manner in which they are placed are detailed in this last section of the Minor Tractates.

Though having no specific connection to the Talmudic order in which they appear, these 14 tractates are by no means orphaned from the body of Talmudic study or relevant application to Jewish law. They contain many details that form the basis of modern Jewish practice and are widely cited in literature related to Talmudic logic and debate. Come to think of it—we are going to be exposed to quite a bit of that unique logic and debate as we enter Part 3, "The Spirit of the Talmud." Let's take a look!

The Least You Need to Know

◆ Seder Taharot contains many tractates without Talmudic commentary. They deal primarily with ritual purity laws, most of which are no longer applicable.

◆ Niddah (Separation) is the lone tractate with Talmudic discussion in this order. It covers vital issues involving when marital relations can take place and when a couple must refrain.

- The mikvah is an integral part of the process of purification for a menstruating woman, as well as for others who needed ritual purification.

- The Talmud also contains 14 minor tractates that do not belong to any order, yet contain very relevant teachings.

Part 3

The Spirit of the Talmud

The Talmud has a style all its own. Far from being dry, legalistic discourse, it's full of logical debates, tangential discussions, stories, contradictions, and unresolved disputes. It's also an amazing repository of the principles of mystical thinking and practices, punctuated with tales of dreams and visions and a good dose of humor and wit.

Astrology, numerology, psychology, even potions and remedies—no subject was off limits to the facile minds of the Talmudic sages. These ancient scholars were delighted and fascinated with the world around them. Their keen observations on it are what give the Talmud not only a style of its own, but its own unique spirit.

Chapter 11

Talmudic Logic and Debate

In This Chapter

◆ Logical twists and turns

◆ Introducing Talmudic discussion

◆ The seven elements of Talmudic discussions

◆ Rabbi Jeremiah's hairsplitting logic

Full of debates, tangents, stories, contradictions, and unresolved disputes, the Talmud definitely has a logic system all its own. People sometimes use the term "Talmudic logic" in a negative way to describe what they feel is needless arguing and hairsplitting over minute details. What they don't understand is that such attack and counterattack, even over hairsplitting concepts, is what makes Talmudic discussions come alive. Follow them carefully, and you can almost hear the voices of the great sages who made them.

Talmudic discourse revels a profound truth about how the sages thought, and by extension, about Judaism itself—that the conclusion is more important than the process.

In this chapter, we'll take a look at Talmudic logic, and you'll get a taste of what it's like to step inside the minds of Judaism's great lawmakers.

Introducing Talmudic Discussion

Before we start our exploration of Talmudic logic and debate, let's pause for a story that illustrates just how far Talmudicly honed minds can go, using the elements of logic and reasoning:

After months of negotiation, a Jewish scholar from Odessa was granted permission to visit Moscow. He boarded the train and found an empty seat.

At the next stop a young man got on and sat next to him. The scholar looked at the young man and thought, "This fellow doesn't look like a peasant. If he isn't a peasant he probably comes from this district. If he comes from this district, he must be Jewish because this is, after all, the Jewish district. On the other hand, if he is a Jew, where could he be going? I'm the only one in our district who has permission to travel to Moscow.

"Wait … just outside Moscow there is a little village called Samvet, and you don't need special permission to go there. But why would he be going to Samvet? He's probably going to visit one of the Jewish families there, but how many Jewish families are there in Samvet? Only two—the Bernsteins and the Steinbergs. The Bernsteins are a terrible family, so he must be visiting the Steinbergs. But why is he going? The Steinbergs have only girls, so maybe he's their son-in-law. But if he is, then which daughter did he marry?

"Sarah married that nice lawyer from Budapest and Esther married a businessman from Zhadomir, so it must be Sarah's husband. Which means that his name is Alexander Cohen, if I'm not mistaken. But if he comes from Budapest, with all the anti-Semitism they have there, he must have changed his name. What's the Hungarian equivalent of Cohen? Kovacs. But if he changed his name he must have some special status. What could it be? A doctorate from the University."

At this point the scholar turned to the young man and said, "How do you do, Dr. Kovacs?"

"Very well, thank you, sir," replied the startled passenger. "But how is it that you know my name?"

"Oh," replied the scholar, "it was obvious."

Would you have made all the logical twists and turns that the young Talmud scholar in this story did? Most people wouldn't unless they had the requisite training for doing so, and they were extremely skilled in it. But chasing the logic, as was done in this story, is exactly what intrigues people about Talmud study.

Virtually every Talmudic discussion begins with a statement of fact. That is the starting point and a given, the summation of the oral tradition from Mt. Sinai. As mentioned earlier, Rabbi Judah, the Prince, enlivened the discussion by recording not only the prevailing law, but the minority opinions as well. You could say that by doing so, he set a precedent, and the tone of Talmudic debate and discourse for all time.

According to Rabbi Moshe Chaim Luzzatto, an outstanding eighteenth-century Italian scholar and teacher, virtually every Talmudic discussion is built from seven principal elements of logical reasoning:

1. Statement—The speaker states a simple statement of fact.

2. Question—A sage asks for information, often from the original speaker.

3. Answer—The original speaker responds to the question directly, or

4. Contradiction—He will disprove a statement and contradict or refute it.

5. Proof—The original speaker presents evidence from which the truth of a statement or idea is made obvious.

6. Difficulty—A sage points out something untrue in a statement or idea.

7. Resolution—The original speaker or some other sage reconciles the difficulty raised against a statement or idea, and everyone goes home happy.

Every written or spoken statement in the Talmud will have one of these seven components. However, not all Talmudic debates or discussions end neatly with all contradictions and refutations reconciled. As mentioned in Chapter 1, there is a thing called "taiku," which practically speaking means "a tie." Taiku happens when it's impossible to decide who is correct based on the information presented.

What happens when a taiku arises? According to Maimonides, when a question can't be answered, it is appropriate to take a more stringent position if the matter in question is a Biblical precept, and a lenient one when it is rabbinic in nature.

Some disputes are left unresolved, and the term taiku is not used. In these matters, if a majority of opinions from the sages exists, it is

> **Talmud Trivia**
>
> Rabbi Moshe Chaim Luzzatto, also known as the Ramchal (an acronym for his name Rabbi Moshe Chayim Luzzatto), wrote a book called *The Way of Reason* that took up the challenge of making Talmudic learning accessible to everyone.

Talmud Tidbits

The literal translation of taiku, is either "sealed," "let it stand," or an acronym for the Hebrew phrase "Tishbi (Elijah) will come and answer difficulties and questions."

traditional to side with the majority, in keeping with the Biblical pronouncement specifically directed toward such occurrences—"You shall incline after a majority." (Exodus 23:2) Yet, every stated opinion is treated with respect and assumed to be valid until proven otherwise. Even in the case when majority rule sides with one opinion over another, the Talmud affirms the minority opinion with the statement, "these and those are the words of the Living God."

The message of the Talmud is that not only that a correct understanding and reconciliation of opposing positions is relevant and a desired goal, but careful analysis and evidence-based argument are crucial. This was assured by Rabbi Judah, the codifier of the Oral Laws, who made sure that diverse opinions, divergent opinions, and even rejected opinions were given voice and recorded.

Now, let's take a look at some real Talmudic discussions.

Storekeepers and Nuts

First, a simple one. This selection is from Baba Metzia, "The Middle Gate," in the Order of Damages (Nezikin), and the subject at hand deals with monetary matters.

According to Rabbi Yehudah, a storekeeper "should not distribute parched corn and nuts to the children because he habituates them to frequent his store." In their commentary, however, the sages permit this behavior.

At this point, the Talmud asks, "What is the reasoning of the sages?" The answer? "For the storekeeper can say 'I will distribute nuts and you can distribute dried fruits.'" In other words, there's nothing wrong with a storekeeper offering nuts when another can offer something else. It's a fair business practice and open to all.

End of discussion. This example has three of the seven elements previously discussed: statement, question, and answer.

Let's look at another discussion.

Gamblers and Judges

The third chapter of Sanhedrin, also in the Order of Nezikin, deals with matters of judges, witnesses and testimony in a Jewish court. As it is written:

> "And these are the ones ineligible (to be judges or witnesses)—One who plays with dice (gambler), one who lends on interest, pigeon racers (also a form of gambling, though some say this is a person who use his pigeons as decoys to steal his neighbor's pigeons), and merchants who illegally trade in produce of the sabbatical year …"

First, a sage asks a question: "A dice-player, what has he done (to be considered disqualified)?"

Next, several commentators weigh in with their opinions. Rami bar Chama says that the dice player is disqualified because the wager agreement (we call it betting today) is considered a "reliance," meaning that neither side expects to lose. Therefore, the eventual loser unwillingly surrenders his money, and the winner is considered to be stealing by collecting the wager. So, a successful dice player would be a thief, and wouldn't be allowed to be a witness or judge.

Rabbi Sheishes, on the other hand, disagreed and held that such an agreement was not considered a reliance. He considered such a wager binding. Since each side entertains the hope of bettering their opponent with their "skill" at this game, they accept that dice throwing is ultimately governed by chance and they are resigned to coughing up their money—hence no claim of theft.

Rather, Rabbi Sheishes holds that the reason a gambler is invalid for purposes of testimony is because as a professional gambler he is not engaged in furthering the general welfare of society.

The Talmud asks, since they both agree that a dice-player is disqualified, what practical difference is there in their disagreement? The answer—the gambler has an occupation and is merely playing dice for entertainment. That is, according to Rami bar Chama, such a person is still a thief and disqualified to testify, while according to Rabbi Sheishes, who held that gambling was not an issue of theft but of dereliction, the man can still be a valid witness or judge.

Let's Get Talmudic

It happened that a silver goblet was stolen from Mar Zutra the Pious, when he was in a hotel; in the meantime he saw a young man who dried his hands, after washing, with the garment of another, and he thought, this man does not care for his neighbor's money, and he accused him until he confessed that he stole the goblet. Being that most people of his time were respectful of another's property, Mar Zutra deduced from this young man's actions that he indeed was the thief and extracted a confession. (Baba Metzia 24a)

The Argumentative Rabbi Jeremiah

Here's another example that illustrates just how hairsplitting Talmudic discussions can get.

Rabbi Jeremiah was a notorious agitator in the fourth-century Talmudic academies. He had an unusual penchant for questioning the rationality of the various measurements that were used to define the limits within different categories of Jewish law. The rabbis who opposed Rabbi Jeremiah argued that without such fixed measurements there would be no consistent way of formulating and enforcing laws. Anarchy would become a predicable outcome.

Let's Get Talmudic

"I considered my path, and my legs returned me to the guarding of Your law." (Psalms 119:59) Said King David: "Master of the Universe: each day I would consider going to a particular place, or a certain house, indeed I would be on my way, yet, my legs would bring me to the Synagogues and Houses of Study." (Midrash Leviticus Rabbah, 35:1)

Using a modern analogy, Rabbi Jeremiah's protestations might be comparable to a sharp-witted attorney who defends a client against a moving violation charge by arguing the laws are unfairly applied. For instance, he might have harped on the absurdity of differentiating between stopping behind the white line, or inches over it. Is it logical that one should be legal and the other culpable for punishment? Where's common sense when nobody was injured?

Once Rabbi Jeremiah went too far and it cost him dearly. The proverbial final straw occurred during a discussion of a ruling regarding pigeons, which states that when a young pigeon is found on the ground, if it is within 100 feet of a dovecote it is presumed to be from the dovecote, and must be returned to its owner. However, if the distance is greater than 100 feet, the pigeon is assumed to have come from elsewhere, and hence the finder, keeps it.

Talmud Trivia

Rabbi Jeremiah eventually repented of his ways, respecting the need for consistent guidelines in legal measurements, and was readmitted to the academy.

When Rabbi Jeremiah's students began discussing this law, he posed the following question: If the pigeon was found positioned so that one of its feet was inside the 100-foot range and the other beyond it, who does it belong to?

At this point, the Talmud curtly reports, "It was on this occasion that they unceremoniously removed Rabbi Jeremiah from the academy."

Lost Items and New Vessels

Let's move on to a sample taken from "The Middle Gate." (Baba Metzia) Here, the sages discuss the law of returning lost items to their rightful owners. There is a list of the types of items the finder is obligated to announce, and which he may keep, either because there is no discerning mark, or it is assumed the owner has given up hope of recovery. During the course of the discussion, Rabbi Shimon ben Elazar is quoted as saying, "New vessels (that are found) are not required to be announced."

What constitutes "new vessels"? The Talmud seeks a number of clarifications of Rabbi Shimon's law. The following is a segment of that discussion. As you read it, take note of the flow of logic and use of questions to get to the desired point.

What does he mean by the expression new vessels? Said R. Judah in the name of Samuel: "By the word new he means that the eye was not acquainted with it."

What is this case? If the vessels had a mark what does it matter if he is not acquainted with it? If it doesn't have a mark, what good does it do if he is acquainted with it? Actually, we are speaking of a case where it doesn't have a mark.

The Talmud answers its own inquiry; "It can be used to return it to a seasoned scholar who claims that he recognized them upon sight. If the eye was acquainted with them, we do return it, if not, we don't."

The Talmud now wants to know why a seasoned scholar is an exception to the rule.

As R. Judah said, in the name of Samuel in the following three things, the rabbis "are wont to avoid the truth when being questioned"—concerning a tractate, and concerning issues of intimate relations between him and his wife, and also when asked about the hospitality of an individual, they usually answer in the negative, although it is not so.

Talmud Tidbits _____

Why would these three things cause a scholar to deviate from the absolute truth? If someone asked if a rabbi could repeat a certain tractate by heart, they answered no out of modesty. The same thing was true regarding questions of a more intimate nature. And, when asked about the hospitality of an individual, they answered in the negative so that people would not abuse the man's generosity and bring him to poverty.

And when it was questioned to what purpose did Samuel declare the above, Mar Zutra answered: "It was said with regard to returning a lost thing to one of the rabbis, if he recognized it with his eye, if we know that only in the above three things he hesitates to tell the truth, but in all other things he speaks 100 percent truth, then the article in question is to be returned to him, but not otherwise."

Watching Another's Property

The Talmud tractate Baba Metzia contains a discussion about the obligation of a watchman of another's property. In this case, a man deposited money with a custodian. The custodian then gave it to his mother for safekeeping. She put it in a chest, and it was stolen.

The sage Rava asks, "How shall the judges rule in this case? If we say (to the custodian) 'Go and pay,' he will claim that anyone who makes a deposit does so with the understanding that the custodian may transfer it to his wife and older children, and, by extension, his mother, too.

"If we tell the mother to pay [since the only way to safeguard money is to bury it], she may claim that he didn't tell me that the money was not his. Had he done so, she would have buried it. If we ask the custodian why he did not tell his mother that the money was not his, he can claim that he thought that she would take even better care of his money than of someone else's."

> ### Talmud Trivia
>
> According to Torah law, when a person was prepared to take an oath, invoking the ineffable name of God while holding a Torah Scroll, it was assumed that the person was telling this truth. This is the origin of placing a hand on the Bible today in secular court.

Rava ruled that he (the custodian) takes an oath that he gave the money to his mother, and she must take an oath that she put the money in a chest and it was stolen, and they are not liable.

What are the sages getting at here? The custodian is not liable because depositors accept the possibility that the custodian will transfer care of the money to close family members. Plus, the mother is not liable, even though she did not keep the money "in her hand," e.g. visible, because storage in a chest is an acceptable form of safeguarding money that she thought was her son's, with the understanding that he might need it soon.

The Least You Need to Know

◆ Hairsplitting logic that reveals a truth about the world or of the law given to us by God characterizes Talmudic logic and debate.

◆ There are seven principle components to every Talmudic discussion.

◆ Talmudic discussions often go off on tangents as memory aids, to teach moral lessons, or offer ethical advice.

◆ Talmudic debate is healthy in that it allows divergent opinions, even erroneous ones in the discussion and demonstrates that the process is at least as important as the conclusion.

Chapter 12

Getting Mystical

In This Chapter

- Things revealed and hidden
- Mystical secrets
- Reading the numbers
- The vessels of creation
- Practical Kabbalah and magic
- Kabbalistic astrology

Among its many pearls of wisdom, the Talmud is also a repository of the principles of mystical thinking and practices. No, this isn't about wizardry and magic, although the sages certainly dabbled in some of this. Instead, we're talking about God-consciousness turned up a notch.

There is a dimension to understanding the Torah and Jewish practice that scratches beneath the surface and opens vistas of profound meaning. Issues such as "How did God create the world?" "What was the process of divine inspiration and prophecy?" "What is the deeper meaning behind customs and rituals?" "What hidden meanings are imbedded in the verses of scripture?" and much more, are discussed in the tractates of the Talmud. Let's take a look at some of them.

Things Revealed and Hidden

The entire purpose of our world cries out to be revealed. Take God's first words, "Let there be light!" It seems from that moment onward, we see nothing but creation cascading into one revelation after another. All is revealed. Or is it?

In reality, there is something in the midst of all this revelation that hints to just the opposite. Yes, the world is revealed, but what remains secret is its very creation. At the very center of the world is a mystery, something like the sweetness of a cactus fruit concealed under a shell of prickly skin. It's tough to penetrate, but once you're there, what a treat!

> ### Let's Get Talmudic
>
> The Talmud often comments that certain wise scholars "cover two hand-breadths and reveal just one." This implies that much information in their teachings and proclamations is concealed.

> ### Let's Get Talmudic
>
> Talmudic nitpicking may seem trivial, but it is very important. The sages took divine commands very seriously. For this reason, it was essential to know things like the earliest times that prayers should commence, as well as the latest.

The Talmud itself contains both hidden and revealed things. Because the sages were so cryptic in their writings, those who study them have to dig really deep and be quite skilled in order to uncover the Talmud's concealed gems.

Here's an example of just how hidden the Talmud's meanings can be. The very first discussion in the very first tractate of the Talmud deals with how to fulfill an important biblical commandment called the Kriat Shma. It concerns the recital of several passages that begin with the words "Hear O' Israel, The Lord is our God, The Lord is One." (Deut. 6:4) It also says "… you shall speak of them (words of Torah) when you retire [at night] and arise [morning]." (Deut. 6:7)

Well, "night" is a rather long period. In addition, fulfilling this commandment raises an important question: Does night begin when the sun sets, when there are three visible stars in the sky, or when it is pitch black out?

The Talmudic discussion that follows is involved and technical, so we won't get into it here. There is, however, a part of it that seems a bit out of place:

> Rabbi Eliezer said, "There are three 'watches in the night.'" At the first watch a donkey brays. At the second, dogs bark. At the third, an infant suckles from its mother's breast and a woman converses with her husband." (Berachot 3a)

What is Eliezer getting at? Why does the Talmud mention the concept of "three watches," in such a fashion? Why not just say there are three periods of time dividing the night, then go on with the question of when to pray? What the sages are doing here is cloaking a profound moral lesson under seemingly mundane facts of nature. Their discussion has more to do with the nature of human existence than with determining the correct times to say evening prayers.

Let's take a deeper look, based on the teachings of the Vilna Gaon, an outstanding eighteenth-century commentator on the Talmud. As he explained it, the world of physical existence is the "night," blocking out the light of the divine presence. Further, the three watches are three stages in our human existence. First is youth, when our existence is dominated by our physical needs and creature comforts. This stage is represented by the donkey braying.

> **Talmud Trivia**
>
> Chomer, the Hebrew word for donkey, is the same as (the word for) physicality.

The dog is the next stage—an animal that has companions, but demands a good deal of attention for itself. Similarly, when we marry and start making a living we allow nothing to get in the way. The dog is a great metaphor for this because it is seen often as the boldest of the domestic animals. We establish ourselves in society, but also we want to make our mark on the world and have other people serve our needs.

The third period is old age, represented by the suckling babe and the intimate relationship (there is disagreement among the sages on the meaning of the word converse, with some saying it refers to sexual intercourse and others saying it simply means talking) between wife and husband. The babe represents innocence and return to the source of life, while the wife and husband represent our relationship with God. This is the phase of life when the concerns of the soul take precedence. In the autumn of our lives, regardless of how far we have strayed, many of us desire to return to the source and tend to spiritual needs.

There are countless examples of Talmudic passages similar to the one you just read that conceal hidden messages and lessons on life in this fashion. The sages wished to preserve these pearls of wisdom, yet they weren't going to do so in an obvious way. The approach they took did indeed conceal more than they revealed, but that was the idea. When students came across them, they would pique the curiosity and stimulate the mind, as well as stimulate discussions with their teachers and mentors.

Talmud Tutor

Gematria is an ancient system by which hidden truths and meanings are discovered within words. It is formed from the Greek words ge, meaning earth, and matria, meaning measurement.

Playing the Numbers

One of the ways in which the Talmud's hidden truths and meanings are discovered is through *gematria*, which assigns a numerical value to each Hebrew letter.

Jewish tradition teaches that this system was transmitted along with the Oral Tradition from Mt. Sinai. The basic premise is that each letter of the Hebrew alphabet corresponds to a number, as detailed on this chart.

Gematria Chart

Order	Hebrew Letter	English	Numerical Value	Name of Letter
1	א	A	1	Aleph
2	ב	B	2	Beth
3	ג	G	3	Gimel
4	ד	D	4	Daleth
5	ה	H	5	Heh
6	ו	V	6	Vav
7	ז	Z	7	Zayin
8	ח	Ch	8	Chet
9	ט	T	9	Tet
10	י	I	10	Yud
11	ך , כ	K	20	Kaph
12	ל	L	30	Lamed
13	ם , מ	M	40	Mem
14	ן , נ	N	50	Nun
15	ס	S	60	Samech
16	ע	O	70	Ayin
17	ף , פ	Ph	80	Peh
18	ץ , צ	Tz	90	Tzadee
19	ק	Q	100	Kuf
20	ר	R	200	Resh
21	ש	Sh	300	Shin
22	ת	Th	400	Taf

As you can see, the Hebrew alphabet has 22 letters, with numerical values from 1 to 400. Using the gematria chart, it is possible to total up the numerical values of words. These words may then correspond with other words that contain the same numerical value, or simply hint to an idea.

Through gematria one can observe secret insights and unique connections that are imbedded within the Talmud. These hidden messages and wisdom come to life and sometimes teach practical lessons.

Let's Get Talmudic

The description of the classification of Hebrew alphabet was first recorded in a 4,000-year-old book called the Sefer Yetzirah, or The Book of Formation, which is attributed to Abraham. This book, which has been translated into English, also contains mystical teachings about an ancient form of astrology that is no longer practiced today. According to at least one ancient source, Abraham was indeed an astrologer, and taught it to the Phoenicians and the Egyptians.

Gematria is a hotly discussed and debated topic in some circles. Let's see how it works.

You recall the Biblical story of how Jacob sends his sons down to Egypt to buy food. (Exodus 42:2) Jacob used the word redu, meaning "go down." Using gematria, this word contains a hint to this hidden fact about the sojourn of the Israelites in Egypt.

Looking at the left column of the chart, locate the twentieth, fourth, and sixth letters ordered. The numerical equivalents are found in the fourth column. These three letters yield:

$$\text{ו} + \text{ד} + \text{ר} = \text{רדו}$$
$$6 + 4 + 200 \ (210)$$

The gematria (numerical equivalent) of the redu is 210. This is the exact amount of years that the Children of Israel dwelt in Egypt before their redemption.

Let's try another example, this one related to the tradition that 613 biblical commandments were conveyed to Moses. The tradition traces to Rabbi Simlai, who wrote in Makkos 23b in the Talmud that the commandments are, "… 365 prohibitions corresponding to the days of the solar year, and 248 positive commandments corresponding to the limbs [bones] in the human body" (by the way, this number has been scientifically confirmed).

Another great ancient sage, Rabbi Hamnuna, found a hint to this sum from a gematria based on the verse, "Moses commanded us the Torah as a heritage." (Deuteronomy 33:4) Rabbi Hamnuna taught, "The numerical equivalent of the word Torah is 611. To this total one must add the first two commandments of the Decalogue (Ten Commandments), because they are distinct inasmuch we heard them directly."

Let's do the math, shall we?

$$\text{ת} = 400$$
$$\text{ו} = 6$$
$$\text{ר} = 200$$
$$\text{ה} = 5$$
$$\overline{611}$$
$$+ \quad 2 \quad \text{(For the first two Commandments,}$$
$$\text{which were heard by all at Mt. Sinai)}$$
$$\overline{613} \quad \text{Total Commandments}$$

Mystical Writings

When people talk about Jewish mysticism, they are almost always referring to a group of writings called the *Kabbalah*. These writings are based on the teachings of Rabbi Shimon Bar Yochai (you met him in Chapter 4), who spent 13 years delving into the deepest mystical secrets contained in the Torah with his son while hiding from Roman authorities in a cave.

Talmud Tidbits

When Rabbi Shimon's teachings were revealed, it was said that the revelations of this "concealed law," were comparable to the revelation of the revealed law by Moses at Mt. Sinai.

For 1,500 years, this wisdom was transmitted strictly orally to the most elite of the scholars. After bar Yochai's death, however, it was systematically recorded into a work known as the Zohar, which forms the backbone of the mystical teachings, or Kabbalah, that are based on the Torah. The Zohar is

written in Aramaic in a dialect similar to that
of the Talmud. It is formatted as a commentary on the five books of Moses.

Many consider the Torah as the "how," of
Judaism, while the Zohar forms the "why."
That is a bit simplistic, for the Torah itself contains many of the kabbalistic principles laid out
by the Zohar. Still, most people who study the
Torah interpret it as a narrative and basis of
divine instruction of the "do's and don'ts,"
while mystics typically look for the hidden signs
and symbols that reveal the secrets of God.

Talmud Tutor

Kabbalah means
"receiving," as in accepting
and transmitting a tradition that
has been handed down from
generation to generation. **Zohar**
translates as "splendor" or "radiance."

Throughout the centuries, Torah scholars and devout Jews used what could be called
Kabbalistic concepts for what would be today called self-transformation: to turn
themselves into purer vessels for serving God. The intellectual study of Kabbalah—
the philosophy of it—helped by outlining the various levels of existence known to the
scholars.

What the Kabbalah Is and Isn't

Kabbalah is perhaps the most tragically misunderstood part of Judaism. In fact, the
word Kabbalah didn't even exist until the Middle Ages. It was then, in medieval
Europe, that the English word cabal, meaning secretive councils, was coined to
connote a secretive (implied "nefarious") council or intrigue. Fueled by various dark
superstition phobias and tinged with anti-Semitism, such concepts led to persecution
of quiet, unassuming rabbinic leaders for alleged occult practices.

More recently, everything from tarot cards to astrological readings have distorted and
usurped basic Kabbalistic teachings, ripping them entirely out of context. It is now
trendy for a fraternity of both Jewish and non-Jewish celebrities to dabble in its study.

As previously mentioned, there are revealed and hidden things about the world we
live in. By analogy, you can think of the invisible forces behind physical reality as we
know it today—electromagnetism, gravity, the strong and weak nuclear forces. There
are also invisible forces behind social reality, such as the emotions we feel toward others that unconsciously affect our behavior. Kabbalah says there are even more esoteric
realities behind these, and they all are traceable to the ongoing creative activity of
God.

The study of Kabbalah aims to bring some of these hidden spiritual forces to awareness. Certain people could exercise some control over them—this would be what was referred to as kabbalistic "magic." Yet control was not the ultimate ideal, because the highest spiritual forces can never be brought to awareness—and certainly not controlled—while a person is still in physical form. Through study and prayer, however, people could become more receptive to the Divine, and a better vehicle through which God could act.

Talmud Tidbits

Although the Kabbalah is often referred to as being one work, it is actually a body of mystical writings. They include interpretations of mystical visions of prophets like Ezekial, and a lengthy work called Etz HaChaim, or the Tree of Life, which is the most famous, and perhaps, most studied of all Kabbalistic texts. It includes eight sections, called the Eight Gates, which range from commentary on some Zohar passages to explaining and describing the doctrine of transmigration (the soul's passage into another human body at or after death).

Talmud Tutor

Literally, a **pardes** means an orchard of grapevines or other fruit-bearing trees. Just as a vineyard can produce much enjoyment this word is used figuratively to allude to the higher levels of knowledge and understanding of the Divine.

Talmud Trivia

Developing the required level of egolessness for Kabbalah study took some time. Forty was typically the minimum age at which an already seasoned scholar was inducted into the study of Kabbalah and its mystical secrets.

To illustrate this concept, let's explore a story about four sages of the Talmud who were attempting to comprehend the deep secrets of the essence of God. The Talmud (Chagigah 14b) tells us that these four entered an orchard, or *pardes*, of mystical revelation, a Garden of Eden on high, by invoking the Divine Name.

These were four renowned scholars and pious men: Ben Zoma, Ben Azzai, Elisha ben Avuya, and Rabbi Akiva. They prepared themselves extensively with prayer, fasting and immersion in the mikvah. Nevertheless, after the experience one died, one went mad, and one became an apostate. Only one, Rabbi Akiva, came out unscathed, as "he entered in peace and left in peace."

The point is clear: These men, wise and thoughtful though they were, nevertheless took a gamble. While sometimes the experience "from above" may be a positive influence, one can't count on it—even if you're a profoundly religious person.

Dipping into the well of divine secrets was a regular pastime of the sages of the Talmud. But they were very patient and did not boast of this ability. Humility was, in fact, a prerequisite for Kabbalah study. The sages who did so disciplined themselves in the spirit of Moses who, the Torah tells us, was "the most humble man that ever lived."

The Vessels of Creation

To illustrate a mystical secret that emerges from studying the Kabbalah, let's turn to Rabbi Yitzchak Luria, a Talmudist and Kabbalist par excellence from the sixteenth century. Also known as "the Arizal," his account of the creation story is at the core of all mystical Jewish movements today and has influenced modern Jews of all philosophies.

First, a shortened form of the creation story, taken from the book of Genesis:

> In the beginning of God's creating of the heavens and the earth—when the earth was profoundly empty with darkness over the face of depths, the Divine Presence hovered upon the face of the waters—God said, "Let there be light!" and there was light."

Here's the Arizal's take:

> Originally, there was only Ain Sof, the Infinite—all of reality was God. In order for the universe to exist, God had to "withdraw" from some part of that reality. This metaphorical withdrawal (tzimtzum) left a "place" bereft of God's presence, allowing the cosmos to come into being.

> Now God did not forsake this empty space, but projected a beam of light, which became a mass without form inside that space. From that mass, all levels of reality came into existence. God at that point injected another beam of light, which began to create "vessels"; (in typical Talmudic fashion, the Arizal speaks in symbols and metaphors in his analysis. For instance, he interprets "light" is a metaphor or a hint to something more than the physical form) these represent facets of God's activity and God's qualities, and each contains a portion of that light from Ain Sof. This process could not reach completion and was halted. Some of the vessels were not strong enough to contain the divine light. These vessels were shattered into bits.

> While the vessels fell and became the world of reality and material, this ray of light returned to Ain Sof. A residue of the divine light adhered to the shattered vessels, much as oil adheres to a vessel even after it is poured out. Thus there are sparks of God's light trapped in every piece of reality. God left an "imperfect unity" of His own creation. Through prayer and correct action, a person

liberates and elevates these sparks and "repairs" God's unity, so to speak. That process is known as *Tikkun Olam*, or repair of the world or universe.

Talmud Tutor

Tikkun Olam translates to repair of the world, or repair of the universe.

What is the Arizal getting at here? When you look at the world around you, you notice a great deal of fragmentation. Wars, social inequalities, political parties, divorce, so many things that cause pain. This is because, in the Arizal's terms, "the vessels were shattered."

Our job as human beings is to pick up the pieces and rearrange them in harmonious forms, to heal the pain and to "mend the world." Whatever your profession or place in life, you have the opportunity every day to make tikkun, and this contributes to the reunification of all the lights of creation

Practical Kabbalah and Magic

The Talmud and other sources ascribe supernatural activities to many great rabbis. Their magic incantations indeed accomplished great deeds for the sake of the community. According to the Sanhedrin, they were even able to create a calf when they needed food.

The rabbis even occasionally used white magic to counteract black. Using clever subterfuge and practical kabbalistic wisdom, Rabbi Simon ben Shetah hanged eighty witches who were wreaking havoc on the community, ridding the Land of Israel of a serious threat in a single day. (Sanhedrin 45b) We even find scholars capable of pulverizing miscreants with a mere glance, or reduced them to a heap of bones.

How did they do this? Almost no one knows today, at least not precisely how it was done in ancient times. We do know that the sages intoned certain mystical names of God and offered petitions to the Heavenly Abode while in deep meditative states.

Taking the Name of God (Not in Vain)

God's name itself is believed to have immense mystical power. For this reason, the Jewish people refer to God in several ways, but they never use his name directly. The holiest name of God, which is used in study and prayer, is known as the Tetragrammaton and is based on four Hebrew letters, yud, heh, vav, and heh (YHVH). It could only be pronounced safely in the Holy Temple, as the immense physical and ritual structure of the Temple was the only place that could contain its power.

Kabbalists also refer to the 42-lettered name of God. This is a name formed through permutations of seven groups of six Hebrew letters taken from words in the Torah. In a mystical way, the actual name of 42 words emerges before the first letter of the Torah, alluding to God's "work" before the creation. This is one of the most obscure names of God. Rashi comments that "this name was not given over to us." (Kiddushin 71b)

Talmud Tidbits

Out of respect, devout Jews to this day do not pronounce the name YVHV, either when reciting out loud or when reading to themselves. Instead, they substitute Adonai (Lord).

The origin of this name is not well known. It is mentioned many times in mystical literature, and is also cryptically eluded to in a meditative prayer found in the Sabbath evening prayers. It is believed that one who truly understood the name could manipulate God's creation with it. If one was ill tempered, too young, given over to substance abuse and particular when insulted, he lacked the proper restraint when, or when not, to use the 42-lettered name of God. Such a person would cause more harm than good.

Tradition has it that the High Priest was the only one familiar with and knew how to accurately pronounce what also known as the Shem Hameforash, the "Detailed Explicit Name." Thus, this name was never documented and was lost after the destruction of the Second Temple with the end of the priesthood.

Let's Get Talmudic

Rav Judah said in Rav's name: The forty-two lettered Name (of God) is entrusted only to him who is discreet, meek, middle-aged, free from bad temper, sober and not insistent on his rights. And he who knows it, is careful and observes it in purity, is beloved above and popular below, feared by man and inherits two worlds, this world and the future world. (Talmud Kiddushin 71a)

Spiritual Healing and the Kabbalah

In addition to countering black magic, spiritual healing using kabbalistic techniques was fairly common among the sages. These practices are similar to the miracles performed by the prophets, which included expelling demons through exorcism. As historians have pointed out, the late classical world in the entire Mediterranean region were engrossed and fascinated by the subject of spiritual healing by means of amulets and special incantations. Every sage of the Talmud was an expert in this field.

The Talmud notes three incidents of exorcism by rabbis. The following story is told about Rabbi Hanina ben Dosa, who lived in the first century:

> Once Rabbi Hanina ben Dosa went to immerse himself in [the water of] a cave. Kuthim (Samaritans) came and placed a large rock over the mouth of the cave. The spirits came and removed it. Subsequently, an evil spirit haunted a poor woman in Rabbi Hanina's neighborhood.

> His students said to him: Rabbi, see how this poor woman suffers grief from the evil spirit. Rabbi Hanina addressed the spirit: Why do you cause grief to the daughter of Abraham? The spirit responded: Are you not the one who went down to dip in the cave, and so on, ... till I came with my brothers and my father's household and removed the rock. Is this how you pay me for the favor I did you? He answered her: I decree ...!

The passage abruptly ends here but we are told elsewhere that indeed the spirit fled and the woman was cured, revealing the power of Rabbi Hanina.

Talmud Tidbits

The line between the physical and the spiritual was fluid in the ancient world, and most people believed that spirits that entered the body caused sickness. Just as with other "magical" accomplishments, however, healing had to be performed through the power of God, generally by calling upon the name of God.

Even healing would be forbidden if it involved idolatry or pagan worship. The Talmud tells us that the nephew of a great sage suffered death rather than resort to an idolatrous ritual of the pagans that was known to cure his aliment. (Avodah Zarah 27b) In addition, some passages in the Talmud that excoriate novice wizards and extol occult arts where useful and prudently applied.

Women and the Kabbalah

Young Jewish women seem to have become involved in magical practices during Talmudic times. Indeed, the rabbis were concerned about women dabbling in magic merely to alleviate their boredom, so they issued decrees urging women to remain active in community life. (Eruvin 64b) Of course, women were very much involved in caring for infants and mothers, the sick and the elderly, so they would naturally have turned to mystical teachings that might offer potential for healing. The sages had no objection to using traditional folk medicine treatments that were proven effective. But, since women rarely had opportunity to learn Torah deeply, the rabbis were concerned that they might misuse their knowledge or even cross over into paganism.

The Talmud describes a woman, the mother of Rabbi Ahadbuy ben Ammi, as making a potion of roses and strong liquor for a man, which caused the poison of a snake to come out of his body. (Shabbat 109b) Many other remedies are also described in the Talmud. However, as mentioned above, the line between treatments for physical illness and treatments for demonic attack was fluid, so that antidotes for magic were also prescribed. The sage Ameimar was even taught a protective chant against other sorceresses by a head sorceress. (Pesachim 110a–b)

The Kabbalah and the Community

The multitudes used protective omens, went to wizards for spells and amulets, and warned against numerous dangers. It is not surprising that the Talmud, too, records some of these things. For example, the sages recommended avoiding the shade of certain trees believed to be the hiding places of demons. They discussed at length the folk belief that doing things in pairs was dangerous because the "king of the demons" ruled pairs. (Even today, folk traditions allude to this ancient belief; "natural gardening" books sometimes advise not setting out plants in even numbers.)

Yet, the sages were also concerned about the proliferation of magical beliefs and practices, and warned their people of the consequences of relying too heavily on them. They declared that "Adultery and sorcery have destroyed everything," (Sotah 9:13) and that the majesty of God departed from Israel and His wrath came upon the world when the wizards became too numerous. (Tosefta Sotah, 14:3) In this way, the sages of the Talmud brought a balanced perspective to the world through their faith in the blessings of God canceling the power of evil.

The Least You Need to Know

- Hidden messages and deeper teachings are imbedded in many Talmud teachings. In many cases the rabbis "concealed more than they revealed."

- Mystical teachings, or Kabbalah, are part of the oral tradition handed down to Moses at Mt. Sinai but only shared among a privileged few.

- Mystical teachings on such subjects as the creation and on how God deals with his world add a much deeper meaning to the Torah.

- Magic and practical Kabbalah were discouraged for the masses, yet had positive uses in the hands of the sages. Cures and community needs were affected through these techniques.

Dreams and Visions

In This Chapter

◆ The importance of dreams

◆ Dreams and prophecy

◆ Interpreting dreams

◆ Making a bad dream good

Most people are intrigued by their dreams, and no wonder! Dreams are often bizarre or mysterious. We spend nearly a third of our lives sleeping, and much of that dreaming, so there must be some purpose in dreams.

Psychologists believe there is much to be learned from dreams. Some believe that every part of a dream contains a subconscious message about the dreamer. Others theorize that dreams serve to "clean" the files of the brain and allow people to forget disturbing experiences, images, and events.

The Talmudic sages were also very much aware of the importance of dreams, and spent a good amount of time discussing and analyzing them. While they didn't always agree (when did they ever?) as to exactly how dreams should be taken, or whether everything that a dream contains was

Talmud Trivia

In the Talmud, a person who went without dreaming for long periods of time was seen as unwell, a viewpoint that has been backed up by modern science. Researchers at the University of Cape Town found that patients who had sustained damage to a certain part of their brain could no longer dream.

Talmud Tidbits

Many of the sages of the Talmud believed that dreams are valuable. So much so, in fact, that several pages of a chapter in tractate Berachot (found in the order Zeraim) discuss dreams. There are also mentions of it in such mystical writings as the Zohar.

to be taken seriously, they, too, were clearly fascinated by what happens when the mind and body are at rest.

The Value of Dreams

The ancient Hebrews understood that dreaming was healthy. The prophet Isaiah even petitioned God to "… make me dream and give me life." (Isaiah 38:16)

But it was also understood that there was more to dreams than good mental health. Dreams could convey messages and information, and illuminate the mind and soul of the dreamer.

Yet, the very nature of dreams makes it difficult to know exactly what they're all about and to determine their meaning and significance. Still, this didn't discourage the sages from offering their interpretations of dreams. In fact, it would be possible to write a book on their dream interpretation alone.

Even though the sages do offer their interpretations of dreams, Talmudic literature gives a caveat emptor, encouraging one to err on the side of caution when it comes to dream interpretation.

Unlocking the Meaning of Dreams

Why does the Talmud urge caution when it comes to assigning meaning to dream imagery? As mentioned, the sages saw dreams as conveyers of information, but they didn't believe that all parts of every dream held equal weight, or were equally important.

Some sages believed that dreams must be interpreted to unlock their meaning. Rav Chisda, a third-century sage wrote, "A dream that is not interpreted is like a letter that has not been read." While his words clearly underscore his belief that dreams should be investigated, Rav Chisda also warned that dreams should not be taken as authoritative statements. No good dreams, nor bad dreams, he said, were ever fulfilled completely.

Wandering into the Bizarre

Rabbi Shimon Bar Yochai, the author of the Zohar, wrote that there is no dream without some nonsense in it. In other words, when one is sleeping, the mind easily can wander into the bizarre. In general, the Talmudists recognize that the mind can sometimes latch onto things that have no meaning, so it's not necessary to be obsessed with interpreting every part of a dream.

The sages believed that dreams are associated with the part of the mind that's responsible for imagination, and that one's imagination can become quite lively during sleep, a belief that modern science has proven to be true. When we sleep, logic and reason recede into the background, ordinary sight and hearing are muted, and gross motor movements are usually shut down as well. Even the metabolic rate is subdued so that a sleeping person is in a sort of suspended animation. However, one component of the mind—the imagination—does not retire. It remains very busy, creating images that we seem to "see" and sounds we seem to "hear."

Further experts believe that sleep loosens the bond between the body and the soul, and sometimes, allows one's mind to travel to places not possible in a waking state. This, too, was a belief of the Talmudists, who considered sleep to be "a sixtieth part of death." (Brachot 57b)

Dreams and Symbolism

So are dreams to be believed? Or are they to be seen as products of an overly vivid imagination at work inside of a resting brain, and not taken seriously? Even the sages weren't quite sure on this one. When he would experience a negative dream, the sage Shmuel would recite a verse from Zechariah 10:2, "Dreams speak falsely." When he saw a positive dream he would reference another biblical verse (Numbers 12:6), and proclaim, "But do dreams speak falsely? Surely it is written, 'through a dream I shall speak to him.'" (This biblical verse portrays dreams as a vehicle to convey truthful information from God through the prophets, so Shmuel is suggesting that the verse may also apply to other dreams.)

On one point a minority opinion in the Talmud seems to side with the great psychoanalyst Sigmund Freud, who believed that dreams held great symbolism, and that all details of a dream, even the most absurd, are meaningful. Rabbi Yonatan said that dreams show only what is in a person's own heart or mind. The sage Rava applauded that sentiment, stating, "Know that this is so, for in a dream one never sees a palm tree of gold or an elephant passing through the eye of a needle!" (Brachot 55b)

This statement seems a bit odd; because our minds do sometimes yield dream images that one would never see in reality. But the main point is that dreams can sometimes be (and according to Rabbi Yonatan always are) merely expressions of one's desires or fears.

Let's Get Talmudic

The Talmud cites a clever story of psychological suggestibility and dreams. The Roman emperor Hadrian, in one of several exchanges with the first-century sage Rabbi Yehoshua ben Chananya, demanded, "You Jews claim that you are very wise. If so, then tell me what I am going to see in my dream tonight!" The rabbi answered, "In your dream you will see that the Persians will induce you into the service of their king (the reference is probably to the Sassanids, heirs of the Persian empire who warred periodically with the Romans during Talmudic times). They will abduct you and force you to shepherd unclean animals with a staff of gold."

Hadrian was transfixed by this disturbing prediction the entire day and indeed dreamed this exact vision when he went to bed that evening. (Brachot 56a)

Such dreams would certainly be regarded as mundane or psychological dreams, easily explained. But not all dreams are of this sort. In contrast to Freud, the Talmud regards dreams as potential vehicles for a special kind of knowledge. They can tell us what the future holds.

Dreams and Prophecy

Dream prophecies are mentioned quite a few times in scripture. Abraham had an important dream about the future enslavement and liberation of his descendants. The story of Joseph sharing his dreams with his brothers (and paying the consequences for doing so) is well known.

So, too, were the people of Israel aided through the medium of dreams. Joseph became viceroy of Egypt through Pharaoh's dreams. The prophet Daniel's rise to a place of influence during the Babylonian exile was partially affected through his interpretation of the dreams of King Nebuchadnezzar.

Let's Get Talmudic

"A good dream should be kept in mind and not forgotten, so that it will be fulfilled. ... Therefore Joseph mentioned his dream [to his family], so that it would come to be. He would always anticipate its fulfillment." (The Zohar, based on Genesis 37:11)

The Oral Law teaches that all prophets, except for Moses, experienced their prophetic messages through dreams and their interpretation. Prophecy, in Maimonides' words, occurred exclusively through a "dream, a night vision," or, if by day, through a "deep sleep." Regardless, a prophetic dream was accompanied by "tremulous limbs, an exhausted body, and disrupted thoughts," leaving the mind "free to understand what it sees." (Mishna Torah, Foundations of the Torah, 7:2)

> **Talmud Trivia**
>
> Sometimes help was sought in dreams but it was not forthcoming, as in the case of the first king of Israel, Saul: "And Saul inquired of the Lord, neither by dreams (was he answered). (I Samuel 28:6)

However, after the destruction of the first temple in Jerusalem, prophecy came to a grinding halt. Nonetheless, the Talmud teaches that the world would not be entirely without this form of communication from God for indeed, "Although I hide My face from them, I shall speak to them in a dream." (Chagigah 5b)

The majority of the sages held that all dreams contain at least a kernel of discernible truth. Given this, are there ways to know whether a particular dream contains prophecy? The Talmud takes note of three types of dreams that are likely to be fulfilled:

- A dream occurring just before waking in the morning

- A dream that a friend dreams about you

- A dream interpreted within the dream itself

> **Talmud Tidbits**
>
> Some later Talmud commentaries state that the degree of excitement generated by a dream is a measure of its veracity. Rabbi Yehudah Patiah, a great Kabbalist of the nineteenth century, insisted that hearing one of God's names in any language during a dream is a sign that the dream will come true.

Another type of dream that might possibly be fulfilled is one that is repeated, such as Pharaoh's double dream that was later interpreted by Joseph (found in Genesis 41:7).

A Dream Is Only as Good as Its Interpreter

As previously mentioned, the sages believed that dreams had to be interpreted to unlock their meaning. But interpretation puts a human spin on dream symbolism. And, such spin can never be entirely without bias—a point that later sages were well aware of when they concluded, "The realization of all dreams goes after the mouth."

But if a dream were truly prophetic, would the whims of a subjective interpreter make it any less so? Rabbi Bana'ah said "I took my dream to the twenty-four dream interpreters in Jerusalem and each one interpreted my dream differently, and they all came true!"

How could this be? Could the interpretation "cause" the dream? Or is the dream a set of possibilities, any of which could be actualized, and the interpretation anchors one of them to reality?

The Talmud tries to answer by bringing scriptural proof. Rabbi Bana'ah, the author of this principle that "all dreams follow the mouth," relies on Rabbi Elazar, who points to a story about Joseph (Genesis 41:13) that goes like this: Two chamberlains of the Pharaoh are both thrown into the slammer with Joseph over some indiscretion. On the same night these servants have similar dreams. Joseph hears them out. For the baker he proclaims that the meaning of the dream is that he would be executed. The wine butler was fortunate to hear that he would be pardoned and reinstated. Indeed, that is precisely what happened.

About this story, Rabbi Elazar writes, "Just as he interpreted it for us, so did it happen." He links Joseph's interpretation to the outcome.

Rules for Interpreters

While the meaning of dreams was clearly up to one's interpretation, there were some do's and don'ts. Giving way-out explanations that don't relate to the dream as told was frowned upon. According to the sage Rava, the interpreter must interpret in a way that approximates what the dreamer saw in the vision. In the above example, the wine bearer saw a specific vision in his dream—"a grapevine with three tendrils, and its blossoms bloomed and its clusters ripened into grapes." Joseph interpreted this as portentous to good tidings in three days, using the number and the sense of time elapsed as clues to interpretation.

Dealing With Ambivalent Dreams

Ambivalence is common in many dreams that contain neutral information. If someone dreamt of, say, a head of lettuce (the Talmud cites such a dream), one possible interpretation would be to view the layered leaves as a multiplying of profits. Another interpreter might assert that the bitterness of the vegetable implies a souring of one's business affairs. We could say that either interpretation was latent in the dream. Or, other images in the dream might hint what direction the interpretation should take.

The Talmudic sages believed that dreams containing an ambivalent message may emanate from a demon, or from one's secret desires or fears, and had no intrinsic meaning. With these dreams, the interpretation rules.

However, there is another type of dream whose interpretation is beyond doubt. It is too specific to be given over to chance and cannot be influenced by someone's subjective take. This type of dream, says the sage Rava, is a dream sent through the proxy of an angel. While these dreams must also be interpreted, any interpretation given can be considered accurate.

Pick Your Interpreter Well

If you want to have a dream interpreted, says the Zohar, share it only with a friend, lest an unscrupulous individual ruin your day with a negative twist. Good advice, right? But sometimes even the sages didn't follow their own wise words.

The Talmud tells a story of an ancient charlatan who victimized the sage Rava. This wizard, named Bar Hedya, exacted a handsome price for dream interpretations. Abbaye, Rava's companion, also had dealings with him, but came out unscathed. How? Rava failed to pay Bar Hedya his fee, and thus several dreams were interpreted negatively, while Abbaye paid the fee and his life turned out okay.

It gets pretty wild in this Talmudic episode. Rava is arrested and incarcerated by the Roman authorities on trumped-up charges. He loses a significant amount of livelihood and his wife dies. Meanwhile, Abbaye flourishes. The last straw for Rava was when he told this Bar Hedya, "In my dream I saw two heads of turnips." Bar Hedya responded, "You will receive two blows with clubs today." In order to protect himself from such an outcome, Rava spent the entire day in the Beit Midrash (house of learning).

Toward the evening, Rava saw two blind people fighting with one another. They were in the midst of exchanging blows when Rava interceded to break it up. Unappreciative of his peaceful gesture, they turned on Rava and dealt him two blows with their clubs.

When Rava eventually had the money to pay for Bar Hedya's services, he noticed a change in the tenor of the interpretations. Rava would report, "I saw the walls of my house collapsing." Bar Hedya told him, "You will acquire abundant property without boundaries." Rava would say, "I saw my entire mansion in ruins and people taking it away brick by brick." To this Bar Hedya responded, "Your teachings will spread far and wide."

Eventually the two happened to be traveling together on a ship. Bar Hedya was uncomfortable traveling with Rava and tried to disembark at the nearest port. In his rush, a book fell from his belongings and Rava picked it up. He found written inside, "All dreams follow their interpretation." Rava sternly rebuked him "It was within your power to interpret these dreams one way or the other and you chose to make them harbingers of misfortune?" He prayed that Bar Hedya be handed over to "a regime that would have no pity on him."

And that's exactly what happened when Bar Hedya tried interpreting dreams in Rome. A royal guard of the emperor's wardrobe had a dream that a worm bore a hole through his hand. Bar Hedya interpreted it as a sign that silk garments of the caesar would be eaten by worms. Sure enough, the caesar's royal silk garments were eaten by worms.

The punishment meted out to Bar Hedya is too gruesome to describe.

Turning a Dream to Good

What clues does the Talmud give for interpreting dreams? Interestingly, the sages perceived more than 1,500 years ago what Sigmund Freud would make so famous later: Dreams speak in a coded language, full of twists and turns, especially that oddity of human communication called puns.

For example, say the sages, if a person dreams of a cat in a place where a certain word means "cat," the dream-cat means something different than if you dream it where a different dialect is spoken and a different word is used for "cat."

In another story, a man dreamed of a place called Cappadocia. "Did you live in Cappadocia?" queried the sage who was asked to interpret the dream. The man said no. "Did you plan to go to Cappadocia? Did your father do business in Cappadocia?" Each time, the answer was no. "Then," the interpreter said, "it means you will discover a treasure of coins in the tenth beam of your house."

Here, the interpreter first tried to discover whether this was a mundane dream, having to do with current or past events in the person's life. Since it wasn't, he interpreted Cappadocia symbolically and prophetically, and went with a play on two parts of the word—"capa," which means beam in Greek, and "deka," which means ten. Then he combined the symbolism in these words with a little free-form fortune telling about future wealth.

Talmud Tidbits

If a person had a frightening dream, he could even bring it to a "dream court" of three friends. They would recite auspicious biblical verses that suggest turning the dream toward a good future outcome, and then an affirmation stating, "You have dreamed a good dream. Seven times may it be declared from heaven that it is good."

Since "the dream follows the mouth," and contains possibilities that might be fulfilled, it was important to make an effort to give a positive interpretation.

In addition, the sages formulated a prayer asking God to direct the dream's possibilities toward a good outcome. It still appears in traditional prayer books and is usually recited in an undertone during the public formal chanting of the Priestly Blessing. This prayer tells us the importance the sages attached to seeing one's dreams in a good light.

Let's Get Talmudic

The following prayer is the one coined by the Talmudic sages to be recited when one has had a disturbing dream:

"Master of the Universe, I am Yours and my dream is Yours, I have dreamt a dream but I do not know its meaning. Whether I have dreamt a dream about myself, or whether my friends have dreamt about me, or if I have dreamt about others; if these dreams are positive ones, strengthen them and fortify them like the dreams of Joseph the Righteous. But if they require healing [for they portend evil], heal them as You healed the bitter waters, through the hand of Moses our Teacher; as You healed Miriam from her leprosy; and as You healed Hezekiah from his illness; as like You (healed) the waters of Jericho through Elisha—and just as You inverted the curse of the wicked Balaam into a blessing—may You transform all of my dreams concerning myself for goodness." (Brachot 55b)

Divine Guidance and Dreams

One final aspect of dreams discussed by the sages is the propriety of using dreams to request divine guidance. The idea was to shed light on a subject. The sage Rav, says tractate Baba Metziah 107b, was capable of passing over individual gravesites at the cemetery and receiving a dream vision telling him who died of what cause. The Jerusalem Talmud records that the sage Rav Yose fasted 80 days in order to merit seeing Rabbi Chiyah in a dream. (Kilayim 9:3) In 1572 Rabbi Menachem di Lonzano wrote an entire book about Talmudic subjects on the basis of his dreams. The great Yosef Caro, who wrote the classic Code of Jewish Law, discussed legal problems with a "maggid," or teacher in his dreams.

On the flip side come the rabbis who discourage basing decisions, let alone entire legal works, on the content of dreams. Asking for divine guidance for which marriage partner to choose or business partnership to enter is also frowned upon. Early authorities base this on Biblical passages, such as "Thou shall be wholehearted with the

Lord, your God," (Deuteronomy 18:13) meaning that one should live in simplicity of faith, not searching out hidden knowledge. Similarly, "It (supernatural knowledge) is not in heaven for you to say, 'Who can ascend to the heaven for us and take it for us.'" (Deuteronomy 30:12)

Taking actions such as choosing to prescribe or withhold medical treatment based on what one receives in a dream is also strongly cautioned against. In situations like these, the codifiers of Jewish law encourage healers to carefully examine the situation; if one is confident that no harm will come to the patient, the dream should be ignored. If not, it might be a good idea for a colleague to handle it.

Let's Get Talmudic

According to the Talmud (Brachot 5a), reciting the Shema immediately before going to sleep provides protection against the perils of the night. The sages also drafted a prayer meditation called "Hamapil" that appears in every prayer book:

Blessed are you Lord, our God, King of the universe, Who casts the bonds of sleep upon my eyes and slumber upon my eyelids. May it be your will, O Lord my God, and the God of my fathers that you lay me down to sleep in peace and allow me to arise in peace. May any idea, bad dream or bad notion not confound me; may my offspring be perfect before you and may you illuminate my eyes lest I die in sleep, for it is you who illuminates the pupil of the eye. Blessed are you Lord who illuminates the entire world with His glory.

Sweet Dreams—The River, the Kettle, and the Bird

In closing, I'd like to share with you one of the most beautiful Talmudic metaphors on dreams, and the interpretation of its symbolism. First, the metaphor:

> "One who sees these three things in a dream will see peace, a river, a kettle, and a bird." (Brachot 56b)

The Vilna Gaon suggests these items are all related to domestic tranquility of ascending degrees. The river, he says, is the classic symbol of civil cooperation. Neighboring cities often took residence near the banks of rivers. What one did upstream, affected the flora, fauna, and commerce downstream. This is the minimum attitude when seeking cooperation, and the lowest level of cooperation that will support peaceful coexistence in a marriage. Not flaming passion, but it works.

The kettle, a very useful vessel indeed, symbolizes the second level. Fire and water are opposites that cannot coexist as is. But, add the medium of a kettle and voilà, we have a cup of tea! In marriage, a higher level is achieved when a couple takes their often clashing attributes and find ways to make them meet and intertwine. Not a bad relationship, but it gets better.

The highest level is the peace of the bird. Not only is the dove a ubiquitous symbol of peace, it represents something even more significant. The bird, unlike land or water-based creatures, is equally at home in diverse environments. It can seamlessly transition from land to air and back again. Couples who achieve closeness and love where it matters not who is receiving or who is giving, have reached the peace of the bird and the "Dream Relationship."

The Least You Need to Know

◆ The Talmud disagreed with Sigmund Freud's belief that every part of a dream contains a subconscious message about the dreamer.

◆ Certain dreams were understood as potentially containing prophetic information coming from a divine source.

◆ Dreams could also be of ambivalent nature and depend on the interpretation of others to indicate how they might play out. The source of these dreams may be demonic or mundane.

◆ The rabbis discouraged people from seeking divine guidance for mundane and even significant issues by inquiring through the medium of dreams.

Chapter 14

Meaning and Metaphors

In This Chapter

- ◆ Unlocking scriptural meaning
- ◆ Talmudic interpretation
- ◆ Understanding Biblical exaggeration
- ◆ Dining with an emperor

A good portion of the Talmud deals with exploring the meaning of Biblical verses. Like all great adventurers, the sages dove headlong into Biblical passages to find the written source of all Jewish practice and philosophy. As they did, they used what they found as the basis of the Oral Torah that they taught to others.

In this chapter, we'll take a look at a specific approach that the sages took to unlock the messages in scripture, and how they used metaphors and parables based on their studies to teach lessons based on them.

Extracting Meaning from Biblical Texts

Let's start by talking about why some scripture doesn't make sense, because it includes words that are extraneous or seemingly out of context.

Knowing how to "read" a verse of scripture is an art. What is true about the Talmud concealing more than it reveals applies to scripture as well. Plus, more often than not, the literal translations found in versions of the Bible are erroneous or misleading.

For example, Moses was told to write in the Bible "But if there shall be a fatality, then you should award a life for a life ... and eye for an eye ..." (Exodus 21:23-24) One can imagine him turning his eyes to the heavens and protesting, "God, is that just, should a man lose his eye for accidentally goring out someone else's?"

> **Talmud Tidbits**
>
> The origins of the techniques that the sages used to unlock the meaning behind scripture, according to most authorities, began at Mt. Sinai. In other words, just as the content of the Oral Law was conveyed to Moses, so were the principles and techniques for deriving meaning from them also given.

In the Talmud (tractate Baba Kamma 85a), the sages, through an ancient principle of interpretation, link two scriptural verses together to appease Moses' fears. God's message is that Moses shouldn't worry, and that the punishment for involuntary manslaughter and causing loss of limb will be monetary compensation.

A good portion of all Talmudic content deals primarily with three things:

- ◆ Figuring out the meaning behind certain parts of scripture that seemingly don't make sense.

- ◆ Reconciling apparent contradictions between scriptural passages.

- ◆ Tracing the origin or source of the Oral Law back to the scriptural passage.

This process of exploration and reconciliation is called *midrash*.

Because the rabbis believed that every word in the Torah is from God, no words were regarded as superfluous. When they came upon a word or expression that seemed superfluous, they sought to understand what new idea or nuance the Bible wished to convey by using it. Here's an example:

> **Talmud Tutor**
>
> The word **midrash** derives from doresh, which means "to search" or "seek." The word also implies a search for the positive and necessary. The plural is "midrashim." The term can also apply to a book that compiles midrashic teachings.

In Exodus 24:7, the Torah teaches that the Israelites at the revelation at Mt. Sinai proclaimed, "Everything that God has said we will do and we will hear." However, a question emerges as to this seemingly superfluous verse, since the Israelites already agreed to follow the Torah just four verses earlier; "And the entire people responded with one voice and they said 'all the words that God has spoken we will do.'" (Exodus 24:3)

The late rabbinic leader Rabbi Moshe Feinstein explained the reason for this repetition. He said that when the Jewish people made the first declaration, they agreed only to accept those utterances that they knew to be said by God. God, in His infinite wisdom, however, knew this declaration to be insufficient since in later generations, teachings might be forgotten or their essential rationale might become vague. Therefore, God desired that the Jewish people accept also what would be said by the sages of each generation. Hence the extra verse.

The sages believed that one of the main goals of studying the Talmud was finding harmony between the written and oral traditions through discovering where all the laws were alluded to in scripture. As the eighteenth-century scholar Rabbi Chaim ben Attar put it:

> I wish to resolve certain declarations of the sages concerning the unity of the Written and Oral Law. They say that this entire law was conveyed to Moses at Mt. Sinai, including all the novel insights that scholars would ever expound in the Torah. However, they also taught that Rabbi Akiva explained insights that even Moses was not aware of. It appears that the resolution of this paradox is this. It is true that the entirety of the Torah (Written and Oral) was transmitted to Moses, and not even the most seasoned scholar can attain more. "There is nothing new under the sun." The reconciliation though is that when God gave Moses the Torah, He inscribed the entire Oral teaching within the Written one. But He did not inform Moses where everything was encoded. This would become the holy task of the Jewish people in every generation, to find the places where various laws and mysteries that were transmitted orally to Moses could be traced to the Written text.

Midrash doesn't attempt to explain the plain literal meaning of the text as much as it works to extract teachings from it. At times it offers a rationale behind one of the 613 precepts contained in Jewish law. It might even focus on details about the lives of Talmudic sages and the authors of scripture—the prophets themselves.

Two Types of Midrash

The Talmudic sages utilize two types of "exploration of the scriptures." A midrash that deals strictly with legal matters is called midrash halacha; while a midrash aggadah is often comprised of stories and legends that teach values, ethics, religious outlook, and so on.

Talmud Tidbits

Many midrashim are found directly in the Talmud. However, there are collections of midrashim outside the Talmud that were written during the Tannaitic (Mishna) period and from the Amoraic (Talmud) period.

Midrash aggadah might not even be based on a specific scriptural verse, as it deals with a wide range of fundamental issues such as immortality of the soul, the world to come, the nature and identity of the Messiah, and other principles of Judaism that are not explicitly mentioned in the Written Law.

Midrash Halacha

As previously mentioned, midrash halacha is a teaching related to a Jewish law. As an example:

> Leviticus 19:3 commands, "Every man (Ish, in Hebrew): Your mother and father shall you revere …"

Some people might incorrectly view this statement as implying that women are exempt from honoring their parents. If we were to read the Bible literally, this would be an obvious conclusion, as the verse above does not specifically mention women. But does this make sense? How do we know otherwise? Let's see what the sages had to say.

The Talmud tractate Kiddushin deals, in part, with laws pertaining to honoring one's parents. It asks for clarity on a very ambiguous first statement found in the laws, identifying which expressions of honor are due a parent, or more specifically a son to a father.

The sages ask, "What does 'All commandments of the father *upon* the son' mean? If we say that it means, 'All of the commandments that a son is obligated to do for his father,' is it true that women are exempt? Did we not learn (in another place) … ?"

The Talmud then answers its own question: "When the Torah uses the word "Ish" (i.e. man) [in Leviticus 19:3], it seems to imply males alone. From where do we know that the verse implies women, as well? When that very verse says, "you [plural] shall revere," that indicates two [types of people—male and female]."

In this way, the Talmud clarifies an ambiguously worded piece of scripture and clarifies the law. The Torah commands a man (Ish) to show reverence for his parent, which might be taken to exclude women. However, careful analysis of the text reveals that two people (the plural "You shall revere") are implied. By deduction, this includes a woman. (At this point, the Talmud continues on to discuss why logically we might have thought women should be exempt from honoring parents—one of the Ten Commandments—but we won't get into that here.)

Here's another illustration of midrash halacha:

> What can learn from the superfluous passage found in the creation story of Adam and Eve in Genesis 5:2; "Male and female he created them?" We already know they were both created from earlier scripture. (Genesis 2:22)

Looking into the Talmud (Yevamoth 61b) we find this teaching; "A man should not cease from attempting to fulfill the commandment of procreation ('be fruitful and multiply') until he has (a minimum number of) children. The School of Shammai says that minimum is 'two boys.' The School of Hillel however says, 'A boy and a girl, as it is written, Male and female he created them.'"

Now we understand why that extra verse was conveyed to Moses. It actually serves the purpose of teaching a legal ruling. Thus according to the School of Hillel, it teaches that siring a boy and a girl minimally fulfills the mitzvah of procreation. And that is the halacha, or law, in this case.

Midrash Aggadah

As previously mentioned, the brilliance of midrash aggadah lies in its ability to fill in the gaps and bring biblical text alive. Scripture often leaves out the details. It's hard to know what the people involved are thinking and feeling, or why they respond the way they do. It can be hard to tell what certain phrases really mean, or get a handle on the moral lessons that can be derived from them.

Here's an example:

> In Job's second soliloquy (speech to himself) he speaks in parables. One of them is "The blessings of the lost would be upon me, and I would bring joyous song to a widow's heart." (Job 29:13) From this passage we have no idea what blessings he is referring to, who the "lost" are, or how those blessings would help him bring joy to a widow.

Without clarification from the Talmud, we would have no idea what Job was talking about. So the Talmudic sages present a midrash aggadah (in Baba Batra 16a) to fill in the gaps. Job would "steal" the fields of orphans (the lost) improve them until they were ready to yield produce, and return them to the orphans. Can you imagine what people must have thought while he was apparently doing such a heartless thing? Right, they cursed him. That is where the expression "Blessing of the lost would be upon me," comes from. The Hebrew word "birchat," though literally meaning "blessing," is often used in the Talmud as a euphemism for just the opposite—cursing! That is what it means in this passage, too.

As for rejoicing the widow, we also learn from this Talmudic passage that Job, when he learned of a widow who could not remarry, would announce that she was his relative. Being a pious and wealthy man, this would cause men to aspire to marry such a woman, which would then bring joy to her heart.

Midrash aggadah does not necessarily give authoritative answers to these perplexities, but proposes likely answers and inspires the reader to engage the text more deeply. It is not uncommon to have several midrashim answering the same question in almost contradictory ways. This is perfectly all right as long as the midrash doesn't contradict scripture, or established Torah practice, but instead is supported by the specific text and the spirit of scripture as a whole.

Let's Get Talmudic

The great Rabbi Judah Loew, also called the Maharal of Prague, was one of the most influential thinkers in the post-medieval period. It is likely that no previous author devoted so much space to interpreting the nonlegal thought of the rabbis of the Talmud.

Rabbi Loew developed an entirely new approach to the aggadah of the Talmud. He explained how it is possible for seemingly contradictory Talmudic teachings to emerge from the Torah if all was given to Moses at Mt. Sinai. Torah is similar to nature, he said, where dichotomy exists. A lemon, for instance, can at the same time taste sweet as it tastes sour.

When correct methods of derivation are applied to many Torah teachings, they yield "Godly truth," even if two sages come up with paradoxical conclusions. This is what is meant in the phrase, "These and those are the words of the Living God."

Here's an example of how two contradictory midrashim that explore Biblical passages dealing with a nocturnal wrestling match. As it is written:

> "Jacob was left alone and a 'man' wrestled with him until the break of dawn … Then Jacob inquired, and he said, 'Tell me, please, what is your name.'"(Genesis 32:25,28)

In the first midrash (Midrash Tanchuma, Vayishlach 7), the "man" that Jacob wrestles with is identified as the angel Michael. This midrash has Michael asking Jacob why he is afraid of his brother Esav, inasmuch as, he has prevailed against such an angel as himself.

The second midrash (Genesis Rabbah 78:4) also takes the "man" to be an angel, but this angel has no fixed name. The midrash explains that angels' names depend on their missions, and that as their missions change, so, too, their names.

Does there seem to be a contradiction here? Perhaps these two midrashim are identifying two aspects of Jacob's encounter. What seems to be implicit in the second midrash is that angels actually have no fixed identity: as their missions change, so, too, do their identities change; and it is precisely because of this that their names change. This midrash thus clarifies the angel's answer when Jacob asks him his name: "Why is this, you will ask for my name?"(Genesis 32:30) The angel is telling Jacob that his name is not going to convey any more information about his identity than his presence does, since what he is today may not be what he is tomorrow. And thus we have here a Jacob who is face to face with the embodiment of one of his greatest fears; identity and mission in life.

The first midrash implies that Jacob knows the identity of his sparring partner, and teaches another lesson. By realizing he has fought and prevailed over one of God's most powerful messengers, he can surely overcome his vengeful brother. Thus, there are no problems in these seemingly contradictory midrashim. They both teach valuable lessons, and in the words of the Talmud, "these and these are the words of the living God."

Since we're on the subject of Jacob, let's take a look at an example where two verses in the same story seem to contradict each other and are reconciled by the Talmud. When fleeing from his brother, Jacob arrives at a place that tradition says was Mt. Sinai. God communicates with him in a dream and promises, "behold, I am with you, I will guard you wherever you go ..." (Genesis 28:15) However, verse 17 says, "And he became frightened ..." What's going on over here, didn't the Lord just promised him divine protection? Rabbi Yaakov bar Idi reconciles these verses by teaching that Jacob was worried lest some unforeseen transgression or sinfulness cause that promise to be abrogated.

Finally, an example of midrash where the sages were able to intuit where a specific word contained a hidden message that explains elements missing from a story.

Here's the scripture: "'And Haran (brother of Abraham) died in the presence of his father Terach in the land of his nativity, in Ur Kasdim." (Genesis 11:28)

Pretty straightforward, right? Haran died in the presence of his father. Make sense? Well, maybe not. Maybe there's a hidden story here. The midrash aggadah on this scripture tells us there is. Here we go:

> The Hebrew term for "in the presence of" is "al pnei." However, it also has an alternative meaning of "because of." Midrashically (so to speak), the use of this phrase could mean that Haran died as a result of something his father did, either directly or indirectly.

Here's the midrash aggadah: Terach, the father of Abraham and Haran, was a manufacturer and seller of graven images as well as a worshipper of them. Once, he gave Abraham his stock of idols to sell in his absence. In the course of the day an elderly man came to make a purchase. Abraham asked him his age, and the man gave it as between fifty and sixty years. Abraham taunted him with logic, pointing out that these manmade idols were produced perhaps in a few hours, and that the man shouldn't worship anything so much younger than he was. The fellow placed Abraham's words to heart and gave up idol worship.

Then a woman came with a handful of fine flour to offer to Terach's idols. In her presence, Abraham took a stick and broke all the images except the largest one. He then placed the stick in the hand of this idol.

When his father returned and saw the havoc wreaked on his "gods" he demanded an explanation from his son. Abraham sarcastically explained that when an offering of fine flour was brought to these divinities, they quarreled with each other as to who should be the recipient. The largest took up a stick to chastise the offenders, and in so doing reduced them to rubble.

Terach, not satisfied with this explanation, took it as a piece of mockery. When he thought of all the customers he had lost under Abraham's supervision, he grew more than a little angry. So, he took Abraham to have a little talk with the world leader and master idolater, Nimrod.

Nimrod suggested to Abraham that since he refused to worship his father's idols because of their lack of power, he should worship fire, which is very powerful: Abraham pointed out that water has power over fire. "Well," said Nimrod, "let us declare water god." "But," replied Abraham, "the clouds absorb the water and even they are dispersed by the wind. "Then let us declare the wind our god." "Bear in mind," continued Abraham, "that man is stronger than wind, and can resist it and stand against it."

Nimrod also became weary of arguing with Abraham and decided to cast him before his "god"—the god of fire—challenging the God of Abraham to deliver him. God indeed saved him out of the fiery furnace. Witnessing this event, his brother Haran was also challenged to declare his god, but wavered between two opinions and delayed his answer until he saw Abraham's fate.

When he saw the latter saved he declared himself on the side of Abraham's God, thinking that he, too, having now become an adherent of that God, would be saved by the same miracle. Nimrod cast him into the fire as well, but since his faith was not authentic and depended on a miracle, he perished.

In this way, Terach's actions dealing with Abraham indirectly lead to the death of his son Haran. The entire episode is hinted to in the words "in the presence of," where the midrash has indicated an alternative interpretation of this phrase.

Midrashic Hyperbole "How Tall Was Adam, Anyway?"

If you're familiar with scripture at all, you probably know that it contains some stories that are somewhat ... well, unbelievable, especially in modern times. Seas part, the earth opens, buildings tumble down due to trumpet blasts. Pretty amazing stuff, all of it. But did these things really happen as written?

The Talmudic line is that all these things actually happened. However, there are other events that are not directly alluded to in Biblical verses that are considered *hyperbole*. In other words, at times accounts in the Bible might be a bit exaggerated to make a point.

> **Talmud Tutor**
>
> **Hyperbole** is the deliberate and obvious exaggeration used for effect; i.e. "She cried buckets of tears."

Examples of Biblical hyperbole include:

- Moses' height being given as 20 feet or so.

- Bitya, the daughter of Pharoah, having her arm increase by a few feet to pull Moses out of the Nile.

- Moses asserting after the well dried up and the people were begging for water "just a little more and they will all stone me."

In a sense, scriptural hyperbole offers a source as well as a point of departure for the same practice in the Talmud, and the sages used hyperbole to make their points as well. The following is an illustration of an aggadah that imparts a mystical idea in an overtly exaggerated statement, "The height of Adam, the first man, reached from earth all the way to heaven .... But when he sinned, the Holy One, blessed be He, placed His hand on him and made him shorter." (Talmud Chagigah 12a) Superficially, this statement is very bizarre. Could Adam really have been that tall? And how can you imagine God placing His hand on Adam's head and shrinking him!

Later commentaries insist that this midrash aggadah, like all midrashim of this type, should not be taken literally. Rabbi Chaim of Volozhin, the chief disciple of the Vilna Gaon, explains a profound lesson through allegory:

When Adam was created, his intellect was so lucid and comprehensive that he was capable of understanding all the workings of the universe and even fathom the deepest mysteries of the Divine realm. But when he sinned, his power of intellect was diminished, causing his lofty spiritual stature to decline as well. God "reduced him to size," so to speak, in a spiritual and intellectual sense.

Regarding this type of midrashim, the Maharal of Prague wrote that "… most of the words of the Sages were in the form of metaphor and the analogies of the wise … unless they state that a particular story is not a metaphor, it should be assumed that it is a metaphor. The matters of great depth were generally expressed by the Sages using metaphors, and should be understood as metaphors unless they explicitly indicated they to be taken literally. And therefore, one should not be surprised to find matters in the words of the Sages that appear to be illogical and remote from the mind."

Here's an example of what the Maharal was referring to. The holiday of Purim commemorates the miraculous salvation of the Jewish people from their nemesis Haman during the Persian exile. In the Talmud tractate Megillah, which discusses this holiday, we find an unusual statement from the sages concerning an individual named Ahashveros, who, wishing to show off the beauty of his queen before the dignitaries of this banquet, commands his wife Vashti to appear before him wearing nothing except her crown.

Whether she was prepared to do so or not, no one really knows. However, the Talmud teaches (Megillah 12b) that the angel Gabriel descended and planted a tail on her! All the makeup and costumes in the world could not hide such a blemish, so she refuses to come. Her failure to attend the king's banquet cost Vashti her life. End of story? Not so quick.

According to the Maharal, this "tail" episode is really a tall tale. He vehemently protests against anyone assuming that the rabbis of the Talmud meant this literally. Rather, he asserts, they found a colorful way to express what actually happened. The vainglorious Vashti had put on a few extra pounds and was not too inclined to present herself under those circumstances. Why the metaphor of the tail? Simple, just as someone suddenly sporting a new appendage would feel cumbersome, so too, was that extra poundage to Vashti.

Let's take a look at a few more hyperbolic statements:

> In tractate Chulin 90b, the Talmud cites Rabbi Ami, who states that scripture uses hyperbole as we find in Deuteronomy (1:28) "To where shall we ascend? Our brothers have confounded our hearts, saying, 'A people greater and taller than we, cities great and fortified to the heavens, and even children of giants

have we seen there.'" Likewise, Moses, in describing the Land of Israel, exaggerates the wonderful things that will be found there, "a land where you will eat without poverty—you will lack nothing there; a Land whose stones are iron and from whose mountains you will mine copper." (Deuteronomy 8:9)

An example from the prophets is found in the opening verses of the Book of Kings, where Solomon is proclaimed as the successor to his father David; "and all the people then ascended after him, and the people were playing flutes and rejoicing with great joy; the ground burst from their noise." (Kings I, 1:39–40)

Dining with the Emperor

As previously mentioned, many forms of Midrashim contain accounts of the lives of the sages. To end with a nice taste of Talmudic lore, here is an abridged account of one of the Talmud stories that relate encounters between the sages and significant personalities of antiquity. This one has the seal of Rome on it!

Rabbi Judah the Prince invited his friend Marcus Aurelius Antoninus to dine with him on the Sabbath day, when all the food was served cold. After a time the Rabbi again had the pleasure of his friend's company at dinner on a weekday, when warm food was served. Antoninus, however, expressed his preference for the food he had enjoyed at his friend's table on the Sabbath, though it was cold.

"Ah," said the sage, "there is an ingredient missing today which we cannot procure."

Replied Antoninus, "surely my means can procure anything?"

"No," answered the Rabbi, "your means cannot procure the Sabbath; it is the "spice" Sabbath that gives the zest to the food!" (Genesis Rabbah 11)

The Least You Need to Know

◆ There are two major categories of midrashim found in Talmudic literature. Midrash halacha deals with legal rulings and how they are derived from scripture. Misrash aggadah covers everything else, including ethics, business advice, medical counsel, immortality of the soul, etc.

◆ Midrashim fill in much of the white space between verses and allow the reader to even gain a glimpse of the motivations and personalities of the Biblical characters involved, as well as the moral lesson to be gleaned.

◆ Many of the miraculous or illogical parables recorded in the Talmud were intentionally hyperbolic and are not to be taken literally. Some of these, however that deal with events that occurred in the lives of the sages are believed to be literally true.

◆ Scripture utilizes hyperbole to emphasize a point. However, when a miracle is explicitly mentioned in the Torah or Prophets, it is generally assumed to be literal.

Chapter 5

Talmudic Humor and Wit

- ◆ The value of humor
- ◆ Professional clowns
- ◆ Spicing up Talmud study
- ◆ Talmudic one-liners

Although it's almost always folly to make sweeping generalities, this chapter starts with one: As a rule, the Jewish people are known to have a pretty good sense of humor. As it turns out, they can trace their funny bones all the way back to their earliest ancestors.

Flip through the Old Testament, and you'll find more than one place where the scripture within gets downright funny. Sometimes the humor is decidedly on the sly side, but it's definitely there.

The sages of the Talmud very much appreciated the value of humor, and were also known to let loose with quick-witted one-liners and jabs on a fairly regular basis. In this chapter, we'll take a look at the humor and wit of the world's earliest standup comics.

The Importance of Humor

Facing life's challenges with humor allowed the historically persecuted Jew to deal with the harsh realities of exile in a positive way. At almost every turn, the Talmud urges followers of the faith to seek what is beautiful and joyful about life, instead of the ugly and sad. As the Talmud says, "Tears of sadness are bad for the eyes, tears of laughter are beautiful and beneficial to the eyes." (Shabbat, 151b–152a)

Let's Get Talmudic

In a scene from the musical *Fiddler on the Roof*, the villagers of Ana Tevka gather around their beloved rabbi. "Rabbi," one of the villagers cries out, "is there a proper blessing for the Czar?" The rabbi ponders a moment, strokes his beard, and responds, "May God bless and keep the Czar ... far away from us!"

In a way, the rabbi of the fictitious village Ana Tevka epitomized the Talmudic saying, "Tears of sadness are bad tears, tears of laughter are beautiful."

The sages underscored the value of taking a lighthearted approach to life in various Talmud tracts. One relates the story of man who left a will containing a clause that confounded the rabbinic courts: "My son shall not receive his inheritance until he becomes foolish."

Two rabbinical judges could not figure out a solution to the riddle, so they sought out the great scholar Rabbi Joshua ben Korcha to solicit his view as to this unusual stipulation's meaning. Approaching the rabbi's house, they found him crawling on his hands and knees in the yard, a rope dangling from his mouth. The rabbi was playing with his small son, who was leading him about like a horse.

The men said nothing, and retreated to Rabbi Joshua's house to wait for him. When he arrived, they showed him the will. Laughing, Rabbi Joshua commented, "By my life, this issue that you are concerned about, acting like a fool, applied to me just a few minutes ago!" He explained that it was clear that the will's author didn't want his son to literally go crazy in order to inherit. Instead, he wanted to delay his son's inheritance until he married and had a family, for "when a man has children it is not abnormal for him to act like a fool when it comes to them." (Midrash Psalms 93:12)

Let's Get Talmudic

You can gauge a person's true nature by the way he spends money, the way he handles anger, the way he acts when drunk, and some add by how he laughs. (Eruvin 65b)

Let's Get Talmudic
Rabbi Nachman of Bratslav (1772–1810) was also a great Jewish figure who appreciated the significance of timely humor. Although he was himself described by his chief disciple as a "tormented master," he wrote, "There are men who suffer terrible distress and are unable to tell what they feel in their hearts, and they go their way and suffer and suffer. But if they meet one with a laughing face, he can revive them with his joy. And to revive someone is no slight thing."

Clowning About

Another Talmud passage that underscores the value of humor tells the story of Rabbi Baroka of Huza (Babylonia), who was fond of frequenting the marketplace at Lapet. One day, the prophet Elijah appeared to him there. Rabbi Baroka asked Elijah, "Is there anyone among all these people who will have a share in the world to come?" Elijah answered, "Sorry, there is none."

Later, two men came to the marketplace, and Elijah said to Rabbi Baroka, "Those two will have a share in the world to come!" Rabbi Baroka asked the newcomers, "What is your occupation?" They replied, "We are jesters. When we see a person who is sad, we cheer him up. Likewise, when we see two people quarreling, we try to make peace between them."

About this the sage Rashi comments, "Bringing peace between two people is one of those virtues mentioned in the Mishna Peah (1:1) for which a person 'eats of its fruits in this world, and principle of that merit accrues for him in the world-to-come.'"

Here, the Talmud is clearly emphasizing that joy should come with the knowledge of living in God's divine plan; and in not taking oneself too seriously. Therefore, the truly holy man should be joyful, and cause others to absorb that joy by osmosis.

Talmud Tidbits

Jesters, or professional clowns, were (and are) valuable resources to the ancient Jewish community. A certain type of professional clown, known as a badchan, might sing humorous verses (all in jest) to warn the bride of the faults of her husband-to-be. The humor of some badchans bordered on or went beyond satire. Irate in-laws and even a groom or two have been known to chase a badchan who had gone a little overboard off the stage.

Humor and Study

The sages also often used humor as a teaching tool to attract their students' attention, or to sharpen the mind of a lazy disciple. Rabbah, the great Talmudic sage of the third century C.E., would say something humorous before starting his legal discourse to the scholars. They would laugh; after this, he would hunker down to the lecture.

Why was humor so important? The sages believed that it was important to study the Talmud when one was in the proper frame of mind, and they knew through experience that a little levity went a long way to establish it.

Telling lighthearted stories was another tool the sages used to put their students in the right frame of mind. Rabbi Meir would devote a full one-third of his lectures to his "300 fox fables."

Only about three of Rabbi Meir's fables are found in the Talmud and its commentary. Here's one of the most famous:

A sly fox passed a lovely vineyard. A tall, thick fence surrounded the vineyard on all sides. As the fox circled around the fence, he spotted a small hole in the fence, just large enough for him to push his head through. The fox could see that succulent grapes grew in the vineyard, and he began to salivate. But, alas, the opening was too small for him. So what did the sly fox do? He fasted for three days until he became so lean that he managed to squeeze through the hole.

Inside the vineyard the fox began feasting to his heart's content. He grew bigger and fatter than ever before. Then he wanted to get out of the vineyard. But alas! The hole was too small again. So what did he do? He fasted for three days again, and then just about managed to slip through the hole and out again.

Turning his head towards the vineyard, the forlorn fox said: "Vineyard, O, vineyard! How enticing you look, and how luscious are your fruits. But what good are you to me? Just as I came to you, so I leave you?"

The moral, say the sages, "So it is also with this world. It is a beautiful world, but just as man comes into this world empty-handed, so he leaves it. Only the Torah he studied, the mitzvot he performed, and the good deeds he practiced are the real fruits which he can take with him."

Scoffing Is Sinful

While the sages employed humor on a regular basis, even when addressing such serious topics as ethics and religious instruction, they never used it frivolously. They appreciated the value of a good belly laugh, but they drew the line at humor that came at the expense of others, proclaiming, "All forms of mockery are forbidden, except for the mocking of idolatry." (Megillah 25b) In other words, scoffing or amusing oneself at the expense of others is strongly discouraged. In fact, such entertainment is seen as sinful.

On the other hand, the sages say that scoffing can be a virtue when it is done to protect others from the dangers of pagan idolatry. Regardless, they seem to be reluctant to engage in gratuitous unbridled lampooning, even if the object is worthy of scorn. Their concern was over a person developing a generally cynical outlook on life. And as one philosopher put it, "Cynics are the parasites of society."

The basis for this Talmudic guidance is found in Avodah Zarah, which states, "All forms of mockery are forbidden, except for the mocking of idolatry." What is behind this statement is a wonderful piece of scripture that definitely employs sarcasm and humor. In I Kings, Chapter 18, Elijah the Prophet amuses himself during a confrontation with 450 idolatrous prophets who worshipped Baal, whom the Hebrews considered to be a false god.

> **Talmud Trivia**
>
> The earliest and best known example of sarcasm in scripture is found in Exodus 14:11 " ... Moses, were there not enough graves in Egypt that you brought us to the desert to die?" (Exodus 14:11)

Elijah challenges the prophets to prove that Baal was a real god by staging a biblical barbecue. Each side was to take a bull, cut it up, and place it on a dry bed of wood. Then, "you will call on the name of your gods, and I will call on the name of the Lord; and the God who answers by fire, He is God."

The people agree, and go about preparing their bull. Elijah even lets them go first. They call on Baal to prove his power by lighting a fire in the wood that nestles the bull, but to no avail. Hours transpire and the only "fire" coming down from above is the sweltering summer heat of Mount Carmel.

At noon, Elijah "mocked them and said, 'Cry aloud, for he is a god; either he is meditating, or he is busy, or he is on a journey, or perhaps he is sleeping and must be awakened.'"

> **Talmud Trivia**
>
> "Derech lo," the Hebrew words that Elijah used to speculate on Baal's failure to appear, can also be translated as either "he is on his way (e.g. a journey), or "he is relieving himself."

Now, to get the humor in this, understand that Elijah was speaking euphemistically, and used the word "busy" as a pleasant way to say that Baal couldn't make an appearance because he was preoccupied in the bathroom. (Okay, so it's not fall down funny, but there's definitely some humor here.)

A Wedding Prankster

Another example of the wit of the sages comes from the tract Brachot. It involves Rabbi Judah, the Prince, who you'll remember as being the man who took on the awesome task of writing down the oral laws.

Foremost among Rabbi Judah's critics was the maverick scholar Eleazar Ha-Kappar, known simply as Bar Kappara. Bar Kappara's talent as a Torah scholar was characterized by his flair for allegory and poetic expression—on a good day, that is. If he was in a bad mood, or his fury was aroused, his sharp wit would quickly turn into biting satire, and woe to the targets of his cutting wit.

It was the pious and kindhearted Rabbi Judah who figured prominently as the unwitting target of Bar Kappara's taunts. Therefore, it's easy to understand why Rabbi Judah and his wife entertained serious reservations about inviting such a troublemaker to their son's wedding. But, Bar Kappara's preeminence as a scholar made it impossible to exclude him.

Not having received an early invitation, Bar Kappara assumed that Rabbi Judah had deliberately omitted him from the guest list. So, he schemed a pay back. In fact, he resorted to a very effective form of protest—graffiti. He got his message across by scrawling "millions of denarii were spent on this wedding" on the wall of the wedding canopy.

Soon, Bar Kappara discovered that he had been invited after all. Ever the joker, he sought a new reason for taking a jibe at his colleague. This time, he took exception to the fact that Rabbi Judah had allowed his daughter to marry an individual named Bar El'asah, who, while being aristocratic and wealthy, wasn't exactly the sharpest knife in the drawer when it came to brainpower.

Bar Kappara struck up a friendship with Bar El'asah, and was able to convince him that a great way to impress his soon-to-be father-in-law would be to pose ingenious questions to him. Bar Kappara, of course, would be pleased to compose appropriate queries. The next time he saw Rabbi Judah, Bar El'asa began reciting a provocative riddle that Bar Kappara had devised for him. It was a brainteaser replete with vague biblical allusions that were obviously beyond El'asah's modest academic capacities. As he listened, Rabbi Judah observed Bar Kappara grinning widely in the background, and expressed his strong disapproval of the prank.

Rabbi Judah did not appreciate the prank, and was convinced that Bar Kappara's influences on his soon-to-be son in law would only yield negative consequences. In desperation, he offered to pay Bar Kappara forty bushels of wheat if he would only contain his jesting. When the time came to claim the reward for his improved conduct, Bar Kappara approached Rabbi Judah with a basket. But he wasn't carrying the basket; he was wearing it—upside down and on his head. Even the august Rabbi Judah could not restrain from letting out a brief chuckle.

At the same wedding, Bar Kappara bet Bar El'asah that by the end of the night he could get Rabbi Judah to dance (almost unheard of for man of his stature) and his wife to pour him wine. Holding the trump card—his brilliant novel biblical interpretations—he won the bet by refusing to entertain the wedding guests with his insights unless the rabbi and his wife complied. They did, and Bar Kappara won his wager with Bar El'asah.

Comedy Showdown: The Sages vs. the Greeks

The Jews of Talmudic times were not greatly impressed with the philosophy and arts of the Greeks, and considered themselves far superior in wit and wisdom. Some Talmudic literature has preserved debates and mental wrestling matches between the Athenians and the Talmud scholars of what was then Palestine. The tractate Niddah contains detailed accounts of some of these encounters. Here's a couple of them:

One Athenian arrived in Jerusalem and accosted a young Jewish boy. Pressing into the lad's hand a small amount of money, he requested that the boy run off into the marketplace and purchase for him something that would satiate him now and have enough left over for the rest of his trip. So the child went out and brought him some salt!

Another Athenian philosopher came to Jerusalem and spotted a number of young students who were taking recess by amusing themselves with riddles. The Athenian requested they share one with him. A precocious boy threw out the following clues, "Nine pass by, eight come, two pour out, one drinks and twenty-four serve," and told the Athenian to figure out what it was that they described.

The schoolboys stumped the Athenian. Want to try to unravel this bid of Talmud puzzlery yourself? Go ahead. You'll find the answer at the end of this chapter.

Talmud Trivia
There's an old Yiddish expression: "Ah mentch tracht und Got lacht" which translates to: "A person thinks and God laughs." In this spirit, the great physicist Albert Einstein wrote, "Before God we are all equally wise—and equally foolish."

In another episode, found in tractate Bechorot 8b, an Athenian wanted to make sport of a certain Jewish tailor. He handed the tailor a broken mortar and requested that he sew it. Not missing a beat, the tailor handed him some sand and asked him to spin thread out of it so that he could use it to sew the split in the mortar.

Yet another Athenian encounters a boy who brings him several rolls of cheese and some eggs. The Athenian asks the boy if he knows which balls of cheese came from white goats and which come from black goats. The boy, undaunted by the request, agrees to demonstrate but not until the Greek tells him which eggs came from a white hen, and which came from a black one.

"Don't Place Your Money on the Horns of Deer"

The Talmud also is replete with clever aphorisms and one-liners. Here are a few of the pithiest, courtesy of the sages:

> "The house that does not open to the poor shall open to the physician."

> "Give me friendship or give me death." (Perhaps Patrick Henry read the Talmud?)

> "Too many captains sink the ship."

> "Good deeds are better than creeds."

> "The sensible man drinks only when he is thirsty."

> "No person dies having fulfilled half of his desires. If he has 100 he'll want 200."

> "Study is not the essential, rather it is action that counts."

> "We do not see things as they are, we see things as we are."

> "Who is the mighty? One who conquers his (evil) inclination."

> "A container with one coin makes more noise than one that is full."

> "Silence is a fence around wisdom."

> "It is as hard to arrange a good marriage as it was to divide the Red Sea."

And, finally:

> "The mouse is not the thief, the hole is the thief."

The Least You Need to Know

♦ The sages of the Talmud appreciated the virtues of wit and humor as teaching tools to help convey Torah lessons to their charges.

♦ Some sages would actually begin their lessons with a joke or witty parable to catch the attention of their students.

♦ Badchans were professional jesters. Not only did they entertain at weddings and special occasions, many were employed to lift up the spirits of the melancholy and depressed.

♦ The Talmud records many encounters between the Jewish sages and Greeks, where they challenged each other with riddles and witticisms to hone their skills.

♦ The Talmud also records wise and clever ways with which the sages and people solved everyday interpersonal relationship issues with a sense of humor and wit.

The solution to the riddle is: A child. (Nine months of pregnancy, eight days for the circumcision, two breasts, the boy's mouth, and twenty-four months until the child is weaned.)

Part 4

The World According to the Talmud

The Talmud is often compared to the sea, as its waters run very deep and its breadth truly spans the earth. In its pages can be found remarkable discourses on subjects ranging from science and the environment to man's relationship to God and whether there is death after death.

What makes many of these discussions even more intriguing is that the Talmudic sages often present astonishing theories that were not only way ahead of their time, but are still timely and relevant to this day. Even the origins of relatively new discoveries and advances in medicine and technology can be found in obscure passages of the Talmud.

Chapter **16**

The Talmud and Science

In This Chapter

- ◆ Calculating pi
- ◆ The stars, the moon, and beyond
- ◆ Calendar calculations
- ◆ Talmudic animal husbandry

Among the most intriguing things about the Talmud is that aspects of the ancient wisdom it contains have been confirmed through modern research and technology.

The Talmudic sages believed that God created the Torah two thousand years before He created the universe. When the time came to create the universe, God merely "used" the Torah as a blueprint. In other words, the Torah was the blueprint of creation; it dictated what should be created, and how the world should look and function.

Later commentators stated that this blueprint extends to each molecule, scientific fact, and even each individual being on this planet. According to this viewpoint, there is a harmony to be discovered between the Written and Oral traditions and science.

In this chapter, we'll investigate some of scientific discoveries made by the ancients centuries ago that have been preserved in the Talmud.

Have a Slice of Pi

Most school children learn that the ratio between the diameter of a circle and its circumference is 3.1415926 … or π (pi). Using this figure, it's possible to calculate the circumference of a circle by knowing its diameter and multiplying it by π.

This figure employs the wisdom of two disciplines, algebra and gematria, to yield a hidden code found in a passage of scripture.

$$קוה = 100 + 6 + 5 = 111$$
$$קו = 100 + 6 = 106$$
$$\frac{111}{106} \times 30 = 31.415$$

This calculation, one of the most important in mathematics, has been known for so long that it's hard to know exactly who came up with it.

Most of us could care less who gets the credit, but if you remember what we said about scripture being a blueprint for creation, we might just find a clue as to pi's true origin.

In the First Book of Kings (7:23), when King Solomon builds the Temple, we are told:

> "And he made a molten sea, ten cubits from one brim to the other—it was round all about and its height was five cubits—and a line of thirty cubits did circle it round about."

The verse takes the simplest value for the ratio be-tween the diameter and the circumference: 3. "Since the diameter is 10 cubits, the verse seems to say, "it follows that the circumference is 30 cubits. All is fine and well, you say. But the value of 3 was actually a bit off; using it to compute true circumference may yield an object smaller than desired. The Talmud talks about what to do if one wishes to make a circular succah, for example, that complies with the minimum size requirements. The builder is told to multiply the diameter by three. Well if he does that too precisely, he will wind up with a succah that is too small.

So, is the computation given in the Bible inaccurate? Not necessarily. The eighteenth-century Talmud commentator Elijah of Vilna, also known as the Vilna Gaon, wrote that if one takes the numerical equivalent (gematria) of the word for "diameter" as it is written in the verse, and divides it by the gematria of the same word as it is read, and multiply it by the

Let's Get Talmudic

Traditionalists claim that it was the third-century B.C.E. Greek mathematician Archimedes who made the discovery. Others state that the sage Aryabhata used it, and several later Indian mathematicians and even the Arabs adopted it.

value for the circumference provided in the verse (30), it will yield the figure of pi that is accurate to at least four numbers.

It seems that King Solomon might deserve to get the credit for his familiarity with π, and Elijah of Vilna gets the assist!

The Stars, Moon and Beyond

God said to Abraham "Gaze now toward the heavens, and count the stars if you are able to count them … so shall be your progeny." (Genesis 15:5) Abraham might not have bothered to count them all, and relied on the Lord's word instead, but it did not stop the sages of the Talmud from taking a crack at computing the contents of the heavens.

As it is written, "Twelve constellations have I created in the firmament, and for each constellation I have created thirty hosts, and for each host I have created thirty legions, and for each legion I have created thirty cohorts, and for each cohort I have created thirty maniples, and for each maniple I have created thirty camps, and to each camp I have attached three hundred and sixty five thousands of myriads of stars …." (Berachot 32b)

The sages were aware that the stars are not just randomly distributed over the firmament; instead they are clustered (for each constellation I have created thirty hosts, and for each host …). Astronomers confirmed this by stating that galaxies "live" in great clusters, and even super clusters like swarms of bees. They also use the number 30 in describing the number of clusters within clusters of stars.

The number of stars stated in the Talmud is 1.06434×10^{18}. (10 to the 18th power) The number of stars in the universe counted by the best astronomical estimate of somewhere between 10^{18} and 10^{20}, which is amazingly close to the Talmudic count.

> **Talmud Tidbits**
>
> To the best of our knowledge, the sages didn't possess something like the Hubble telescope (or even Isaac Newton's 400 years ago). Yet, their calculation of the number of stars in the heavens this calculation was confirmed by two early discoveries made in 1923 by astronomer Edwin Hubble.

Halley's Comet and the Rabbis

The Jerusalem Talmud relates a story about Rabban Gamliel and Rabbi Joshua. They sailed and lost their way in the sea. Rabban Gamliel's food ran out, but Rabbi Joshua had a lot of food. Rabban Gamliel asked him why he had so much food.

He responded, "Because there is a star that rises every seventy years and misguides the skippers."

Talmud Tidbits

In 1997, NASA reported that the Hale-Bopp comet last appeared about 4,200 years ago. According to traditional sources, a "new" star appeared in the sky some 4,100 years ago. That was around the time the world was destroyed by a flood in Noah's generation. This star, evidently, was actually a comet, and traveled through all the constellations in 30 days. Perhaps it served as an omen for the people in the world to reconsider their wicked lifestyles and practices.

What is fascinating about this brief exchange is Rabbi Joshua's obvious familiarity with astronomy. Indeed, every 70 years or so (actually 76) a comet makes its elliptical orbit around our solar system. It's possible that Rabbi Joshua sighting was not long after Halley's initial sighting, some 2,052 years ago.

Calculating the Calendar

While Rabban Gamliel might not have been the best navigator of the seas, he was skilled in other scientific areas, especially mathematics. The Talmud tractate Eruvin quotes him as saying, "If someone wishes to ascertain the height of a palm tree, let him measure his own height and the length of his shadow as well as that of the shadow of the tree, and he will thus ascertain the height of the palm tree."

It is possible that the Oral Torah, handed down for thousands of years, might contain astronomic statistics that have recently been confirmed by NASA (National Aeronautics and Space Administration) using advanced electronic devices.

The late Carl Sagan, a renowned cosmologist and physicist was chief scientist at NASA. In his book *Broca's Brain*, he describes how twentieth-century scientists calculated the length of the lunar month by reflecting a laser beam back to Earth from a glass prism placed on the moon by American astronauts. With the aid of powerful telescopes connected to an automatic clock, they've computed a time of 29.530388 days.

Talmud Trivia

The "traditional information" that Rabban Gamliel alluded to was orally received on Mt. Sinai with the Written Torah, and was transmitted orally from teacher to pupil for 13 centuries.

This is the same calculation that Rabban Gamliel came up with thousands of years earlier. He is quoted in tractate Rosh Hoshana as saying, "I have received the traditional information from my paternal grandfather that the lunar month can never be less than 29 and a half days [a half-day being 12 hours], two thirds of an hour and 73 divisions."

According to Rabban Gamliel's tradition, there are twenty-nine-and-a-half days, two-thirds of an hour and seventy-three divisions in a lunar month. The total of these two fractions of hours (comprising the ⅔ of an hour and the several minutes over the ⅔ hour which was stated by the sages as 73 divisions), are now converted to a common denominator of divisions. These two fractions of an hour when combined become 793 divisions. In modern terminology our final total of days is stated as 29.530359 days, which is a discrepancy of six-millionths of a day.

Fixing Date Drift

The Torah fixes Jewish holy days according to specific dates as well as specific seasons. Unlike the Christian holiday Easter, for example, they are celebrated on the same day and month of the Jewish calendar every year. As an example, the Passover celebration begins in spring on the fifteenth of Nissan; Sukkot on the fifteenth of Tishrei in the fall.

The Jewish calendar primarily uses the moon to calculate the beginning of each month.

However, because there are more lunar months than solar months (12.4 to 12), a 12-month lunar calendar loses about 11 days every year, while a 13-month lunar calendar gains about 19 days. This causes what is called "calendar drift," which results in lunar months not lining up with a solar calendar. On a 12-month lunar calendar, for example, the month of Nissan occurs 11 days earlier every year. It's supposed to occur in the Spring, but calendar shift moves it back to the Winter, then Fall, then Summer, and eventually back to Spring again.

Since the Jewish holidays must fall during a particular season, the Jewish people must follow a lunar-solar calendar that reconciles the

> **Let's Get Talmudic**
>
> According to Jewish belief, the heavenly bodies were, in part, created to help us determine the dates of the Jewish Holy Days. "And God said: 'Let there be luminous bodies in the firmament of the heavens in order to distinguish between day and night and that they should serve for signs, for festivals, and for days, and for years.'" (Genesis 1:14)

> **Talmud Trivia**
>
> In ancient times, observation determined the beginning of a new month. People anxiously watched the skies for the new moon, and would inform the Sanhedrin when they saw it. When the Sanhedrin received reliable testimony from two people, they declared that a new month had begun, and sent out messengers to tell everyone that it had.

difference between the length of the solar and lunar years. The solution is *intercalation*, an ingenious system of adding an additional month to the calendar seven times every 19 years.

In the fourth century, the sage Hillel II developed a fixed calendar based on earlier mathematical and astronomical calculations found in the Talmud. This calendar, which the Jewish people still use, standardized month length, and called for adding an extra month (much like February 29 is added to the solar calendar) during certain years to make the lunar calendar align with solar years. A month called Adar II is added during certain years. In this way, the months on the Jewish calendar always stay in the season in which they're supposed to fall.

Learning from the Animals

The sages were fascinated with animals, and enjoyed observing animal behavior. They made a number of very perceptive observations about our four-legged friends, and for

that matter, our many-legged creatures, too. One story illustrates the cleverness with which they posited hypotheses, conjured experiments to test their theories, and recorded some of them, in true scientific style.

The Talmud tract Hulin tells us about Rabbi Shimon bar Chalafta, a second-century contemporary of Rabbi Judah the Prince, who was a tinkerer of sorts. He once became fascinated with a passage he had learned in King Solomon's proverbs, "Go to the ant, you lazy one, observe its ways and become wise. Though there is no officer, guard or ruler over it, she prepares her food in the summer and stores it during the harvest." (Proverbs 6:6,7)

Rabbi Shimon wondered how King Solomon knew this about ants, and decided to investigate and see if it was truly so. In the middle of a blazingly hot summer in the arid land of Israel, he found an anthill. Realizing that the ants save their foraging for the cooler hours after the passing of the midday sun, he took his cloak and held it over the entrance to their lair. Sure enough, a nice black ant cautiously emerged from the hole. Rabbi Shimon took a drop of red dye and marked the ant on its back. After many ants exited the hole to scurry around, Rabbi Shimon removed his coat and they hastened back into their protective hill.

Rabbi Shimon waited a few moments and again held his cloak over the hole. As he anticipated, the red-backed ant popped its head from the hole and seemed to motion to the others that the coast was clear.

Just as they had before, a swarm of ants poured out of the entrance. Suddenly, Rabbi Shimon removed his coat. Much to his surprise, all the ants pounced on the red-backed ant, and killed him in a display of anarchy (or would it be ant-archy?). In true scientific observation style, Rabbi Shimon examined the variables of his experiment. Had the ants truly a leader, would they not have taken the law into their own hands and executed an ant that lied to them? Alternatively, he thought, maybe the leader had just died and they hadn't had time to crown a new one. So they resorted to frontier justice in the meantime.

In the end, Rabbi Shimon threw up his hands and concluded that the results were inconclusive and perhaps impossible to prove one way or the other. So one must rely on the wisdom of King Solomon that God imparted to him. Thus, ants must not have any rulers or policeman after all.

Let's Get Talmudic

It should be noted that the Talmudic sages taught kindness to the beasts that serve us. The Torah contains many laws teaching that animals enjoy similar rights as humans do. The Talmud also expounds on laws that demonstrate concern for the physical or psychological suffering of animals in several places. Animals owned by Jews rest on Shabbat as humans do. One is forbidden to muzzle an ox while it is working in the field.

Plowing a field using animals of diverse species is forbidden because this would be a hardship to these creatures that function with varying strengths. The Talmud teaches us that one should feed his flocks and herds in the morning, even before he himself eats. (Gitten 64) The Talmud also says that before people decide to take a work or companion animal into their home, they must first make sure they can feed the animal properly. (Yevamot 15)

Furthermore, one is not permitted to kill a mother animal on the same day as its young. The Torah specifically says that a person who sends away the mother bird will be rewarded with long life, precisely the same reward that is given for honoring mother and father. An entire chapter in the tractate of Chulin is devoted to details of this precept, which indicates the importance of this law.

The same page of the Talmud also mentions Rabbi Shimon's experiments with chickens. He wanted to disprove Rabbi Judah's contention that a kosher bird that lost its feathers should not be considered kosher. Rabbi Shimon insisted that he could regenerate a new set, and that he could make a bird kosher again. So he took such a bird that had lost its wings, bundled it up in cloth, and placed it in a very low temperature oven as an incubator. Lo and behold, after several weeks the chicken grew a new set of feathers and was restored to its kosher status!

Moses, the Zoologist

And God spoke to Moses and Aaron: 'Speak to the Children of Israel and tell them: This is the animal which you may eat, from among all animals on earth—you may eat any animal that is completely cloven-hoofed and that chews its cud.'" (Leviticus 11:1–3).

In the passage that follows, the Torah reveals an amazing law of nature. From among the tens of thousands species of animals in the world, there are only four that possess only one of the signs of being kosher—that is, they ruminate without being cloven-hoofed or that are cloven-hoofed without rumination.

In every other animal, without exception, the conditions of being cloven-hoofed and rumination appear simultaneously, that is either they have both signs of being kosher—or neither of them.

The Torah also lists the names of those animals that show only one sign of kosher fitness, and links these signs one by one to the small group of animals involved:

> "But the following you may not eat from among those that ruminate or those that are cloven-hoofed: the camel, which chews its cud but is not cloven-hoofed, is impure [not kosher] to you; the hyrax, which chews its cud but is not cloven-hoofed, is impure to you; the rock badger (or Syrian coney), which chews its cud but is not cloven-hoofed, is impure to you; and the pig, which is cloven-hoofed but does not chew its cud, is impure to you." (Leviticus 11:4–7)

It is worth devoting more thought to the significance of these passages. What they really mean is that the writer of the Torah pledges to all future generations that any animal that may be discovered, from the Amazon forests to the Australian Outback, must bear either both signs of being kosher—or neither of them, with the sole exception of the four previously mentioned creatures! This subject is expanded in the Talmud where Rav Chanan Bar-Rava wrote, "Was Moses a hunter (some translate Zoologist) or an archer!? This refutes those who maintain that the Torah was not divinely revealed." (Hulin 60b)

In other words, the only way Moses would have known there were no exceptions to the rule, was by divine communication—for he would not have asserted such a bold statement himself, lest he be refuted by later discovery.

From Moses to Rabbi Shimon Bar Chalafta, the sages of Israel were profoundly in tune with the cosmos, nature, and the animal kingdom with which we share this planet. These wise men strove to better understand their nature and shared their wisdom with us. In the next chapter, we will see how other sages studied and "conquered" nature making timeless discoveries that contribute to medical science and our understanding of fabulous workings of the human body.

The Least You Need to Know

◆ Many sages of the Talmud were also noted astronomers.

◆ The sages's knowledge of the number and arrangement of the stars in the universe matches NASA's for its accuracy.

◆ The Jewish calendar is the only one that reconciles the difference between the solar and lunar years.

◆ The sages enjoyed observing the behavior of the animals around them, and taught many precepts concerning their proper treatment.

Medicine and Healing in the Talmud

In This Chapter

- ◆ Sage as physician
- ◆ Talmudic hygiene
- ◆ Ancient medical discoveries
- ◆ Talmudic potions and remedies

As you saw in the previous chapter, the sages of the Talmud were very connected to their environment and were keenly interested in how it functioned. These factors are even more apparent when it comes to the healing arts.

The Talmud is a rich source of information concerning remedies and potions. The sages's knowledge in the area of health, personal hygiene and disease, and their natural curiosity about its origins, also led to a number of discoveries that were way ahead of their time. In this chapter, we'll examine a number of these discoveries, and see if we can detect a pattern of connecting the ancient to the modern.

Talmudic Sage as Physician

During ancient times, religious leaders were often healers. In fact, for many centuries there was little, if any, difference between religion and medicine.

The tractate Baba Batra relates that Abraham himself was no slouch in the healing arts, and could cure people with a certain luminous stone that may have been given to him by Noah. The general healing power of precious stones and crystals, some of which are also mentioned in the Torah, is noted by later commentaries.

Moses was instructed by God to "build a fiery serpent, and put it on a pole" to cure the Israelites of snakebites.

Talmud Tidbits

The caduceus, a figure of snakes entwined around a pole (applied by the Greeks and Romans in their mythology) symbolizes the healing professions even to this day seems to have its origin in the Biblical account involving Moses.

Years later, King Hezekiah ground up Moses' copper snake to keep it away from the children of Israel, who were abusing it. The sages approved of Hezekiah's actions, even though God originally revealed the snake to Moses. Hezekiah also hid a book called the Book of Remedies, purportedly written by Noah, which contained instructions on the healing powers of all the herbs in existence. He did so because people had become so imbalanced in their outlook that they had forgotten God in the equation of healing.

Jewish tradition states that the Book of Remedies is resting in the same place as the Ark of the Covenant, which houses two sets of the tablets that were given to Moses. When the Ark is restored, so, too, will this book be.

For the Jewish people, the study of medicine came to be part of the regular rabbinical curriculum. A long and distinguished line of rabbi/physicians graduated from these academies. Over the centuries that followed, they served as personal physicians to caliphs, emperors, popes, bishops, and priests.

Talmud Tidbits

The Talmud mentions the office of the chief physician in the Temple, whose duty it was to look after the health of the Cohanim (priests). (Shevuot 12a) A later law required every town to include as a permanent resident a physician who supervised the circumcision of children and looked after the communal well being. In fact, a scholar was explicitly forbidden to live in a city where there was no physician. (Sanhedrin 17b)

The Talmud valued the skills and services of a physician with the proclamation, "He who is in pain let him go to the doctor." (Baba Kamma 46b) The sages obviously decried the notion, sometimes ascribed to by the overly pious, that "If God caused the illness, let Him cure it." Not only did the sages encourage one to visit a truly skilled healer, they even insisted that the physician should be duly compensated, "A healing for nothing, is worth nothing." (Baba Kamma 85a)

The Prince's Physician

Several prominent rabbi/physicians are noted in Talmudic literature. Among the early greats, one figure stands out more than all the others. Mar Shmuel, an astronomer/scientist par excellence, was a second-century Babylonian sage. It seems that not only was he intimately familiar with the paths of the stars in the cosmos, but also with the art of the physician.

Shmuel was Rabbi Judah, the Prince's doctor, and, according to the Talmud, quite a skilled one when it came to fine-tuning dosages. Once, the Rabbi had a pain in his eye, which Shmuel wanted to treat with a potion. The potion's strength was more than Rabbi Judah could bear. Shmuel suggested using something to serve as a buffer between the remedy and the Rabbi's eye. Rabbi still refused. Finally, Shmuel prepared the potion so that just enough of its fumes would vaporize from under Rabbi's pillow, and Rabbi was cured. (Baba Metziah 86a)

In another Talmudic story, Shmuel was attempting to cure the sage Rav of his stomach pains. Shmuel took Rav to his home, fed him barley-bread and small fish fried in flour, and gave him specially brewed beer to drink for its laxative properties. The treatment was effective, and apparently, overly so, as it caused Rav much discomfort and embarrassment when he had to spend the entire day in the bathroom.

According to the Talmud, Shmuel was somewhat of a general practitioner, and was skilled in anatomy, blood-letting, cardiology, dermatology, embryology, gastroenterology, gynecology, general medicine, obstetrics, ophthalmology, pediatrics, urology, and wound healing.

> **Let's Get Talmudic**
>
> "… Shmuel brought him (Rav) to his house and fed him barley bread and small fried fish with beer. And he (Rav) did not cease from visiting the bathroom from the intense diarrhea. Rav then uttered a curse 'One who causes so much pain should not sire any children,' and thus it happened (e.g., Shmuel was childless)." (Shabbos 108a)

The Poor Man's Doctor

The most famous physician, scholar, and teacher of post-Talmudic time was Assaf Harofeh, or Assaf the Doctor. His seventh-century work, called Sefer Asaf ha-Rofe or The Book of Asaph the Physician, is the oldest known medical text in the world.

Assaf's treatise on medicine seems to have been a "poor man's medical bible," as it was comprised of cheap and easy remedies. He believed in making medicine accessible to all, and made his pupils swear that they would attend the poor and needy free of charge. His book, which includes descriptions of more 150 plants and herbs and their uses, also contains the first mention of the hereditary nature of certain diseases.

The Sultan's Doctor

The leading Talmudic healer was the universally acclaimed Rabbi Moses ben Maimon, or Maimonides, who served as the personal physician to the Sultan of Egypt.

Moses Maimonides wrote 10 treatises on medicine, covering such diverse topics as hemorrhoids, cohabitation (the Sultan's nephew wanted to increase his sexual prowess), asthma, and epilepsy. He wrote a glossary of drug names, and was the first to identify the difference between two different types of poisons—neurotoxins, which affect the nerves, and hemotoxins, which affect the chemistry of the blood.

> **Talmud Trivia**
>
> During the Middle Ages, the art of the physician was seen a more as a religious metaphysical practice and not true "science," and was thus a profession "tolerated" for Jews living in a very racially discriminating era.

In his medical treatises, Maimonides anticipated modern discoveries such as psychosomatic illnesses, allergies, epilepsy, the nervous system and overall individual constitution. Almost all of his books were written in Arabic and shortly thereafter translated into Hebrew and Latin. Today, they are available in English.

Cleanliness Is Holiness

Personal hygiene, which included frequent hand washings and ablutions for certain ritual practices, was a spiritual duty of Jews in Talmudic times, and continues to be practiced widely today.

The Talmud advises that the hands, legs, and face should be washed every day. (Shabbat 108b) Attention to bathing the body and the eyes was seen as very important. Rabbi Nathan said: "The eye is (like) a princess and it hurts her to be touched by a hand that has not been washed three times." Rabbi Yohanan says: "Puch (a precious stone or a certain herb) applied to the eye, stills its wrath, dries its tears and causes its lashes to grow." Samuel said, that bathing the eye in cold water in the morning and bathing the hands and feet in warm water at night is better than any medicine for the eye in the world." (Shabbat 108b–109a)

To the sages, cleanliness had both aesthetic and healthy aspects. The sophistication of the Talmudic understanding of disease prevention through hygiene cannot be over-stated. The sages considered perspiration especially dangerous, and referred to it as "Som HaMaves" (potion of death). It was therefore forbidden while eating to touch any part of the body that is usually covered, or to hold bread under the arm, where perspiration is usually abundant.

Interestingly enough, based on the Biblical verse "With the sweat of your brow you shall eat your bread," (Genesis 3:19) the sages advised that the sweat of one's brow or head was not detrimental. (Modern medicine today confirms that there is a great difference between the toxicity of the sweat glands of the head and that of the rest of the body.) The Talmud also admonishes against placing coins in the mouth, for fear that they might transmit contagious diseases.

Talmud Tidbits

The sages taught that it was forbidden to eat from unclean vessels or from vessels that had been used for unseemly purposes, or to eat with dirty hands. One was likewise admonished not to eat while in need of evacuating. Gluttony, as well, was expressly proscribed. All of these cautions were based on the Biblical exhortation, "And you shall not make your souls abominable." (Leviticus 20:25)

Healing with Good Scents

Aromatherapy and oil massage, which are making a comeback in today's health practices, also weren't unknown to the sages. Oiling the body was considered a necessity and not a luxury, and was done by a majority of the population in Talmudic times. One of the gestures of hospitality in the homes of the sages was to anoint your visitor with oil, along with washing his feet, giving him a cold cup of water, and/or burning incense in the home to freshen the air. A base of vegetable oils, such as olive oil, almond oil, sesame oil, or even the fat of geese, sheep, goats, or cattle was used. Often, various spices, minerals, salts, milk, and/or honey were added to these blends. Fragrant resins or aromatic flowers were also added to give them a sweet scent.

> ### Let's Get Talmudic
>
> A passage in the Book of Ruth supports the practice of anointing after bathing. Naomi, Ruth's mother-in-law, advises her to "wash, anoint, and put on her finest clothing," in anticipation of her visit to Boaz. (Ruth 3:3) The Talmud comments, "One who bathes without anointing is likened to water on the top of a barrel that remains on top and does not enter." (Shabbat 41a)
>
> Maimonides considered it a healthy practice to bathe after dinner is digested, and to anoint the body with oil following the bath. (Mishna Torah) The benefit of such a regimen is emphasized by Rabbi Chanina, who attributed his vim and vigor in old age to the baths and oil treatments his mother gave him as a child. (Chullin 20b) Modern pediatricians also recommend such a regimen.

Some historians attribute the relatively low level of Jewish casualties during the black plague that decimated Western Europe in the Middle Ages to their greater consciousness toward personal hygiene. Jewish law actually requires one to wash the hands after using the restroom.

Talmudic Hygiene and Surgery

Infectious disease control was also well known to the Talmudic sages. In tractate Shabbat 29, the physician and sage Shmuel ruled that all medical attendants must wash their hands and sterilize their medical implements. Another passage explicitly mentions washing hands when attending more than one patient to guard against disease transfer between them. The Talmud also relates that surgeons were assigned to marble-lined "batei deSha'isha, or operating rooms, to perform their procedures. (Baba Metziah 83b)

Medical Discoveries Ahead of Their Time

Scientific inquiry and discovery often makes tremendous advancements and improvements in our lives. The religious leaders of the Talmud were equally fascinated by the advancements of their time and embraced (and participated) in the scientific method that drove them. The Talmud mentions how the students of the second-century sage Rabbi Ishmael were given permission to dissect the cadavers of criminals executed by the Roman Government. (Bechorot 45a)

Also mentioned in the Talmud are several surgical operations and experiments. The tractate Abodah Zarah gives an account of an operation to cure a fistula. The Talmud also states that Mar Bar Rav Ashi, the son of Rav Ashi, had operated on a man suffering from crushed testicles. (Yebamoth 75a)

The sages of the Talmud agreed with Greek physicians such as Galen (c.131–200 C.E.), who attributed disease to the imbalance of the four humors of the body: phlegm, blood, yellow bile, and black bile. However, there were discoveries and healing philosophies with which they vastly differed. Galen, for example, testified that he once saw a patient remain alive after having his heart removed. He used this as conclusive proof that the seat of life was in the brain, not the heart. The Greeks accepted this, and his other theories as well, as gospel truth.

However, Maimonides, among others, demonstrated just how far off the Greeks were on this and other important medical theories. For example, Greek physicians believed arteries actually contained air. In fact, the Latin term "arteria" means windpipe. The scientific community took a very long time to make the discovery that blood actually flows through the veins. In fact, it wasn't until the work of the early seventeenth-century British physician, William Harvey, that we learned that the blood didn't just sit there, but circulated throughout the body and heart.

The Talmud, however, clearly states that the blood moves internally through the veins and arteries. Rabbi Zeira, an early fourth-century sage, states in Kritut 22a that "at the time of respiration the blood moves from a point in the neck into the heart." Maimonides and other Jewish physician/sages of the twelfth century confirmed his findings.

The sages also shot down several other leading medical theories of the day. Galen wrote that humans and mammals have three pulmonary lobes on both the left and right sides of the lungs. Hippocrates, the father of all Western medicine, taught that there were two on both the left and right sides. The sage Rava, however, spent 18 months of his life living among four-legged creatures to learn their anatomy, and had become an effective authority on kashrut (dietary laws) issues. In tractate Chulin 47a, he correctly states that there are three lobes on the right side, and two on the left.

Galen also categorically stated that conception can only occur through coitus. However, the Talmud in Chagiga 15a, openly entertains the viability of artificial insemination.

Sex and the Unborn Child

Chapter 10 tells the story of Mar Shmuel and how he was able to determine the exact age of an embryo, and the exact day of conception. The tractate Niddah 25b confirms his expertise. Sex determination is an entirely different skill, but here too, the sages reveal an intuition far ahead of medical science.

Modern science has shown that there are 23 base pairs of x and y-chromosomes that comprise the DNA of every cell of our body. These chromosomes determine the sex of a child at conception.

Talmud tractate Brachot 60a states an interesting concept of a "vain prayer." That is, one can only wish or pray for something where there is a chance of what is desired being granted or coming true. Yet, it also states, "Within the first 40 days after conception one is allowed to pray for a boy. However, after 40 days, such a prayer is said in vain." How can this be? Isn't gender assigned at conception?

Maybe not. In an article titled "What Makes a Man a Man?" that appeared in the July 19, 1990, edition of the British journal *Nature*, author, Anne McLaren details research that found enzymes located on the short arm of the Y chromosome that need to be activated for sex differentiation to take place. When does this happen? Between days 42 and 49 of gestation.

In other words, regardless of what occurs at conception, a number of chemical or endocrine reactions must take place for sex determination. So the sages weren't off their rockers after all! Offering prayer to have a boy baby could still have a positive effect until the seventh week or so.

There is actually a Biblical hint to this notion, found in the story of the conception of Leah's daughter Dinah. Genesis 30:21 says, "Afterwards, she bore a daughter and called her name, Dinah." Rav Yosef in the Talmud (Brachot 60a) comments that Leah's daughter's name comes from the word "din" or judgment, for indeed Leah passed judgment on herself. How so? Leah reasoned, "Jacob is destined to sire twelve sons who will comprise the 12 Tribes. I already have six, and each of his two handmaids have two, making a total of ten, thus far. If the child that I am bearing is a male, then my sister Rochel will only beget one and not even be equal to the handmaids."

With the intent of sparing Rochel this degradation, Leah supplicates God to change the sex of the fetus to female. Rav Yosef understood the superfluous word "Afterwards" in the verse to imply that after Leah judged herself and supplicated the Almighty, she bore a girl in place of the boy she was bearing.

The Talmud makes another ahead-of-its-time observation on genetics. The sages rule that if a woman bears two sons who die of bleeding following circumcision, any additional sons that she has should not be circumcised. This bleeding refers to the genetically linked disorder hemophilia. Furthermore, the Talmud states that the sons of her sisters must not be circumcised, whereas the sons of her brothers should be

(Yevamoth 64b), a clear understanding that this disease is transmitted through the female, yet only affects the male.

One more medical discovery for the road. As is well known, Louis Pasteur, one of the giants of medical research, began his experimental research with an effort to cure rabies. His germ theory of disease, while opposed by some schools of thought at the time (and by some advocates of alternative medicine now), is still the basis of prevention and cure of illnesses that have plagued society for millennia.

> **Let's Get Talmudic**
>
> Jewish law prohibits marrying a woman from a family of epileptics or lepers, (Yevamoth 64b; **Shulchan Aruch,** Even Haezer 2:7) lest the illness be genetically transmitted to future generations. According to Rashi (Yebamot 64b), any hereditary disease is included in this category.

Pasteur's revelations in his experiments with rabies serve as a foundation for all types of immunization. But was he the first to toy with the idea of artificially stimulating the immune response? Likewise, the homeopathic approach to the cure of disease, whose premise it to cure ailments by using materials similar to those that cause them, is generally considered to be less than 200 years old. Or is it?

A Hebrew book called Mevo She'arim (An Entry to the Gates) was published in the latter part of the nineteenth century. In it, the author quotes trustworthy witnesses who heard from Pasteur's close friend, rabbi and doctor Israel Michel Rabinowitz, that Pasteur actually discovered the basis for immunizations in the Talmud.

How did this all begin? Rabinowitz, then living in Paris, simply began to translate the Talmud into French. His translation of Seder Moed (Appointed Times) reached Pasteur and piqued his curiosity. Much to his astonishment, Pasteur discovered an extraordinary statement found in the Mishna of tractate Yoma, 83a, which read:

> "If someone was bitten by a mad dog [and affected with rabies], one should have him ingest the lobe of the (infected) dog's liver, perhaps it will help."

Pasteur's fascination with this theory led him to another observation. He noticed that when a full-fledged cholera outbreak occurred, chickens that had previously been exposed to a weakened form of the cholera bacterium were able to withstand the onslaught of the epidemic relatively unscathed.

> **Talmud Trivia**
>
> The five symptoms that characterize a rabid dog—mouth remaining open, drooling saliva, drooping ears, dragging tail, and abnormal gait, are all identified in the Talmud.

Advances in the area of controlled exposure to nonlethal doses of these diseases to stimulate immunity are generally attributed to Pasteur, but it would have been nice if he had given credit—where credit is rightfully due.

Talmudic Potions and Remedies and Health

"Penicillin cures, but wine makes people happy," said Alexander Fleming, the Scottish bacteriologist credited with discovering penicillin in 1928. As the story goes, Fleming noticed that bread mold which had fallen into a Petri dish proceeded to consume and dissolve the culture of staphylococcus bacteria. He won the Nobel Prize in medicine in 1945, and his "discovery" has saved millions of lives since.

It might come as a surprise, but the Talmud is actually the first medical account to recognize the anti-microbial properties of these bread molds, and even mentioned that it could help curb internal infections as well.

Compared with such progressive healing knowledge, some of the Talmud's other recommended medical practices, potions, and remedies seem quite weird and even backward. Consider the Talmud's suggestion for curing a migraine headache; "One should find a wild rooster and slaughter it with a sharpened pure silver coin over the side of the head that aches, allowing the blood to trickle down the side of the head. Then he should take the slaughter rooster and suspend it from the doorpost of his house so that every time he would enter or exit would touch up against the bird." (Gittin 68b) Kind of sounds like a magical potion, doesn't it?

And if that isn't off the wall enough, consider the remedy for nosebleeds: "One should bring the root of a stalk of Aspasta, the rope of an old bed, rag-paper, saffron, and the red part of a palm branch and burn them together until they are reduced to ash. Then he should bring a ball of wool, twist the fiber to form two strands, and immerse the strands in vinegar. Finally, he should roll the strands in the ashes and insert one strand into each nostril."

The position taken by most of today's Torah authorities in regard to the medical procedures found in the Talmud is "don't try this at home," or anywhere else, for that matter. While remedies such as these might have been effective in ancient times, they're not today. Why? Here are a few possible reasons:

♦ Humankind's constitution has gone through considerable change, and so has nature.

♦ The medicinal qualities of plants and herbs have also changed.

♦ We cannot properly identify many of the ingredients of these Talmudic remedies today and how to prepare and administer them.

In addition, the sages were only recommending conventional medical practices of the times, and like much of folk medicine some of it was effective and some of it wasn't. In some cases, though, their advice was right on the mark, as for instance, in the case of certain fevers drinking "a jug of water" was strongly advised. (Gittin 67b)

The post-Talmudic sages posed an additional concern. If one were to try one of the Talmud's remedies and it proved ineffective, or worse, it could lead people to doubt the veracity of the sages on other issues, even on religious and spiritual ones. The medieval Talmudic commentator Rabbi Shlomo Luria Lublin even stated that even if some of these remedies were still effective, they should not be tried as there was still a risk of apostasy or heresy from among the unlettered.

The Sages on Preventative Medicine and Diet

It should be noted, however, that the sages dispensed much advice on nutrition and preventive medicine that is still quite valid today. For example, garlic has been known for years to have antiseptic qualities. The Greeks used garlic to bring strength to their athletes at the Olympic games and in other contests, and employed it, as well, to help heal battle wounds. During World War II, the Russians called garlic "poor man's penicillin." Research suggests that garlic may help protect against heart disease and stroke by lowering blood pressure. The Talmud states, "Our rabbis taught, 'Five things were said concerning garlic: It satiates, it keeps the body warm, it brightens up the face, it increases semen, and it kills parasites in the intestines.'" (Baba Kama 82a)

The Talmudic scholars warned against overeating, because "more people die from eating too much than from eating too little." (Shabbat 33a, Gittin 70a) The Talmud also states the rule to "eat a third [of the capacity of the stomach], drink a third, and leave a third empty." This rule is today accepted by modern science, which confirms that the easiest way to extend life is to simply decrease the number of calories consumed.

The sages also noted that eating too much meat was unhealthy. (Jerusalem Talmud Shekalim 14:15) They warned against eating heavy meals immediately before going to bed, and advised lying first on the left and then on the right side, this being considered good for digestion (a fact substantiated by modern medical research).

In his treatises, Regimen of Health, Maimonides put it this way, "If a person cared for himself the way he cares for his horse he would avoid many serious illnesses. You won't find anyone who gives his horse too much fodder. He measures out only as much as the horse can tolerate. But he himself eats to excess. He makes sure his animal gets proper exercise to keep it healthy. But when it comes to himself he neglects exercise even though this is a fundamental principle in health maintenance and the prevention of most illnesses."

Let's Get Talmudic

Talmudic scholars held that the amount of food a person eats should be warranted by climate, season, occupation, age, sex, body weight, and state of health, (Pesachim 112a, Taanit 11a) which, in light of modern medical science, is a very sophisticated way of looking at nutrition. Additionally, Maimonides laid down certain regulations by which a man should be guided at sexual intercourse in order to preserve his physical well-being; and he promised that those who complied with these precepts will always be well, will never need to consult a physician, and will live to a good old age.

The Talmud contains a plethora of advice on maintaining sound health, such as procuring healthy vegetables; "A disciple of the Sages is not allowed to reside in a city where no vegetables are to be had," and foods that supported good digestion and elimination; "… three things decrease feces, raise the stature and bring light to the eyes: bread made of well-sifted flour, fat meat and old wine." (Pesahin 42a and Erubin 55b)

"An army marches on its stomach," was Napoleon's famous refrain. However, the Talmud goes a step further to teach us that you can measure the health of a nation by the quality of its bread. Rabbi Elazar taught that eating pas shachris, or morning bread, salt, and water prevented 83 afflictions attributed to the bile of the gall bladder. (Baba Metzia 107b) A discussion then unfolds that extols the virtues of "morning bread" in 13 ways, namely that it will:

◆ Protect you from the heat

◆ Protect you from the cold

◆ Protect you from flatulence

◆ Protect you from demons

◆ Make you wise if you are simple, and help you win a legal dispute

◆ Help you learn and teach Torah wisdom

◆ Cause your words to be listened to

◆ Cause your learning to be memorized

◆ Ensure that you do not perspire greatly and have body odor.

◆ Ensure that you will be attached to your wife and not lust after other women

◆ Dispel tapeworms and other parasites from your system

- Banish envy

- Encourage love and benevolence to enter

Ever hear of the advice regarding the best time to approach a superior for a raise? Some experts say to never choose the morning hours before lunch as this high-pressured individual has most likely not eaten a good breakfast, and will be in a better humor once he or she has eaten lunch. The sages put it this way, "Before a man eats and drinks he has two hearts: after he has eaten and drunk he has but one heart." (Baba Batra 12b) In other words, since in Jewish thought the seat of intelligence and emotions is the heart, the saying indicates that an empty stomach and lack of nutrition has a disrupting effect on the mind and emotions, and makes one irritable and in a lousy mood. So just wait until after lunch, and you'll have a better chance for that raise.

The Least You Need to Know

- The healing arts were part of the curriculum of many rabbinic academies from Talmudic times and through the Middle Ages.

- The Talmud is a repository of health-promoting advice from bathing and anointing habits to proper nutrition, and from exercise advice to tips on preserving sexual virility. Many of their teachings are as valid today as when they were recorded 1,500 years ago.

- The level of personal hygiene documented in the Talmud, as well as the physician's attention to sterile conditions, were very sophisticated for the time.

- While many Talmudic potions and remedies may be sensible and effective, they should be avoided for a number of reasons, including limited understanding as to how they are to be prepared, changes in nature and human makeup, and fear of undermining the authority of the sages.

Chapter 18

On Being Holy

In This Chapter

- ◆ Separate and holy
- ◆ The Talmud on original sin
- ◆ Preserving the true beauty of women
- ◆ Keeping a civil tongue

In Chapter 9 we looked at the concept of holiness as one order of the Talmudic tracts that deals with commandments related to sanctifying the physical world. But holiness is actually discussed extensively in other parts of the Talmud as well.

How does the concept of holiness and being holy translate into the everyday thoughts and pursuits of our lives according to the Talmud? We will examine this theme in its many facets within this chapter.

Holiness as Separateness

The literal translation of the Hebrew word kadosh, or holy, is "being separate." For instance, the Sabbath is referred to as a Yom Kadosh, or Holy Day, compared to the other six days of the week. However, the literal translation of the word for holiness only tells part of the story. In practice, separation often plays a role in people gaining balance and following the golden mean of moderation in all their ways.

The conventional understanding of "holiness" or separation seems to suggest that the more a person is separated from the "mundane" material pursuits of the world, the holier he or she is. Indeed, many religious philosophies of both the East and the West suggest that extreme asceticism is the ideal.

On the flip side is the epicurean approach to life. You know, "Let's eat and drink for tomorrow we shall die." Individuals ascribing to this philosophy have basically thrown in the towel. "Why fight city hall?" their thinking goes. "Man can't control his urges."

They insist there is indeed nothing spiritually altruistic worth striving for. Hedonistic pleasure seeking can be a "religion" unto itself, and devotees pursue its doctrine as passionately as those who are devoutly connected to any of the mainstream religious practices. Traditional Judaism, however, teaches a golden mean that rejects both extremes and their definitions of holiness, or lack thereof.

Celibate or Celebrate?

One particular area where the extremes of asceticism and hedonism can be observed is in marriage, and/or sexuality. A well-circulated anecdote punctuates the Talmudic attitude on the subject:

There was a Pope who was greatly loved by all of his followers, a man who led with gentleness, faith and wisdom. His passing was grieved by the entire world, Catholic and not.

As the Pope approached the gates of heaven, Saint Peter greeted him in a firm embrace.

"Welcome your holiness, your dedication and unselfishness in serving your fellow man during your life has earned you great stature in heaven. You may pass through the gates without delay and are granted free access to all parts of heaven."

"You are also granted an open door policy and may at your own discretion meet with any heavenly leader, including the Father without prior appointment."

"Is there anything which your holiness desires?"

"Well yes," the Pope replied, "I have often pondered some of the mysteries which have puzzled and confounded theologians through the ages, are there perhaps any transcripts which recorded the actual conversations between God and the prophets of old? I would love to see what was actually said, without the dimming of memories over time."

Saint Peter immediately ushered the Pope to the heavenly library and explained how to retrieve the various documents. The Pope was thrilled and settled down to review the history of man's relationship with God.

Two years later a scream of anguish pierced the stacks of the library. Immediately, several of the saints and angels game running to the Pope's side to learn the cause of his dismay.

There they found the Pope pointing to a single word on a parchment, repeating over and over, "Look, the word is celebrate, not celibate!"

Ah, such a subtle difference.

Going to Extremes

Though meant tongue-in-cheek, there is a kernel of truth in every joke. Is the viewpoint of celibacy as a religious or Biblical ideal of holiness correct? Let's see. After the creation of Adam, God proclaimed, "It is not good for man to be alone; I will make him a helper parallel to him." (Genesis 2:18) The sages agree; in their view of the world, man should not be alone. Everyone from the High Priest, who was exalted above his brethren and enjoined only to marry a "woman in her virginity," (Leviticus 21:13) to the commoner who has a positive mitzvah to marry—and not exclusively for the purpose of procreation! Yes, it does say celebrate, and it is holy!

This definition of holiness might appear novel. After all, parts of Christendom, for instance, have long insisted that man is "sinful flesh." Rather than succumbing to carnal drives, it is preferable to incline after the other extreme—celibacy.

The Talmud takes issue with this notion. In chapter seven, we discussed the Nazarites, who abstained from drinking wine (and general social interaction), wouldn't cut their hair, or come into contact with a corpse for a period of time.

Nazarites took this vow to dissociate themselves with the world, and become closer with God. But, they could leave the sect if they so desired. If they did, they were commanded, "on the day his abstinence is completed … He shall bring his offering to God, … one unblemished ewe as a sin offering …" [meaning as an atonement for sin]. (Numbers 6:14) About this, Rabbi Elazar Hakappar asks "What is meant by the Torah that upon termination of his Nazarite vow 'he shall provide an atonement for having sinned upon his soul'?" (Ta'anit 11a).

Striking a Balance

Rabbi Elazar goes on to answer his own query "Whereas someone who merely abstained from wine, is nonetheless called a "sinner," one who abstains from all types of pleasure, is it even the more so that he is considered a sinner?"

The rabbi's point is this: God created people with urges and desires. He is not a tyrant who demands complete suppression of those needs and drives. Sex, food, alcohol, money, and possessions are inherently moral-neutral, not necessarily bad or evil. Placed in their proper context, they can be used for the benefit of the individual and society.

Certainly, they can be, and often are, abused. The "eat, drink and be merry for tomorrow we shall die," approach which was advanced by hedonistic Greek epicurean culture, is an extreme. Total abstinence, as in the life of an ascetic monk, is likewise extreme.

The Torah and Talmud advocate balance and prescribe ways for a person to achieve this worthy objective.

Holiness in the Bedroom

A basic Christian philosophy on the matter of sex and marriage is epitomized by the words of Paul in the New Testament: "To the unmarried and the widows I say that it is well for them to remain single as I do. But if they cannot exercise self-control, they should marry. For it is better to marry than to be aflame with passion." (1 Corinthians 7.1–9)

Talmud Tutor

Pharisees were members of an ancient Jewish religious group who followed the Oral Law in addition to the Torah. The early Talmudic sages are identified as Pharisees.

In other words the institution of marriage is viewed as a concession to uncontrolled urges and the temptations of lust implanted by the "Satan" that can be seen as an equivalent to hell. This notion is anathema to Torah and Talmudic principles. Paul, who professed he was a *Pharisee*, had so sharply deviated from the teachings of the Pharisees and Talmudic sages that he is, in fact, in direct contradiction with them.

In contrast to Paul's beliefs, the sages saw a divine link between marital sex and God. In the Zohar, the Talmudic sages interpreted the verse, "And Isaac brought her [Rebekah] into his mother Sarah's tent" (Genesis 24:67) as meaning that the Divine Presence came into Isaac's house along with Rebekah. According to this mystical teaching, the Shechina, or Divine Presence, resides with the man only when the house is in "readiness" and at the time the male and female are conjoined. At such time the Shechina showers blessings upon them. (Zohar, Genesis 101b) Or, if God's presence is to be felt in the home, the most likely place for it to reside is in the bedroom.

The Talmud additionally teaches that a man should cohabit with his wife in response to her desire, whether she is pregnant, incapable of bearing children, or even advanced in age. The attitude toward the marital union is clearly intended to "celebrate," and not to suppress sexual needs and intimacy.

> ### Let's Get Talmudic
>
> He who loves his wife as himself; who honors her more than himself; who rears his children in the right path, and who marries them off at the proper time of their life, concerning him it is written: "And you will know that your home is at peace." (Yebamoth 62) Additionally, a man is forbidden to compel his wife to her marital duty. (Eruvin 100b)

The Talmud on Original Sin

In the Christian faith, original sin refers to humankind's innate state of sinfulness, derived from the disobedience of Adam and Eve, as noted in Romans 5:12 "… just as through one man sin entered the world, and death through sin, and thus death spread to all men, because all sinned." Original sin condemns one to hell for all eternity. The only escape is to accept Jesus Christ as savior.

Jews don't believe in the doctrine of original sin. In a nutshell, the Talmud teaches that no human being is perfect, and all people have sinned many times. A state of sin does not condemn a person to damnation; only a handful of truly grievous sins lead to anything near the Christian idea of damnation.

The Torah and Talmudic conception of God is that of a Creator who tempers justice with mercy. Based on the views of the Baale Tosaphot in the Talmud, (tractate Rosh HaShanah 17b) God is said to be:

1. Merciful before someone sins, even though God knows that a person is capable of sin.

2. Merciful to a sinner even after the person has sinned.

3. Representative of the power to be merciful even in areas that a human would not expect or deserve.

4. Compassionate, and eases the punishment of the guilty.

5. Gracious even to those who are not deserving.

6. Slow to anger.

7. Abundant in kindness.

8. A god of truth, thus we can count on God's promises to forgive repentant sinners.

9. The preserver of kindness for thousands of generations; the deeds of the righteous benefit their offspring far into the future.

10. The forgiver of iniquity; God forgives the intentional sinner, if he or she repents.

11. The forgiver of willful sin; Even those who purposely anger God are allowed to repent.

12. The forgiver of error; sins committed out of carelessness or apathy.

13. The cleanser and eraser of the sins of those who repent.

The Deeper Meaning of Original Sin

Adam and Eve were told to live it up in Eden, they could eat, drink, cohabit to their hearts content, but had to refrain from only one thing—the Tree of Knowledge. But they couldn't resist the temptation posed by something that was forbidden to them, and they questioned why God had indeed done so, saying to each other, "Why do you suppose God doesn't want us to eat from that tree over there? Maybe He is saving it for himself, because one who eats from it becomes God himself!"

If one analyzes the deeper meaning behind the "Original Sin," of Adam and Eve in the Garden of Eden, Adam and Eve are proven to be ingrates. Adam, in response to God's taking him to task, tries to deflect blame for the crime, "The woman that you gave to be with me—she gave me of the tree and I ate." Eve's response was similar, "The serpent deceived me, and I ate." (Genesis 3:12,13) The bottom line was that they could not handle the amazing freedom they were given in the Garden. They showed contempt for the myriad benefits bestowed upon them, and this contempt led them to rebel against their Creator.

There is an element of independence and detachment from authority in every transgression, whether religious or secular. Tinged with the desire for the elicit, "Stolen waters are sweet," (Ecclesiastes 9:17) every rebellion against authority is an act of self-centeredness and selfishness, even to the detriment of the individual. It ultimately leads to the form of ingratitude demonstrated by Adam and Eve.

Holiness in Action

Talmudic thinking intended to rectify ingratitude is to encourage actions of loving-kindness, among other positive deeds. These positive actions are seen as the greatest antidote for the destructive quality of sin. Spreading kindness and emulating the Creator (Imatio Dei) are major principles of Judaism.

While recognizing man's flaws and proclivity to succumbing to the Evil Inclination, the Talmud teaches that one can become holy by proper actions, namely, emulating God's attributes and loving-kindness. A classical rabbinic work, Midrash *Avot de Rabbi Natan*, states:

> One time, when Rabban Yochanan ben Zakkai was walking in Jerusalem with Rabbi Yehosua, they arrived at the place where the Holy Temple now stood in ruins. "Woe to us," cried Rabbi Yehosua, "for this house where atonement was made for Israel's sins now lies in ruins!" Answered Rabban Yochanan, "We have another, equally important source of atonement, the practice of gemilut hasadim (loving kindness), as it is stated 'I desire loving kindness and not sacrifice.'"

The Talmud teaches that "Rabbi Yochanan and Rabbi Eleazar both explain that as long as the Temple stood, the altar helped atone for Israel, but now, one's table atones [when the poor are invited as guests]." (Berachot, 55a)

Let's Get Talmudic

While pursuing holiness is a noble cause, and removing the taint of sin through proper actions is the correct approach, one should not think that once accomplished, he or she is impervious to natural cause and affect. So, it's best not to tempt fate.

A bedrock concept of Judaism is that a man's fate is in the hands of Heaven. As the saying goes "Every bullet has its address." So when a person's time comes, or a person deserves to be taken as a result of his sins, we are taught that there isn't much that can be done to prevent it. For this reason, the Talmud urges one not to place himself in mortal jeopardy or in a life-threatening situation. One may not say, "A miracle will be performed for me," perhaps one is not forthcoming. (Ta'anit 20b)

Holiness Between the Sexes

Found in First Esdras, an ancient collection of *apocrypha*, is an entertaining tale about three young courtiers who debate the question, "What is the strongest thing in the world?"

The debate is held before Darius, King of Persia, and the winner is to get a handsome prize. The first courtier maintains that the strongest thing is wine, as it makes even the wise foolish; the second that it is the king himself, for he was the mightiest in the world (not to mention it always pays to flatter the king); the third argues with some satire and humor that women are stronger than either wine or kings, for their charm and power of seduction can overcome both. However, "truth" is by far the strongest entity. This last young man turns out to be none other than Zerubbabel, or the prophet Daniel, who for his prize receives generous help from the king in rebuilding the Temple in Jerusalem.

Modesty Equals Majesty

The power that women can have over men is well documented in history. Nations have fought wars over desirable woman. It was a woman, Delilah, who brought down one of the mightiest warriors in history. King David's passion for Batsheva almost destroyed his reign as king. So, what's a woman to do about her innate feminine charms? Balance them with her equally innate sense of modesty and virtue. The Talmud expresses the greatest attribute of a woman in these terms: "The grace of the princess is internal (private), her raiment is of gold settings." (Psalms 45:14)

The Talmud advises women to wear modest garments in order not to inflame the men's sensibilities. (Baba Kamma 82b) It also informs us that Israel was redeemed from Egypt because of the righteousness of the women, (Sotah 11b) and that their sexual modesty and virtue played a key role in that redemption. We are also taught that women have greater power of discernment than men, (Niddah 45b) particularly in their keen intuitions concerning personality.

Let's Get Talmudic

Lest one should get the impression that women are to suppress all expression of beauty, it should be noted that the Talmud (Baba Kama 82b) recounts 10 regulations instituted by the scribe Ezra upon leading the Jewish Nation back to Israel in 424 B.C.E. following the Babylonian exile. Among them was the mandate that merchants should travel throughout Israel, selling cosmetics to endear wives to their husbands.

Women, according to Judaism, possess a special trait called binah, loosely translated as "deep understanding." In the Torah, women are exemplified as having a rich internal system, consisting of a unique ability to penetrate deeply into people's true nature.

They are described by the sages as having insight and perception beyond logic, external details and shallow facades.

If women are viewed superficially, devoid of their rich internal character and spirituality, they are stripped of this unique gift called binah. The consequence is that they will be objectified and degraded. In fact, we see that cultures that admire women primarily for their physical characteristics ultimately demean them and take advantage of them.

In view of this reality—coupled with a strong penchant among males to notice the physical and be stimulated visually—women would do well to de-emphasize their bodies in order to accentuate that which is their real beauty—their regal spiritual qualities and superior discernment.

We'll conclude this section with a quick Talmudic anecdote about a maiden who demonstrated a high level of consciousness in this matter. Evidently she was rather attractive and realized her power as a potential unwitting seductive siren of men, poised to causing spiritual shipwrecks on lonely islands of inflamed passions. Rabbi Yochanan actually overheard this young woman, who was habitual in prayer, fall upon her face and exclaim, "Lord of the Universe! You have created Paradise and Gehinnom (purgatory); you have hast created righteous and wicked. May it be Your will that men should not stumble through me." (Sotah 22a)

Give Me Space!

Being that men are visually stimulated and are wired to their carnal appetites, Talmudic teachings are brutally frank and aware of man's flaws. Various regulations were taught to prevent sexual improprieties from sullying a person's holiness and closeness to God.

Recognizing female attraction, and taking into consideration male hormones, the Talmud is quite forthright and blunt regarding how a woman's innate modesty is to be protected. Leviticus 18:6 teaches, "None of you shall approach a female to uncover her nakedness: I am the Lord." From this, the Talmud derives a prohibition against any intimate contact with a person with whom one is forbidden to have sexual relations. This "intimate contact," includes even a handshake, as strange as this may seem. (Of course, physical contact is permissible between grandparents, parents and children.)

Curb Your Hormones!

God created men and women with many differences. One of the most significant differences is how we are wired sexually. So, of course, given our differences, our temptations are not the same. The Evil Inclination, being a veteran strategist, hits us where we are weakest.

While it might seem that the Talmud's directives on modesty apply more to women than to men, both sexes were responsible for behaving appropriately toward each other. Modesty applies to everyone. Here are two Scriptural passages to demonstrate:

> (God) tells you, man, what He requires of you, but to do justice, love kindness and walk modestly with your God. (Micha 6:8)

> … And with the modest ones lies wisdom. (Proverbs 11:2)

And yet, when modesty involves the issue of clothing and covering up, it does have more serious ramifications for the female gender, as it also does, interestingly, for Torah scholars:

> Torah scholars should be extra modest in clothes and in their behavior. (Derech Eretz Zuta 7)

Worshipping Modestly

Such modesty even extends to worship. In Jewish houses of worship, it is traditional to physically separate men and women to set the appropriate mood and decorum for prayer.

There is a structure in the synagogue called a mechitza (a divider) that separates the women from the men and is one of the main fixtures in Orthodox houses of worship today.

Let's Get Talmudic

The Talmudic source for making a separation is connected to the Temple of Solomon at the time of the celebration of the "Water Drawing Ceremony." (Succah 51b) When a good portion of the nation gathered at the Temple Mount during the Festivals, the sages saw that much intermingling and levity between the sexes was taking place. After a bit of trial and error with a number of solutions, they eventually settled on a situation where the women sat high on a very large balcony, above the men.

The late Talmudic scholar Rabbi Joseph ber Soloveitchik explained the rationale of mechitza as a product of concern for setting the appropriate mood and decorum for prayer. In Judaism, the synagogue has been transformed into a place of gathering and meeting, in certain ways similar to that of the Holy Temple celebrations of old. Thus, there is always a danger in losing focus of the essential task at hand—developing and maintaining a personal relationship with God. If we are honest with ourselves, we will admit that one of the greatest distractions for a man is someone from the opposite sex. In order to subdue these social aspects and make it possible to concentrate on praying to the Almighty, it became necessary to institute the rules of the partition.

Separating men from women in prayer may seem old fashioned and perhaps even a bit extreme, but there's also a good Biblical basis for it. Adam and Eve frolicked around the Garden of Eden naked, and were not ashamed until they ate from the Tree of Life. Then, a big change took place in their feelings about nakedness and clothing. As Genesis 3:7 puts it: "And their eyes were opened, and they knew they were naked and they sewed fig leaves."

What caused this revolutionary change in attitude? The answer is rooted in another aspect of the sin of Adam and Eve.

Adam and Eve were in the Garden of Eden, their bodies were a mirror of their souls. Indeed, there was no need to cover up such a pure innocent expression of spirituality—God's image illuminating a human being. However, once evil was assimilated into man, the body came to represent something adversarial to the soul. Looking at the body could now distract the observer from focusing on his or her internal being and instead focus exclusively on the physical—the superficial shell.

God found it necessary to artificially de-emphasize the physical in order to emphasize the spiritual, thus forcing a "cover up" of the body to let the soul shine through. De-emphasizing the physical in a house of worship has the same effect.

Tongue Fu—The Sanctity of Speech

Imagine the following scenario: Someone, maybe an irritable boss or an overwrought spouse, is giving you a tongue-lashing. The diatribe comes to an end, and your very natural inclination is to retaliate. Under normal circumstances, you wouldn't back down from such a stimulating sparring session, but suddenly, for whatever reason, you decide to restrain yourself and not respond in kind. As the moments pass, a certain feeling of empowerment and even serenity over takes you.

"Hey, this feels good, exhilarating, how did I do that?" you say.

What you have just experienced is a tremendous virtuous act of self-control concerning which the great Vilna Gaon revealed, "Each and every minute that a person seals his mouth he merits to see the Ohr Ha'ganuz (hidden light) that no angel or living being can fathom."

It is almost like mental martial arts. Not one "punch" was necessary to diffuse the tension, and you received tremendous reward for the effort! A win/win scenario all around.

Let's Get Talmudic

"All the days that I grew up among the wise, I never found anything more beneficial to the body than silence."

—Rabbi Shimon in Ethics of the Fathers

The last, and arguably most significant area of cultivating holiness is in the area of speech. The sages mince no words to extol the virtue of one who watches his tongue.

The sages understood that man is a speaking creature. The Talmud says that when man received the breath of life, he was also imbued with the spirit of speech.

With such a strong tendency to speak, it is no wonder that the Talmudic sages "spilt much ink" on the subject. Often, they were extremely graphic when discouraging one from enjoying a juicy piece of gossip. For example, the Torah admonishes, "Do not accept a false report." (Exodus 23:1) The Talmud infers from this verse that there is a prohibition to accept or to speak *lashon harah*.

Talmud Tutor

Lashon harah means "evil tongue." The term is often used to describe gossiping or tale bearing.

The Talmud further comments on the placement of this verse. It is preceded by one that says, "You shall not eat flesh of an animal that was torn in the field; to the dogs it shall be thrown." (Exodus 22:30) So, one who speaks or listens to gossip or bears false testimony against his friend is worthy of being thrown to the dogs!

Talmud Tidbits

One of the greatest sages of the previous generation was Rabbi Yisrael Meir Kagan (1838–1933), who wrote extensively on the virtue of guarding one's tongue. He even used the term as the title for one of his books. Rabbi Kagan was became known for another of his epic works, titled Chofetz Chaim, based on the verse in Psalms "Who is the one who desires life (chofetz chaim), guard your tongue from evil and lips from speaking deceit" (34:13–14). In the introduction to this book, Rabbi Kagan enumerates 35 prohibitions and positive commandments one can violate by speaking lashon harah.

Let's conclude this subject with a story that illustrates the consequences of an uncivil tongue.

There was once a Jew who constantly spoke lashon harah. Creating ill will among people seemed to be his mission in life. Suddenly, he seemed snowed under with misfortunes of all sorts. He decided to take stock of his life. He finally admitted to himself and God that he was guilty of speaking lashon hara. As a dutiful Jew, he sought out his Rabbi for advice on how to repent and to rectify the damage he had done.

The rabbi told him succinctly, "Go home and find a pillow, bring it with you to the town square at midnight."

This Jew, while not exactly regaling in the prospects of spending the night sleeping on a park bench, was willing to do anything to atone for his sins. So he followed the rabbi's instructions diligently and met him there precisely at midnight.

"Rabbi," he asked, "what do I do now to finish the atonement process?"

"Take this knife and slit open the pillow and scatter the feathers in the wind," was the rabbi's terse order.

The penitent follower did just that. Assuming it was some symbolic ritual of "letting go of one's sins," he preceded to leave.

"Where are you going?" the rabbi asked. "You have just started. If you sincerely wish to repent, you must now gather all of the feathers you just scattered."

The man stopped in astonishment. "Is the rabbi for real?" he asked himself. "How can I possibly gather up feathers that have blown onto trees, rooftops, and balconies?"

"Ah," the rabbi added. "Just as it is virtually impossible to retrieve thousands of feathers, do you think it will be easy to gather up all the words of lashon hara, and make amends for all the damage you caused over the course of time?"

There are many scriptural verses that speak to the wisdom of clean speech. "Life and death are in the hand of the tongue." (Proverbs 18:21) "The tongue of the wise gives health." (Proverbs 12:18) and, "A wholesome tongue is a tree of life." (Proverbs 15:4) With these verses in mind, perhaps one should add to his/her dietary regimen and workout a bit of Tongue Fu, and avoid "high cholesterol" evil speech.

The Least You Need to Know

◆ The Talmud preaches balance and the "Golden Mean" in terms of achieving holiness on pursuit of material needs. General asceticism and self-mortifications such as constant fasting and the like strongly discouraged.

◆ The concept of original sin and temptation is one directly addressed by the sages. While recognizing man's flaws and proclivity to succumbing to the Evil

Inclination, the Talmud teaches that one can become holy by proper actions, namely, emulating God's attributes and loving-kindness.

◆ Holiness is achieved in gender relationships by healthy separations during specific events, such as community prayer. Both the Torah and Talmud contain teachings that encourage safeguards to uphold a Godly standard of modesty and sexual propriety.

◆ Proper use of speech is viewed by the Talmud as one of the most vital components of living a holy existence. Many pages of the Talmud are devoted to the serious transgression of slandering a person through speech.

Chapter 19

Talmudic Behavior and Conduct

In This Chapter

- ◆ God's laws for all
- ◆ Noah's laws vs. the Ten Commandments
- ◆ The moral responsibilities of Jews and non-Jews
- ◆ God's sensitivity lessons

According to Jewish belief, all of God's people, regardless of how they define Him, or what their relationship is with Him, are governed by a code of conduct that God gave to Adam and Eve. These principles were then handed down to Abraham, then to Noah, and then to Moses.

When the Torah was given at Sinai and explained and taught by Moses over the next forty years, it resulted in a system of laws that is based on the Ten Commandments. This system, according to tradition, contains 613 commandments for Jews. However, when it came to what God expects from the rest of His people, things are a little different.

For the rest of humankind, God only required adherence to a vastly smaller set of laws to gain acceptance to His kingdom.

In this chapter, we'll take a closer look at what this code of conduct is all about, and what the Talmud says about it.

God's Laws

Remember the story of Noah and the Ark? When God decided to cleanse the earth of all corruption, he chose Noah, his family, and pairs of all living creatures to survive the deluge. After the flood, they repopulated the earth.

God made a covenant with Noah and his family just as he had with the children of Israel. When he did so, he gave them seven commandments to observe. These commandments are called the *Seven Noachide Laws*, in keeping with the tradition that all humans are descended from Noah and his family.

Talmud Tutor

The **Seven Noachide Laws** are seven universal principles that form the basis of God's moral expectations of all humankind. They are sometimes called the Seven Universal Laws, or the Seven Laws of the Children of Noah.

The Seven Noachide Laws include six "thou shalt nots":

- ◆ Idolatry
- ◆ Blasphemy
- ◆ Murder
- ◆ Robbery and grand theft
- ◆ Immorality and forbidden sexual relations
- ◆ Removing and eating a limb from a live animal

And one "thou shalt":

- ◆ Establish a judicial system, including courts of law, to ensure the enforcement of the other six.

Although the Bible doesn't specifically mention the Noachide Laws, they all come from specific Bible passages, mostly in the book of Genesis.

Multiple Paths to God

The Seven Noachide Laws should look pretty familiar to you as they are very similar to the Ten Commandments. In fact, there are only slight differences between the two.

They contain a law about eating something taken from a live animal that the Ten Commandments don't. The Noachide laws don't specifically command that you should honor "thy mother and thy father," although it's certainly implied. Nor do they directly address the Sabbath. Why?

In a certain respect, Judaism is mankind's original "Rainbow Coalition." Unlike other religious catechisms or principles that insist that it's, "My way or the highway," Judaism is remarkably accepting to the notion of multiple paths to God.

The Talmud teaches that there are 70 original families with 70 paths within the great "family of man." Each individual has his or her path within a path, yet, there is one unifying entity for all—the Torah, which is considered a blueprint for the life of all humankind.

Talmud Tidbits _____

The 70 original families referred to in the Talmud date back to Noah and the flood.

The gist of the Talmud's attitude in these teachings is that there are complementary roles of Jew and non-Jew integral to the notion of perfecting God's world. In fact, the sages speak of the greatness of a non-Jew occupied in the study of the Torah involving the Noachide laws (Baba Kamma 38a) in terms comparable to that of the service of the High Priest of the Jewish people.

For those who are not Jewish, adhering to the Laws of Noah also gains them God's acceptance as righteous people. Those who choose to live by the Noachide Laws are referred to as *Noachides* in Jewish literature.

Talmud Tutor _____

Noachides are individuals who adhere to the principles of Noachide Law. Another term sometimes used to describe these individuals is b'nai Noah, or children of Noah.

At first glance, it might seem that the gap between Jewish and non-Jewish observance is enormous. But if you look a little more closely, you'll see that it's not as great as it first appears. These seven basic principles all have many implications. In properly observing them, a non-Jew will actually incorporate 66 mitzvot, or religious duties, of the Torah, which specify these items in greater detail. They involve much larger considerations as well; for example, the seventh, which technically reads, "Do not tear a limb from a live animal," implies that one should not practice cruelty to animals.

Moreover, we no longer have a Holy Temple in Jerusalem or a Jewish Supreme Court of 71 elder sages, so many of the 613 mitzvot in the Torah do not apply. As a result, a Jew today can only fulfill 271 possible mitzvot. So there is approximately a four-to-one ratio in the number of commandments a Jew today can fulfill, compared to a non-Jew. In addition, many of the extra mitzvot required of Jews have to do with Shabbat or Jewish holidays or with physical commandments like kosher food, and are not required of the non-Jew.

What's in It for Me?

The commandments were given so that all humans could participate in the boundless good that the Creator wished to bestow on humankind. Maimonides taught that non-Jews who obey the seven commandments out of the conviction of love and respect for God have a portion in the world-to-come (heaven). Although they are worded in the negative ("you shall not …"), that simply emphasizes the importance of avoiding evil. But they have highly positive effects.

Their benefit appears in three distinct areas. The prohibitions against idolatry and blasphemy teach man to revere and worship one Supreme Being, which is the foundation for all ethics, reminding us that all come from one Source. The prohibitions against murder, sexual immorality (primarily adultery and incest), robbery, and perversion of justice serve as the foundations for social morality among human beings. The prohibition against eating flesh from a living animal instills in humans basic instincts of kindness toward lower creatures and reminds him to curb his own animal appetites.

Talmud Tidbits

Because of the distinction between Jewish and non-Jewish observance, it is clear that Judaism teaches tolerance of other legitimate faiths and creeds. It categorically denies that a non-Jew must live by Torah or forever be condemned to "purgatory." In fact, active efforts to convince non-Jews to take on Torah observance or "convert" are considered inappropriate; and are almost a form of racism, saying that our religion is better than yours.

Nonetheless, while Jews do not seek to proselytize, individuals from among the nations of the world who have a spiritual yearning to join the Jewish people and take on all the obligations of Torah, replete with its rituals and observances, may do so by the process of a conversion.

The Talmud contains guidelines as to how a non-Jew might convert. The process varies a little between men and women, but includes an avowed commitment to living according to the Torah ways, ritual circumcision, and immersion in a mikvah, or ritual pool.

Judaism unequivocally proclaims that one who chooses an ethical "Noachide" lifestyle, guided by the moral code described above, is fulfilling his tikkun, or spiritual purpose on Earth. A person who seeks to do more than the mere minimum within the Noachide framework may do so. Some people are more spiritually inclined than others, and would want to develop themselves through prayer or meditation; some are more interested in social service. All such efforts are high callings that the non-Jew can perform, without any negative comparisons to Judaism.

The "chosen-ness" of the Jewish people is therefore not connected with "domination" or "exclusiveness." It signifies the bonding with a level of transcendent godliness expressed through the performance of 613 commandments.

Jew and non-Jew have a partnership to fulfill in which each has a crucially complementary service to perform. Let's take a closer look at what that partnership entails.

Don't Be Cruel

God gave Adam, the first man, vegetation for food. It is written, "And God said, Behold I have given you every herb bearing seed which is upon the face of the whole Earth, and every tree upon which there is fruit of a tree bearing seed, to you these shall be for food." (Genesis 1:29) Though Adam was not forbidden to use meat as a food source, he was not allowed to kill animals. If the animal had died of natural causes, it could be eaten as food.

When Noah immerged from the Ark he was given permission to kill animals for food, but he was restricted by God to eat the flesh of any animal while the animal was still alive.

Let's Get Talmudic

Some of the Talmudic sages express the opinion that even if the animal is now dead, if the limb had been torn while it was still alive, it can't be eaten. Others say that Adam received six of the seven Universal Laws, and had been forbidden to eat the flesh of an animal in any fashion. It was only following the flood that meat eating was instituted.

Why is there such a restriction and why is it worded in this way? Furthermore, how do we infer from this prohibition a general admonishment against cruelty to animals? The Torah commands, "Every moving thing that lives shall be for you for food; just as the green herbs, I have given you everything. But flesh with its living soul, its blood, you shall not eat." (Genesis 9:3–4) The vitalized animal soul is contained within the blood, and when an animal dies, this vitalizing soul departs. However, as long as this vitalizing soul remains within the animal, its flesh is forbidden to man as food. (Leviticus 17:14)

What the Torah is getting at here, perhaps a bit indelicately (after all, how many people would ever tear an animal to bits while its life is still vibrant) is despite our carnal desires, and appetite for flesh, restraint must be exercised lest we become insensitive and calloused toward animated life forms. There are several specific commandments, such as not slaughtering the mother and its young on the same day and sending away the mother bird, that are intended to instill the character trait of mercy while distancing one from cruelty.

Showing respect for the creature we are about to ingest calls for patience and restraint as its life force is ebbing away. The person who would tear legs off gerbils or rabbits is vastly different than one who patiently waits for a cow or sheep to be humanely slaughtered and prepared for the table.

> **Let's Get Talmudic**
>
> Jewish mystical teachings state that the Divine Spirit will never rest on one who considers living creatures as clods of dirt under his feat, and kills even the lowliest insect, without purpose.

Another perspective on this commandment is that exercising restraint in what we eat helps develop refinement in one's diet. Since what we eat is absorbed into our bloodstream and becomes a component of our cellular makeup, we are truly a product of what we eat.

There is at least one major Talmudic opinion stating that Noachides must arrange for the humane slaughter of animals, although they do not have to conform precisely to Jewish ritual slaughter.

Blasphemy

One of the most dramatic and powerful expressions of man's struggles with God appears in the Book of Job. In it, God gives Satan permission to afflict Job with all manner of hardships and misfortune in order to test Job's faith. In turn, Job loses his family and possessions, and is stricken with boils and disease. As Job sits in sheer agony, his close colleagues remark, "Your piety is your foolishness." Even his wife chews him out, saying, "Are you still holding fast to your integrity? Curse God, and die." But Job tells them, "You speak as one who is despicable. Should we accept only the good from God and not also accept the evil?"(Job 2:9–10)

Many lessons can be learned from the story of Job. One is that the definitive revenge that man can take against God is to commit blasphemy—that is, to curse Him.

Blasphemy is an extremely impious and irreverent way of addressing the Divine. One who does so shows utter contempt for the Deity, and deliberately attempts to undermine the respect, honor, admiration and love intended for God as the Supreme

Omnipotent and Omniscient Being. One who resorts to such an extreme, for whatever reason, is engaging in a deliberate act of rebellion against his Creator.

When the Sanhedrin (the Jewish Supreme Court) exercised criminal jurisdiction in the Land of Israel, one who transgressed this commandment was subject to the death penalty. No matter how or in what language, cursing God was simply not done.

Let's Get Talmudic

The Jewish form of this law is based on the case of the blasphemer mentioned in Leviticus 24:10–23. In that case, a person who left with children of Israel from Egypt was heard to blaspheme the ineffable name of God. His punishment was to be taken outside of the camp, and all who heard his blasphemy were to lay their hands on his head and the congregation would stone him to death.

Maimonides adds to this prohibition that anyone who acknowledges idolatry, even though he does not partake in it himself, is considered as if he scorns and blasphemes the Almighty. In other words, according to this logic, whether a person is an idolater or a blasphemer, it is the same in that both deny God.

At the other end of the spectrum, all kindred souls who wish to pursue not only the letter, but spirit of this law are advised to withhold speaking evil about their fellow man as well as against his Creator. For in God's image was man created, and one who reviles his fellow man denigrates God as well.

Theft and Kidnapping

In a gathering in Chicago in the early 1990s, more than 150 religious leaders from all over convened a four-day summit to discuss matters of religious principles. One of their objectives was to see if they could come up with a consensus of a universal code of ethics all could agree on. After much deliberation, they could only agree on three points, and held that murder, blasphemy, and theft were wrong.

What they didn't do, however, is define what they believed constitutes theft. Does it only include tangible property? Intellectual property? Identity theft?

Maybe they should have turned to the sages of the Talmud for their thoughts. If they had, they would have found that the Talmudic sages took a hard line when it came to deception.

The Bible says,

> You shall not steal; you shall not deal deceitfully of falsely with one another …. You shall not defraud your fellow. You shall not commit robbery. The wages of a laborer shall not remain with you until morning. (Leviticus 19:11,13)

And the Talmud observes,

> "Such is the punishment of the liar—even if he tells the truth he is not believed." (Sanhedrin 89b)

Additionally, the Talmud tractate Makkot (23b) teaches that, "theft and illicit cohabitations (are vices) that a person desires and covets all and one who abstains from them will earn merit for himself and for all his generations after him."

Talmud Trivia

Many great religious leaders and philosophers through the centuries have echoed the beliefs of the Talmudic sages. The fifth-century church father Augustine felt any form of falsehood regardless of reason was forbidden, and expressed this rationale for honesty: "When regard for truth has broken down or even slightly weakened, all things remain doubtful." "Without staunch adherence to truth-telling," observed eighteenth-century Scottish philosopher Francis Hutcheson, "all confidence in communication would be lost."

The sages also frowned upon deception, even in mild form. Rabbi Meir wrote, "A man should not cajole his friend to eat with him if he knows very well that he won't. Nor should he offer him any gifts if he knows that he is one who refuses them. He should not make believe that it is for his guest's sake that he is opening barrels of wine [in his honor], when in fact he intends to have them brought to a shopkeeper to be sold …. And he should not invite his guest 'anoint yourself with oil' when he knows that the oil jar is empty." (Talmud Hullin 94a)

Let's look at a contemporary example to illustrate this Talmudic teaching. A person enters a business, and, under the pretense of being interested in buying something, extracts proprietary information from the owner about how the item is made, where he obtains it, or how he conducts his business. The person then leaves without buying anything and uses the information to compete with the business owner.

The Talmud makes it clear that this is a sort of theft that goes beyond "shopping the competition" as it consists of obtaining proprietary information under false pretenses. In Talmudic literature it is referred to as *"genevaat da'at,"* literally "stealing one's mind," or fraud.

Other forms of theft defined by the Talmud include:

♦ Man-stealing (kidnapping). The punishment was death for this one, if the victim was sold.

♦ Stealing by way of falsifying weights and measure.

♦ Misappropriating documents, lands or consecrated property, for which only restitution of the principle has to be made.

Stealing things that are useless or the use of which is forbidden to their owner was not punishable by law.

Establishing Civil Laws and Courts

The Talmud commands the Children of Noah to establish courts of law that will carry out justice and morality by upholding the other six Universal Laws. Any entity that fails to establish a court system, that is, that promotes a lawless society or community bereft of a judicial system, or does nothing to correct a situation over which they have power and authority, is punishable by death. (Sanhedrin 59a) Also, any court system that directly clashed with the Universal Laws was seen an instrument removing God's blessings.

According to Maimonides, the basis for this commandment comes from the story of the biblical city of Shechem. Jacob's sons wiped out the population of the entire city because they were aware that Hamor, the son of the city's leader, had kidnapped Jacob's daughter, raped her, and failed to bring him to justice. (Genesis 34: 1–31). The collective lack of moral outrage by tolerating evil exhibited by the people who lived in Shechem indicated a serious breach in their social fabric. Thus, the Torah itself justifies the actions of Jacob's family by saying they only resorted to such draconian measures "because he had defiled their sister." (Midrashic source)

> ### Let's Get Talmudic
>
> "Just as Israelites must establish a court of law in each city and hamlet, so the Noachides must establish a court system in each city and hamlet." (Tosefta Avodah Zara, Chapter 9)

In civil matters between individual parties, later authorities question whether Noachides are commanded to follow the same principles as Jewish law and Jewish courts, or whether they are to follow rulings established by their own Noachide court system and laws.

Coming Forward

An important distinction between civil and Torah law is found in the issue of subpoenaed testimony. Under American law, you are obligated to testify in a court proceeding only if you're subpoenaed. Under Jewish law, whether or not a court summons you, or even knows of your existence, you are obliged to come forward with relevant information.

This is particularly so when your testimony might exonerate an innocent person. This concept is based on a Talmudic teaching, "From where do we learn that if you are in a position to offer testimony on someone's behalf, you are not permitted to remain silent? From 'Do not stand by while your neighbor's blood is shed.'" (Sifra Leviticus on Leviticus 19:16)

The Talmud and the Death Penalty

In Exodus 23:7, it states "and the innocent and the righteous do not kill." From this verse, the sages derive that a Jewish court cannot give a death sentence unless witnesses testify that they actually witnessed the defendant commit the alleged crime. If the Torah were to allow the death penalty based upon compelling circumstantial evidence, then the likelihood would increase that someone would be put to death for a crime he did not commit.

One Talmudic argument discusses a case where two people saw a Jew pursuing another Jew, with the intent to kill him. The prospective witnesses warned the assailant that he would be subject to the death penalty if he were to carry out the deed. The witnesses briefly lose track of the pursuer as he entered a cave. A few moments later, he emerged holding a bloody dagger.

Although it is reasonable to assume that the pursuer committed murder and deserves the death penalty, the Torah exonerates him because no one saw the crime being committed. It is now up to God to punish him.

Talmud Tidbits _____

Much of Anglo-American law has been influenced by and is based on, unwittingly or not, Talmudic law. Many of the founding fathers of the United States, from John Adams to Thomas Jefferson, were familiar with the Talmud and scholars have written extensively on this connection. In 1991, the U.S. Congress even passed a public law (P.L. 102–14) recognizing the "ethical values and principles [that] have been the bedrock of society from the dawn of civilization, when they were known as the Seven Noachide Laws."

While the Torah supports the death penalty in principle, it places formidable obstacles to its implementation, and it was rarely implemented. The court would always seek ways to exonerate the defendant. If witnesses were cross-examined with questions they could not answer, the witnesses were disqualified.

The Talmud even quotes two rabbis as saying, "had we been part of a Sanhedrin at the time they were empowered to execute criminals, no person would ever have been executed."

Murder

God explicitly states to Noah the commandment prohibiting murder: "Whoever sheds the blood of man, by man shall his blood be shed, for He made man in the image of God." (Genesis 9:6) The Talmud takes this a step further, and proclaims that a Noachide who kills even a fetus in the womb of its mother was liable to the death penalty.

The sages derived this ruling from an alternative wording of the above verse. Technically, the passage reads "Whoever sheds the blood of man, in man …") The implication of "blood of man in man," hints to a fetus. (Talmud Sanhedrin 59a)

We will discuss the Talmud's take on abortion in more detail in Chapter 25.

Let's Get Talmudic

The Talmud states that if one is faced with an option to embarrass someone publicly, or suffer death, he should choose the latter. This philosophy is derived from the story of Tamar and Judah (Genesis 38:1–26), where the former was prepared to be thrown into fire rather than to publicly humiliate her father-in-law. The reason given by the Talmud is that extreme embarrassment, where a person's face turns white, is tantamount to death. Thus one must avoid "murdering" someone in this situation at all costs—even if it means sacrificing one's own life.

Here are more details on the Noachide prohibition regarding murder:

◆ If a Noachide kills someone through a messenger; e.g. a "hit man," both the messenger and the one who sent him are liable for punishment as murderers.

◆ A Noachide, like a Jewish person, is commanded to allow himself to be killed rather than kill. This means that if people try to compel a person on pain of death to murder someone, he must remain passive and not act regardless of the consequences.

- If a Noachide causes the indirect death of a person, for instance, he pushes him onto railway tracks and a train subsequently comes and kills him, he is liable for the death penalty. Likewise, if he leaves a person in a situation where he will surely starve to death, although this action only indirectly causes the person's death, it is an act of murder and punishable by the courts.

- Mercy killing or euthanasia is squarely in the category of murder according to Talmudic sources. One may not hasten another's death.

- Suicide is forbidden under the Universal Laws.

Worshipping Idols

The commandment prohibiting idolatry teaches that one should serve no created thing as a deity. That means no angelic worship, not the stars, no living creatures and nothing composed of, earth, water, fire, and air. Even if the worshiper acknowledges God as the Supreme Being and intends to glorify God's greatness through these practices, nevertheless this is idolatry.

There is perhaps no greater expression of a Noachide's love for God than his or her rejection of idolatry and its pagan implications. Maimonides stated that a person who guards himself against idolatry demonstrates belief in God and affirms the entirety of the Seven Universal Laws.

According to some Jewish legal authorities, a Noachide is not prohibited from forming a "partnership with God." The notion of such partnership is the acknowledgment of the existence of the God of Israel while placing belief in the possibility and existence of another entity other than God.

So long as ascribing power to a deity other than the Creator remains conceptual, it is permissible to the Children of Noah. However, worshiping this being independently constitutes idolatry. Accordingly, according to these authorities, Noachides are permitted to swear by the name of an intermediary in combination with God. For instance, one is allowed to swear in the name of the Lord of Hosts and a Vishnu deity.

Sexual Immorality

The Torah expresses virtually all forbidden relations in one loaded verse; "Therefore a man shall leave his father and his mother and shall cling to his wife and they shall become one flesh." (Genesis 2:24)

The phrase, "cling to his wife," teaches us that a man shall have relations with his own wife and not another man's wife. "To his wife" comes to teach us that he shall have relations with one who can become a wife, e.g. the opposite sex, but not with a male. "And they shall be of one flesh" comes to exclude any animal, for an animal is not of one flesh with a man for they cannot reproduce.

A Noachide is forbidden to have sexual relationships with certain relatives and others to whom he or she is not related, including his or her:

- Mother (even if his birth had been the result of her having been seduced or raped)

- Father

- Daughter

- Father's sister

- Mother's sister

Under the Seven Universal Laws, one is permitted to have relations with individuals related through marriage after the death of the relative. According to some opinions, this even includes a man's father's wife (not his mother) after his father dies. Included in this category are a father's wife (if not the individual's mother), a brother's wife, a wife's sister, a daughter-in-law, and a stepdaughter.

The Least You Need to Know

- God offers both Jews and non-Jews many ways to bring spiritual reality into the world through our physical efforts, through the ethical way we live, and through our relationships with others.

- According to the Talmud, the practice of Judaism is not the only way to approach and worship God.

- A system called the Seven Universal Noachide Laws that all mankind should follow to attain holiness.

- The Seven Noachide Laws incorporate 66 commandments of the Torah. That means that both Jews and non-Jews are included in many of same laws.

- The sages of the Talmud show that even intellectual property, and "stealing one's mind," or fraud, is also considered stealing.

Chapter 20

Man and God

In This Chapter

◆ Free will vs. God's control

◆ The hand of providence

◆ Understanding the fear of heaven

◆ Why bad things happen to good people

If you had to guess what was the most asked religious question, what would your answer be? Do a Google search on this subject, and you'll probably come up with "Does man have ultimate free will, or is God in control of everything?" or "Why do bad things seem to happen to good people?"

Man's relationship to God has puzzled humankind since the beginning of time, and if these intriguing questions aren't at the top of the "most-asked list," they have to be somewhere near it!

As you might have guessed, the Talmudic sages have much to say on the subject as well. Let's take a look.

Destiny and Predetermination

Western religious beliefs cover a broad spectrum, ranging from Calvinistic Baptist congregations who adhere to the teachings of the French theologian John Calvin, who believed in strict *predetermination*, to Deism, a faith that grants creation of the world by God, yet believes that he is not interested anymore, and doesn't direct the affairs of man.

Somewhere in the middle of these two polar extremes falls traditional Judaism based on Talmudic teachings. Here's a Talmudic discussion that illustrates these beliefs.

King Hezekiah learned through prophecy that his prodigy would be evil. (Talmud Brachot 10a–b) As a result, he failed to sire children and was eventually afflicted with illness. The prophet Isaiah came to visit King Hezekiah at what appeared to be his deathbed and told him, "You shall die, and not live."

> **Talmud Tutor**
>
> The concept of predetermination is built on the premise that absolutely nothing happens in the world, or to the individual, except through divine providence or guidance. This notion virtually rules out free will or accountability, as its basic tenet considers people's actions nothing more than a marionette manipulated by a puppeteer.

The sages of the Talmud, in tractate Sanhedrin, find this statement of Isaiah very perplexing and redundant. Therefore, they derive a hidden message in these words. Isaiah was telling the otherwise righteous King Hezekiah, that he was being taken to task for not procreating and "doing his job." The prophet admonished him that it was not up to him to challenge fate. At that point Hezekiah decided to comply with the prophet and was given a 15-year lease on life.

So, as it turns out, the wicked Menashe, who succeeded his father Hezekiah as king, might not have had free choice in becoming evil. His evil state, in fact, might have been preordained by his father's actions.

The commentary Tosafot use this story as an example of the possibility that freedom of choice is not necessarily universal. In fact the Tosafot go so far as to cite another passage from the Talmud Shabbat (156a) where it mentions that a person who is born under the influence of planet Jupiter will be righteous, and whoever is born on the Shabbat is called

> **Let's Get Talmudic**
>
> "For against your will were you formed, and against your own will were you born, and against your will do you live, and against your own will do you die, and perforce you to give account and reckoning before the Supreme King of kings, the Holy One, Blessed be He."
> (Mishnah, Ethics of the Fathers Chapter 4:29)

holy. However, one born at a time when the influence of Mars (the blood planet) is predominant will be inclined to spill blood.

At this point, you might be thinking, "Wait a minute rabbi! What you are saying doesn't sound much like middle ground. On the contrary, these sources clearly support a concept of predestiny. King Menashe is preprogrammed to do evil, and my neighbor who was born on the Sabbath is the holiest person on the block! What gives? Is it possible that certain people do not have freedom of choice? How is this determined, randomly? Does it always apply? Are politicians hopelessly condemned to lie? Is it possible that each person sometimes has freedom of choice and sometimes acts as an automaton or robot?"

These are all good questions, and there is a great source for understanding the attitude of the sages on this important issue. In his epic work Guide to the Perplexed (you've got to love the title, don't you?) Maimonides unlocks this mystery by emphatically stating, "It's God's will that we have free choice."

What this means is that the sources in the Talmud above are teaching that man might be born with a proclivity toward one extreme or the other. Certain people, no matter how hard they try, will never become rocket scientists.

Likewise, a person born into a family of thieves and drug dealers and has been grossly neglected, might very well be destined for a career washing dishes in the state penitentiary. Nonetheless, he is not robbed of his free choice to become one who fears heaven. Granted he (or she) has started with two hands tied behind the back and the vast majority of such individuals will continue down the road of misery. However, according to Maimonides, one can change.

So, what is this "fear of heaven"?

Fearing God

Fear of heaven is another way of saying "fear of God." As the Bible says in Deuteronomy 10, "And now, Israel what does God your Lord ask of you, but only to fear him."

Does this verse imply that fear of heaven is an easy matter? It depends. The sage Rabbi Chanina said (in the name of Rabbi Yochanan Ben Zakkai), "The Holy One has hidden in His treasury *only* a storehouse of the merit of Fear of Heaven, as it says (Isaiah 33) 'The fear of Heaven is his treasury.'"

> **Let's Get Talmudic**
>
> Rabbi Chanina says, "Everything is in the Hands of Heaven except for—Fear of Heaven."

To this, the Talmud says, "Yes, for Moses fear of Heaven was an easy thing," as Rabbi Chanina says this is analogous to asking someone for a big utensil. If he possesses it he considers it small. However, if you ask him for a small utensil which he does not posses he considers it a big utensil. So it is with fear of heaven, for people who do not possess it, it is a very big issue. (Brachot 33b)

This concept appears a few more times in the Talmud and forms a central theme in Judaism's concept of God consciousness. Simply put, there are many things in life over which we have absolutely no control, including:

◆ The circumstances into which we're born

◆ How wealthy we'll be

◆ How smart we'll be

◆ What our genetic programming will be

Nonetheless, we are taught to behave in the most righteous way, to try to follow divine will, and to show respect to God. In other words, we are taught to fear Heaven.

God Is Everywhere

The Jewish concept of God is that of a being who transcends time and space. He created these entities, yet is not governed by them. Accordingly, past, present, and future are simultaneously taking place from God's vantage point. Since there are no restrictions, he is already aware of what is going to happen.

However, God's omniscience doesn't really affect our free will. Our orientation toward the world is like that of quantum physics where all eventualities of a given event are possible. Man, in fact, possesses ultimate free will. In other words the best suggestion is to act as though we have total freedom of choice and leave God's decrees up to Him.

Rabbi Bachya ben Joseph ibn Pakuda, a great Jewish philosopher and thinker, once expressed it like this:

"The right way is to act in the belief that man's actions are entrusted to him, so that he earns reward or punishment, and to try to do everything that may benefit him before God both in this world and the next. On the other hand, one should rely on Him with the submission of one who knows that all actions, movements, benefits, and misfortunes ultimately lie under God's rule and power, depending on His permission and decree, for He has the decisive argument against man, but man has no argument against his Creator."

Talmud Tidbits

Rabbi Bachya ben Joseph ibn Pakuda was a Talmudist and philosopher who lived at Saragossa, Spain, in the first half of the eleventh century. He was the author of the first Jewish system of ethics, written in Arabic in 1040 under the title "Al Hidayah ila Faraid al-hulub" (Guide to the Duties of the Heart), and translated into Hebrew by Judah ibn Tibbon in the years 1161–80 under the title "Chovot ha-Levavot." (Duties of the Heart)

In a nutshell, the Jewish attitude to the dilemma of providence versus free will is that God's jurisdiction extends over all of creation—"He created their hearts as one and understands all their deeds."

Nonetheless, one must act according to reason and logic. God created natural phenomena to function with the laws of nature. He decreed fire to burn, water to flow rapidly, avalanches to move heaps of snow rapidly, and gravity to cause stones to fall on a man's head and break a skull if he (or the thrower) isn't careful. There is no contradiction between free will and divine foreknowledge, they always function simultaneously.

Based on the above thought, Maimonides also wrote in *Guide to the Perplexed* (3:20), that someone who defies the laws of nature, such as needlessly picking a fight with a lion, jumping head first into a 100-foot "perfect wave," or walking through fire is asking for trouble and could die before his appointed time. The Torah warned against thinking that life expectancy is already predetermined—the notion that if God wants you to live, you'll live, and if it's your time, you'll die—with the verse, "Do not try the Lord your God ... "

Likewise, the rabbis would frown on such things as the pseudo-piety of a parent lamenting the tragic death of an infant who was left in a car for two hours with the windows up in 90-degree weather by saying, "Everything is in God's hands, it was meant to be." Such thinking is a false indictment against God, and blames

Let's Get Talmudic

The issue of whether or not a person has a predetermined life-expectancy or not is addressed more than once by the Talmudic sages. Rabbi Akiva and his group of sages held that there is a predestined "length of days," for a person. Further, Rabbi Akiva held that one's merits will allow a person to fill those set days, while the sages felt that positive deeds could even extend them.

him for something he didn't do. One who fails to protect himself or his child from the ravages of nature cannot accuse God for not making a miracle.

Take Good Care of Yourself

As weird as this notion may seem, the Torah actually commands a person to take, "Exceedingly take heed of yourselves and guard your souls diligently (from self-inflicted harm.)" (Deuteronomy 4:9)

It is with this passage that a Roman nobleman rebuked a pious person who had stopped by the roadside to pray. The Talmud relates that this nobleman greeted a Jew so absorbed in prayer that he made no reply. Taking this as a slight, the nobleman reprimanded him.

"You fool! Doesn't your Torah say to 'be very diligent to guard your souls?' Why did you fail to return my greeting? For such an impudent and rude act I would be justified to lop off your head with my sword. And there would be nobody around to protect you!" (Brachot 32b)

The pious man answered him sincerely and calmly, saying that it was forbidden to interrupt one's prayers to the King of Kings even for a nobleman inasmuch as it would be an even greater insult. The nobleman's anger was appeased and he went his merry way. But the point the Talmud makes here is that a person can't rely on providence to take care of him. He must be vigilant concerning potential dangers, and take measures to protect his physical well-being.

> **Let's Get Talmudic**
>
> Rabbi Akiva ... used to say: Everything is observed; and permission is granted; and the world is judged for good; and all is in accordance with the majority of deeds. (Mishnah Ethics of the Fathers 3:15)

Not to belabor the point, but here is another example that demonstrates how the Talmudic sages understood the extent of license granted a person from Above over his own body and personal affairs ....

Rabbi Chanina said, "Everything is in the Hands of Heaven except for thorns and snares (tzinim u'pachim), as it is written 'Thorns and snares are placed in the way of a stubborn person, he who guards his soul will distance himself from them.'" (Proverbs 22:5)

One of the commentaries on Rabbi Chanina's statement makes a play on words, and relates tzinim to the word tzinah, which means cold. Pachim is related to a similar-sounding word meaning hot. Thus a "stubborn person" is also one who is derelict with his health by not protecting him/herself from becoming chilled or overheated—either which can tax the system, compromise immunity, and bring on illness.

To bolster this sentiment, the Jerusalem Talmud makes a similar assertion in the name of both Rabbi Chanina and a famous physican named Mar Shmuel. "Ninety-nine die from cold and one from natural causes." The rabbis said it differently, "Ninety-nine die out of negligence and one because it was decreed from Above." Regardless, they are on the same page on this issue, and couldn't be more emphatic. A major later commentary stated "These (99) take no precaution against the cold or heat, sexual excesses, uncontrolled anger, overeating and indulgence, and the like."

So there we have it. According to all these opinions, man has been given free choice as to whether he will inflict self-damage, abuse or even bring death upon himself by neglecting basic rules of nature and common sense. In other words, we have only ourselves to blame if we catch a cold!

Why Bad Things Happen to Good People

There is no better way to tackle this most difficult topic than with famous stories of Jewish lore. Moses Mendelssohn, the grandfather of the well-known German-Jewish composer of the nineteenth century, was far from being handsome. Along with a rather short stature, he was cursed with a noticeable hunchback.

One day he visited a merchant in Hamburg who had a lovely daughter named Frummie. Moses fell hopelessly in love with her. But Frummie was repulsed by his misshapen appearance.

When it came time for him to leave, Moses gathered his courage and climbed the stairs to Frummie's room to make one last effort to speak with her. She was a strikingly beautiful young woman, but caused him intense sorrow by her refusal to look at him. After several attempts at conversation, Moses shyly asked, "Do you believe marriages are made in heaven?"

"Yes," she answered, still looking at the floor. "And do you?"

"Yes I do," he replied. "You see, in heaven at the birth of each boy, God announces which girl he will marry. When I was born, my future bride was pointed out to my soul. Then God added, "But your wife will be humpbacked."

"Right then and there I implored God, 'Oh Lord, a humpbacked woman would be a real tragedy. Please, God, give me the hump and let her be beautiful.'"

Then Frummie looked up into his eyes and was stirred by some deep distant memory. She accepted Mendelssohn's heartfelt gesture and later became his devoted wife.

All for Good?

There are certain things that happen in life that we can't conceive of as being good. Assuming that the above story is at least somewhat accurate, one might wonder how young Moses Mendelssohn dealt with his disfigured body until he met Frummie. Did he criticize God over this condition? Or, did he piously announce, "This, too is for the good."

Try as we may to adopt a new perspective, to look from this angle, or from that vantage point, when things don't appear as they should (or as we think they should), we become frustrated. It's all too easy to fall into the trap of thinking, "Good people suffer, and the wicked prosper."

Differing Points of View

One way to understand things that sometimes seem unjust is to remember that our point of view is different from God's. Think of a pair of telescopes. One has a magnification of 50x while the other is infinitely magnified. We're using the 50x telescope, while God is looking through the other one. Guess which one is able to see deeper and with more detail? This analogy works well with the way the sages tell us how to view God's works. He's looking through one lens, and we are looking through another.

I think the following story illustrates this idea better than any explanation. Sit tight, it's a bit lengthy.

Once, when Rabbi Yehoshua ben Levi encountered Elijah the Prophet (or Eliyahu in Hebrew), he asked Eliyahu if he could accompany him so that he could learn from his unique conduct. Eliyahu flatly refused, explaining that Rabbi Yehoshua would not understand what he would experience. On the contrary, his mortal mind would raise countless questions and theological doubts.

Nevertheless, Rabbi Yehoshua pleaded and promised he would not ask any questions. Eliyahu finally agreed on the condition that as soon as Rabbi Yehoshua began to ask questions, the game was over and they would part company.

And so they ventured out together. Toward evening, they reached an old, flimsy hut. An elderly couple was sitting outside. While they appeared to be very dignified folk, they were hopelessly poor. But their poverty did not dampen their spirits or their hospitality. As soon as they saw the travelers, they ran to greet them and eagerly invited them into their home. They offered a modest meal and lodgings.

The accommodations were less than stellar, shall we say, and very meager for this couple did not have much at all. But whatever they had, they shared freely; doing the best they could to fulfill the mitzvah (good deed) of taking in wayfarers and showing hospitality to guests.

The next morning, the two travelers bade their hosts farewell and set out for the road. Shortly after they had departed, Rabbi Yehoshua saw that Eliyahu was actually whispering into the ear of a cow that was the elderly couple's only valuable possession, and their only source of income. The cow immediately keeled over and died.

Rabbi Yehoshua was shocked. The couple had been so nice to them. Why did they deserve that their cow should die? He was about to blurt out against this injustice but remembered he could not ask any questions. A deal is a deal.

The two men talked as they proceeded on their journey. Rabbi Yehoshua hoped that Eliyahu would offer some hint as to what happened. Eliyahu deflected the conversation to other divine issues. Just before evening, they came to a beautiful mansion. Although many members of the household saw them, not one came out to offer them hospitality.

They approached the owner of the house, a very wealthy man, to ask if he had lodgings in his home for the night. Seeing that he was facing two very scholarly sages, the man could not refuse. But he was very cold to them; he offered them no food, and he hardly said a word to them.

Again the next morning, Rabbi Yehoshua noticed that Eliyahu was praying. What was he praying for? One of the walls in this rich man's house was cracked and weak. Eliyahu prayed to the almighty that the wall should be restored and remain whole and solid.

Rabbi Yehoshua could not believe what he heard. Here the person was a miser who had not acted kindly to them at all. And yet Eliyahu was praying for him, entreating God that his cracked wall should become strong again. Yet, the kindly poor couple that bestowed only kindness and warm hospitality saw their source of income dry up from something Eliyahu did to it. But once more, he was compelled to abide by the terms of his agreement: no questions asked.

Eventually, the two travelers arrived in a beautiful city. Everything about the place reflected prosperity and opulence. They made their way to the synagogue. It was a magnificent structure, designed with elegance and taste. Everything, even the benches, was beautiful.

Rabbi Yehoshua ben Levi thought that they would have no problem receiving hospitality in such a town. But it did not work out that way. The people were not very kind. When the prayers were over, nobody approached them to ask where they planned to eat or if they had lodgings. In the end, they were forced to spend the night in the synagogue, sleeping on sparse wooden benches, and ate no supper.

In the morning, when they were ready to leave, Eliyahu blessed the inhabitants of the city, wishing them that they should all become leaders. Rabbi Yehoshua was beside himself with indignation. Why did the righteous Eliyahu bless such people who obviously lacked even a smidgen of class?

That evening, they came to another city. It was not nearly as wealthy a community as the first; the synagogue was barely standing. But the people were all refined, warm and kindhearted. They went out of their way to make the two travelers comfortable. Before leaving that city, Eliyahu blessed them, "May God help that only one of you becomes a leader."

Rabbi Yehoshua had reached his wit's end and could no longer constrain his consternation. He told Eliyahu, "I know that by asking questions I will forfeit my right to continue the journey with you, but I cannot go on like this. You must please, explain these four incidents to me."

And so Eliyahu explained …

"The elderly couple whom we met first; they were wonderful people who performed acts of great kindness. So I wanted to give them a blessing. It was destined for the woman to pass away that day; it was to be the last day of her life.

"By accommodating us, she was given the opportunity to perform a mitzvah. And the merit of the mitzvah of hospitality that she performed was so magnanimous that the decree was lifted, but not entirely. So I prayed that their cow, which meant so much to them and which was their main source of income, should die. This sacrifice, so to speak, allowed the woman to have a new lease on live. So the cow's death was indeed a blessing for them.

"Now, about the miser's house. In that wall, a very great treasure lay buried. But the wall was weak and would soon break. Because he was a miser and conducted himself so crudely, I prayed that the wall should become strong again so that he would never be able to benefit from the treasure.

"What about the people in the prosperous city?" Eliyahu asked.

"My prayer that they should all become leaders in the city is not a blessing at all; if anything, it is quite the opposite. For the most detrimental thing that can happen in a city is that everybody becomes a leader.

"In the other city, where the people were kind, I gave them a real blessing: that one, and only one, of them should become a true leader." (Seder HaDorot)

This story contains a powerful lesson for us all. We have to realize that life contains a pair of telescopes with separate lenses. We were given the one that can only reveal part of the picture and it's very fuzzy. So, of course, we have questions. It's natural.

What we know about ourselves, about others, and the world is extremely limited. Only God "sees" with a completely focused lens. Will people ever be able to see as God does? Jewish belief holds that in the future to come, at the time of the long awaited Messiah, He will share His telescope with us, and everything will be clear.

The Least You Need to Know

- The Talmudic sages taught that while many circumstances are "pre-programmed," fear of Heaven and the free inclination to do what is right are given to all of us.

- Matters of personal safety and well-being are primarily a person's own responsibility. The sages teach that many who "die before their time" are the orchestrators of their own fate due to negligence and poor decisions. One cannot expect a miracle to bail him out when a choice was made to defy nature.

- There is some discussion among the Talmudic and post-Talmudic Sages as to whether a person is allotted a set amount of years and days to live. Maimonides was clearly of the opinion that one's merit, or lack thereof, can lengthen or shorten this allotment, accordingly.

- With our limited intellects and mental abilities we cannot fathom the awesome issue of why bad things happen to good people, and vice versa. As a great philosopher once put it, "If I *knew* God, I would *be* God."

Chapter **21**

The Talmud and the Land

In This Chapter

- ◆ Talmudic ecology
- ◆ The Talmud on preserving natural resources
- ◆ Order and Balance: The Talmud and Feng Shui
- ◆ Seeing the world with "a good eye"
- ◆ The law of the land is law

The Talmud contains quite a few passages that show a keen awareness for the environment and how to treat it with respect. Prohibitions against wonton destruction of nature or property are clearly mentioned in the Torah and Talmudic literature. This concept spills over into stern advice against wasteful behaviors and respect for the "law of the land."

The Talmud even goes so far as to assert that mankind's role is to enhance the world as "co-partners with God in the work of creation." (based on Ethics of the Fathers 1:2) Let's take a closer look at how the sages viewed man and nature.

Talmudic Ecology

There is a Talmud passage that beautifully expresses the idea that God invites people to help tend his creation, the world:

In the hour when the Holy one, blessed be He, created the Adam, He took him around (so to speak) and let him pass before all the trees of the Garden of Eden and proclaimed: "See my works, how beautiful and splendid they are! Now, all that I have created; only for you have I created. Contemplate this and do not corrupt and desolate My World. Indeed, if you corrupt it, there is no one else to repair it after you." (Ecclesiastes Rabbah 7:28)

This sentiment basically sums up what should become man's attitude toward this beautiful playground called Mother Earth that we were given. Or as the Bible puts it, "Be fruitful and multiply, fill the earth and subdue it …" (Genesis 1:28) "Subdue it" might seem like an odd choice of a term here, but God is essentially telling Adam, "Use it, but don't abuse it."

Let's Get Talmudic

There are many other requirements for ecological soundness found in the Torah, including God's commandment to Moses at Mt. Sinai that every seventh year there should be no sowing, pruning, reaping or gathering in the Holy land, as it says, "the seventh year shall be a Sabbath of rest unto the land," (Leviticus 25:4) Although the nature of this rest, according to traditional commentators, ranges from "giving the land its due," to recognizing the Creator's control over the land, there is an undeniable tangible benefit that has been acknowledged by agriculture experts for centuries—allowing the land to lie fallow replenishes the soil.

Although the term "subdue it" is a bit vague, we do have a "user's manual"—the Talmud!—to tell us how this invitation is to be followed. Let's see what specifics the Talmud provides in making sure we preserve the world in God's way.

For starters, the Talmudic sages clearly indicated that preserving the environment and preventing pollution are vitally important. They taught, for instance, that tanneries had to be kept at least 75 to 100 feet from a town's borders and could be placed only on the east side of a town, so that foul odors would not be carried downwind from the west. (Baba Batra 2:8–9) Threshing floors had to be placed far enough from a town so that it would not be sullied by chaff carried by the winds. (Baba Batra 2:8)

The source of this concept is actually found in the Bible itself where sensitivity to environmental cleanliness is illustrated by a law, which commands disposal of human waste, even in wartime, by burial in the ground.

"Thou shalt have a place outside the military camp, whither thou shalt go forth abroad. And thou shalt have a spade among thy weapons; and it shalt be when thou sittest down outside, thou shalt dig therewith, and shalt turn back and cover that which cometh from thee." (Deuteronomy 23:13–15)

Concerning natural esthetics, "It is forbidden to live in a town which has no garden or greenery." (Kiddushin 4:12) What a concept! But even such an obvious and simple environmental amenity that enhances the quality of life is subject to a legal issue. Specifically, cities in the land of Israel were to be surrounded by an area of about 1,500 to 2,000 feet left for public enjoyment in which nothing may intrude, including cultivated fields, for it would blemish the beauty of the city. Accordingly, trees were to be kept 40 to 100 feet from the city wall. (The range given varies depending on the variety of tree and the amount of shade it has).

Talmud Tidbits

As the holiest of cities, Jerusalem had special environmental legislation intended to protect its distinctive atmosphere for its inhabitants, as well as frequent visitors. The restrictions were so great that all garbage was to be removed from the city and no kilns were allowed to operate within its borders. In this way pests and noxious smoke were kept out of the city and the quality of life greatly enhanced. (Talmud— Baba Kama 82b)

Reuse and Recycle

There is a Biblical commandment generically referred to as *"bal tashchit"*—not to destroy, without purpose, any object from which someone might derive benefit. The source of the prohibition is the Biblical command that soldiers at war not cut down fruit trees to use their wood in besieging an enemy. They were required to seek nonfruit bearing trees first for their fuel, weaponry, or building purposes. (Deuteronomy 20:19–20)

Talmud Tutor

Bal tashchit means "don't destroy."

Nonetheless, though fruit trees, in general, may not be destroyed, they may in fact, be cut down if the value of the wood is greater than the value of the fruit, or if the tree is rotting or causing damage to other property. (Baba Kama 91b)

Giving Thanks for Trees

The Jewish people express respect and appreciation for how much they are indebted to the creator for trees in quite a few ways. In the early spring, there is a minor holiday called Tu B'shvat (15th day of the month of Shvat), or the New Year of the Trees. (Mishna Rosh Hoshana 1:1) Some have the custom to sample new fruits in season and recite a special blessing over it. Jewish school children are generally given a taste of nature by going on a field trip. Some even plant saplings to commemorate this "Jewish Arbor Day," although there is no Talmudic source for this custom.

Preserving Natural Resources

The sages also placed an emphasis on preserving resources with their statement; "One should not discard his well water, while others might need it." This concept is particularly meaningful when one considers the almost constant drought conditions in arid climates around the world. For the general environment, reduce; reuse and recycle are three ways of avoiding bal tashchit.

Maimonides includes a great number of destructive activities that are included in this precept;" Whoever breaks vessels, or tears garments, or destroys a building, or clogs a well, or does away with food in a destructive manner violates the prohibition bal tash-chit." (Mishna Torah, Laws of Kings 6:10)

A creative way of recycling resources is found in the Talmudic dictum "Since it was used for one mitzvah, allow it to be utilized for another." As an example, although one may discard the lulav, or palm branch, used to observe the Succot holiday, Jewish tradition suggests one save it until the next major holiday, Passover, where the dried up branch makes excellent fuel for a fire customarily used to burn pieces of leaven restricted on Passover.

The worn out breeches worn by the Cohanim (Priests) in the service of the Holy Temple in Jerusalem, were also recycled for another observance, and fashioned into wicks for lighting the lamps of the menorah. (Succah 51a)

Preserving the Body's Resources

The sages even extended the concept of preservation to the human body. The sage Rav advises his son Chiya in the Talmud, "Do not take drugs, as the addiction to them will take its toll." (Pesachim 113a) Rashi comments that Rav was teaching his son, "Don't be accustomed to ingest drugs for your addiction to them will consume your money."

Recreational smoking and drug taking, in addition to their obvious negative side effects, is proscribed because it leads to habituation and wasting of resources.

Let's Get Talmudic

"The purpose of this mitzvah (bal tashchit) is to teach us to love that which is good and worthwhile and to cling to it, so that good becomes a part of us and we will avoid all that is evil and destructive. This is the way of the righteous and those who improve society, who love peace and rejoice in the good in people and bring them close to Torah: that nothing, not even a grain of mustard, should be lost to the world, that they should regret any loss or destruction that they see, and if possible they will prevent any destruction that they can. Not so are the wicked, who are like demons, who rejoice in destruction of the world, and they are destroying themselves." (*Sefer Ha-Hinukh*, Book of Education #529)

Dying to Live

But the sages also realized that there were times when it was necessary to suspend concerns over Bal Taschit, especially when preserving one's own health. The following Talmud passages illustrate when concerns over health justify destroying natural resources:

"It was stated, R. Hiyya b. Abin said in Mar Shmuel's name: If one lets blood and catches a chill, a fire is made for him on Shabbat even on the summer solstice. An expensive teak chair was broken up for Shmuel to be used for firewood. A table [made] of juniper-wood was broken up for Rav Yehudah. A footstool was broken up for the sage Rabbah, whereupon Abaye said to Rabbah, But you are infringing, Bal Tashchit! "'Destruction' in respect to my own body is more important to me, he responded." (Talmud Shabbat 129a)

Let's Get Talmudic

R. Eleazar said, "I heard that he who rends [his garments] too much for a dead person transgresses the command Bal Tashchit, and it seems that this should be the more so in the case of injuring his own body." (Bava Kamma 91b)

R. Hisda also said: "When one can eat barley bread but eats wheat bread he violates 'Bal Tashchit.'" (The assumption was that wheat bread was more expensive). R. Papa said: "When one can drink beer but drinks wine, he violates, 'Bal Tashchit.'" (Same reasoning) He continued his own thought, "But this is incorrect: Bal Tashchit, as applied to one's own person, stands higher." (Shabbat 140b)

In other words, the importance of properly nourishing and sustaining one's health is a value deemed more important than "wasting" resources.

Order and Balance: The Talmud and Feng Shui

Feng Shui is more than its New Age image that has made many people feel good about spending a lot of money on interior design, housekeeping, and self-improvement. The concept actually takes human/environment interactions imbued with a bit of Eastern traditional spiritual system and offers a way to organize and align the energy flowing through a person's living or working environment. It's the Eastern version of sacred geometry that seems to attract many New Agers to this discipline, but there is a practical side to it as well.

> **Talmud Trivia**
>
> The rabbis express a sense of sanctity toward the environment: "the atmosphere (air) of the land of Israel makes one wise." (Baba Batra 158b) It is for this reason, among others, that many consider the air "quality" of the holy city of Safed, in Northern Israel, as the best in the world.

Positioning and Procreation

The sages even went so far as to suggest there is a link between bed positioning and procreation. However, they don't seem to agree on the correct bed alignment. The Talmud and the Zohar have an interesting dispute concerning how one should align the bed of the master bedroom. According to the Talmud, it should be placed facing north and south, while east and west is the choice of Jewish mysticism. For what reason did they suggest this? Both sources say that a couple positioning their bed, or beds, in this fashion will result in a balance of girls and boys in their offspring—literally, that couples who do so will have male children, because the "default" sex was female.

The medieval commentator Nachmanides sheds some light on this enigma. He tells us that the sages here are actually hinting to a greater issue with this strange notion. According to Nachmanides, they were merely alluding to the need for balance between extremes. Taking the Talmud's example, for instance, north and south represent extremes in temperature—the south being hot and the north being cold. Hence, one is being advised to take note of one's temperament, physical activities, diet, and even sexual habits, to make sure they are balanced and suited to one's body type and general constitution. It's a strange way of putting it, but that's what it means. No need to rearrange the room!

Sleep and Energy Flow

According to Feng Shui, one should not sleep with your head facing the door. It's considered the worst position for the bed as it allows too much energy flow into and out of the room. In fact, Feng Shui teaches that one's bedroom door should not even swing directly open where a person's head would normally rest on a bed, as this positioning creates too much "traffic," symbolized by the entering and exiting of the doorway, over a person's head.

In Judaism, there is one concept related to customary practice concerning head positioning in sleep that agrees with Feng Shui. According to Feng Shui, sleeping with one's feet facing the door (the "coffin position") is a big no-no as well, because this is the same position in which a deceased person is placed in the house before the funeral. That is precisely what the Jewish sages teach and it is considered negative mazal, or fortune, to sleep in such a fashion.

Seeing the World with "A Good Eye"

Learning how to appreciate the world we were given is related to what Judaism refers to as the *ayin tovah*, or "the good eye." It goes something like this. When a person is truly in sync with his or her world and sees everything as a blessing, even when someone else is getting that blessing, we say that he or she has a "good eye."

Being happy for another person is a nice thing. However, there's an entirely different dimension to this concept and it relates to God's creation.

People are often puzzled as to why God decided to create certain creatures that do not seem to fulfill any practical purpose, and that really appear more like illogical nuisances. In fact, we might even think to ourselves, "What possessed him?" Nonetheless, there's a teaching that even creatures one might think completely useless, such as fleas, gnats and the like, are included for the goodness of the earth. Each creature is needed for the maintenance of the God's universe. As the Talmud

> **Talmud Tutor**
>
> The Hebrew expression **ayin tovah** translates as "a good eye." The term is commonly used in to describe someone who is generous or open hearted. The flip side of ayin tovah is "ayin harah," or "the evil eye."

says "The Living God did not create a single thing without a purpose." (Talmud Shabbat 77b)

There's a story from the commentary on the Talmud that illustrates this:

> King David tried to fathom the meaning behind each animal and its creation and he succeeded—with two notable exceptions! One was the spider and the other was the wasp. God, in His infinite wisdom, felt that the best way to demonstrate the purpose of their creation was to show King David just how great is his need for those two creatures.
>
> With King Saul in hot pursuit, David hid in a cave to save his life. King Saul and his soldiers were searching everywhere. God sent a spider to spin a web over the opening of the cave in which David was hiding. When the soldiers arrived at his cave and saw it was covered with a spider's web, they moved right on, not even imagining that the web was freshly made!
>
> On another occasion David clandestinely entered King Saul's military camp at night. King Saul's huge general, Avner, turned over in his sleep and, unwittingly, trapped David with a vise-like clamp of his legs. Just at that time a wasp came and stung Avner just hard enough to cause him to open his legs, but didn't waken him. This allowed David to escape with his life!

David was eternally grateful to the wasp and the spider for these two assists.

The Land and Law

The third chapter of the Talmudic tractate Baba Batra is one of the most complex in the entire Talmud. In it, the sages launch into a lengthy discussion over land ownership. The very first Mishna takes up an interesting concept found in secular law—that a person can seize ownership from a neighbor merely by "playing owner" for a few years, either by occupying the property, e.g. "squatters rights," or by paying its property taxes. This is commonly referred to as "adverse possession rule." (It should be obvious, however, that nowhere do the sages endorse a person dishonestly seizing another's property—claiming it as his own.)

Is this an ethical practice or not? Let's see.

In secular law, for instance, the court could confer possession of a walkway used by a next-door neighbor, who after many years of trampling on it decides to incorporate it into his permanent property. Our good "Samaritan" who tolerated his neighbor using this strip of land that was originally part of his real estate, cries foul in court. But he can be overruled in his claim by the judge declaring, "Yeah, it might have been yours, but why didn't you speak up about it years ago?" His silence is now perceived as a tacit agreement to relinquish ownership to his neighbor.

Talmudic law, as found in Baba Batra, also gives special rights to a long-time possessor or squatter. Generally this is established by occupying land without protest for three years, even without tangible proof—either a contract or witnesses. But there's a catch. If the previous owner can prove the land is still his, he gets it back no matter how long he remained silent over the squatter's occupation, or how many improvements the squatter has made.

> **Talmud Tidbits**
>
> A basic principle of Jewish law is that of "dina demalchuta dina" (literally, the law of the land is law)—that is, the secular government is to be recognized for its authority to establish consistent guidelines for social law and order. (Bava Batra 54b, among many other places in Talmud)

Jewish Law vs. Secular Law

The law of adverse possession in secular law contains a negative connotation. It can deny a person of his real property without his consent or knowledge. Regardless of these obvious problems with adverse possession, Jewish law explicitly recognizes the legality of secular law intended to establish everything from preventing anti-trust monopolies, to regulations of real estate development, to preservation of sacred or historic lands.

Using the Land to Fulfill God's Purpose

The Talmudic way of looking at land ownership can be put into perspective by seeing it as a sacred trust given by God; as with all benefits bestowed on a person, and one should use it to fulfill God's purposes. As the Bible explains:

> "The land must not be sold permanently, because the land is mine and you are but aliens and my tenants. In the entire land of your ancestral heritage you must provide for the redemption of the land. If one of your brethren becomes poor and sells some of his ancestral property, his nearest relative is to come and redeem his

> **Talmud Trivia**
>
> The Biblical law of the Jubilee Year instructed Jews living in the land of Israel to revert even duly "purchased" land back to its original owner, family, or tribe every 50 years. It was to be celebrated when the majority of Jewish people live in Israel. Since there are so many Jews in exile today, it isn't celebrated, and it is no longer calculated.

brother's sale. If, however, a man has no one to redeem it for him but he himself prospers and acquires means to redeem it, he is to determine the value for the years since he sold it and refund the balance to the man to whom he sold it; he can then go back to his ancestral property. But if he does not acquire the means to repay him, what he sold will remain in the possession of the buyer until the Year of Jubilee. It will be returned in the Jubilee, and he can then go back to his property." (Leviticus 25:23–28)

In a sense, no person has absolute or exclusive control over his or her possessions. Every physical entity is temporary and transitory. There is an old Jewish saying "There are no pockets in the shrouds." So we can't take it with us.

The Ground Speaks!

The concept that people have custodial care of the earth, as opposed to ownership, is illustrated by the following humorous true story:

Rabbi Lipele of Bialystock, Russia, lived 150 years ago. He was known far and wide as both a clever and fair judge. Two friends came to the rabbi with a dispute over a plot of land. Their dispute turned nasty and every effort by Rabbi Lipele to resolve the matter ended in more fighting. Great animosity arose over this bitter dispute. It spilled over to their families, and eventually the entire community became embroiled in the quarrel with factions being formed on both sides.

It pained the good rabbi to no end seeing otherwise good neighbors consumed in a tiff over a piece of land. Resolved to end this bickering, the rabbi invited the litigants to go over and examine with him the disputed property once more and try to settle the matter on the spot.

Arriving to the plot in question with supporters in tow, the townsfolk watched as Rabbi Lipele took meticulous measurements and calculations and came up with a compromise he felt was fair. But the parties in question were not thrilled with his solution. In desperation, the rabbi suddenly kneeled down and put his ear to the ground. He waited a moment, then arose and proclaimed, "I've got it!"

By now, those present weren't too sure of their rabbi's sanity, and asked him what he meant. "Well," he responded. "I thought it a good idea to consult with the disputed land itself and asked it to tell me who it really belongs to."

Any doubts of his sanity were probably now cleared up, so more in jest than sincerity they laughed, "Rabbi, and what did the ground say to you?"

"The ground told me," the rabbi replied, "I do not belong to either of these fellows, however they belong to me! For is it not written "For you are dust, and to dust shall you return." (Genesis 3:19)

Rabbi Lipele's extraordinary response woke up the litigants to the folly of their dispute and motivated them to settle their differences right then and there. With their compromise, peace reigned once again in the city of Bialystock.

The Least You Need To Know

- The Talmud teaches sensitivity to the environment that requires one to take steps to insure that obnoxious odors, scenery, and sound are kept away from habitation.

- Esthetics are also appreciated, and laws concerning beautification of one's city are found in the Torah and Talmud.

- Even at times of war, the Torah legislates that one must not destroy fruit bearing trees.

- There are a few Talmudic teachings that indicate an awareness of maintaining orderliness in our living space. Instructions as to how one should even arrange his or her bed are also found in Talmudic literature.

- Even that which is dear to most of us, our plot of land, should be seen in the context of "belonging to God."

Chapter 22

The Talmud on Death and the Afterlife

In This Chapter

- Levels of the soul
- The Talmudic concept of hell
- The Talmudic concept of heaven
- The soul and the mourner
- Recycling the soul

As long as humankind's veins have pulsed with blood, people have sought answers to the profound questions about the true nature of the soul. Does the soul survive earthly existence? What happens? Is there such a thing as "heaven" or "hell"? Do souls travel between worlds after the body is dead? Is there such a thing as reincarnation?

While the concept of an afterlife isn't specifically mentioned in scripture, the Talmud teaches it. In fact, an entire chapter in the Talmud tractate Sanhedrin is devoted to demonstrating where this concept is alluded to in scripture, as well as detailing many of its facets.

Most of the concepts presented in this chapter come from Kabbalistic sources, and might seem a bit "out there" at first. But they're not meant to scare us with Marquis De Sade-like torment and barbarism. Rather, these concepts are to be perceived as a way—perhaps one that's a bit on the somber side—to express our need to reckon with the uncertainties in our lives, connect now with the Creator, and take a spiritual inventory.

Life After Life

For the Jewish people, death is not something to be frightened of. Instead, it's simply a transition from one life to another.

Traditionally, Judaism has held that our life on Earth does not comprise our complete human experience, and that there is life after death. The "next world" or *"World to Come"* is seen as a more complete world, or a "world of truth," a realm where answers to questions such as why bad things happen to good people and the reasons behind the mysteries of our lives and world will be revealed.

Jewish custom also holds that our experiences on Earth will shape what our afterlife will be. Here's how Rabbi Moshe Chaim Luzatto put it:

> "The principle of the matter is, that man was not created for the experience of this world, but for his role in the World To Come. Only, his experience in this world is a means for the achievement of his experience in the World To Come—which is his ultimate purpose. As the Talmud states, 'Whoever labored on the eve of Shabbat, will have what to eat on the Shabbat (when no labor is permitted). Whoever did not labor on the eve of Shabbat (this world), what will he eat on the Shabbat (the World To Come).'" (Babylonian Talmud, *Shabbat* 119a)

Talmud Tutor

The term **World to Come** is sometimes used to refer to an afterlife following death, but can also mean the world of perfection and completion where the Messiah (God's anointed) will lead the world to a "new heaven and a new earth," and the dead will be resurrected. Among some of the mystics, it also seems to mean a state of awareness beyond the ordinary, of which we can only have glimpses in this life.

Rabbi Luzatto goes on to explain that this is virtually a necessary conclusion from the basic principle of the existence of God. Life on Earth is full of trials and tribulations, suffering, problems, pain, illnesses, worries, and so on. But God doesn't mean for our lives to be limited to these experiences, so there has to be something more.

Everything that we go through in life helps to refine and perfect both our own "vessel"—our body, emotions, and mind—as well as the world around us. But a soul's journey doesn't end at death. What happens during and after death continues the purification process.

Talmud Tidbits

The afterlife process is different from life on Earth, and involves more intense experiences than we can imagine in earthly life. So when Jewish writers speak of the World to Come as also referring to an experience following each person's earthly life, they are suggesting that we can have an experience after death that will be a foretaste of the eventual total redemption of the world.

Jewish sources hint at several stages beyond the death of the personal body, stages of experience that enable the personality to be brought to completion. Based on the teachings in Chapter 11 of Talmud tractate Sanhedrin, that complete persona is being readied for the ultimate World to Come, after the resurrection of the dead.

Body and Soul

Thanks to science, we have a pretty good idea of what the human body is all about, and what makes it tick. When it comes to the soul, however, it's a different ballgame. For the most part, all we can really do is guess at its nature. It remains largely a mystery, although the world's religions have come up with some interesting takes on the subject.

Judaism holds that there is one, unified soul, but with different levels, or characteristics. The Talmud describes three major characteristics facets of the soul:

- Nefesh
- Ruach
- Neshama

Nefesh, the first level of the soul, is closest to the physical. It is the vital life force that sustains the body. In a certain sense, the nefesh is the living body. If a person tried to argue that his body was merely a complex combination of chemicals, most listeners would respond, "Yes, but that's not all." The missing factor—nefesh—is what unites the body, and makes it function as a single organism.

The Vilna Gaon taught that the nature of the nefesh, the natural traits of the vital soul, is determined by one's deeds in previous incarnations. Because its main purpose is animating and organizing the body for action, the nefesh is oriented toward survival in the world.

Ruach, meaning "wind," "spirit," or "breath," is the second level of the soul. It involves the passions and dynamic emotions that drive a person. Ruach can be very powerful. The chief danger for the ruach is that it may become out of balance.

The ruach also contains the motive power that can enable a person to change. Even if a person is born with negative traits and temperament at the nefesh level, they can change if the ruach motivation is strong. In fact, Judaism holds that while it is true that a person's heredity or early environment are extremely influential on how one develops, a person always has the possibility of choosing for good or bad, better or worse.

Neshama, the third level of the soul, has to do with the supra-rational powers of the soul. These powers supersede the simple mental functions of, for example, calculation and logic.

Such computer-like functions are not enough to give a human being form and personality. If the brain is a computer, it must have a programmer, one who decides the direction and purpose of the program. Ideally, the programmer is the neshama. With its intellectual potency, it organizes the lower levels, the life force and motive powers, into a personality with an identity. It gives the soul its unique, personal form.

Jewish mystical writings, such as those found in the Zohar, identify two additional levels of the soul. These exalted levels are not ones that everyone develops, and are reserved for more highly evolved and spiritually attuned individuals. These levels are:

- Chaya
- Yechida

Chaya, which means "living one" and is identified with the origin of wisdom, higher even than the consciousness associated with the understanding of the neshama. Chaya is said to reside in the air fluid above the brain, beneath the skull, and it influences a person above even the highest thoughts of the intellect.

Chaya leads a person toward divine service, selflessness, and devotion to God and humanity. But it is beyond ordinary thought. Rabbi Nachman of Breslov describes this level of the soul as "wild" or even "reckless"—like a person suddenly running into a burning building or diving into the water to save a child. Moreover, it is said that the level of chaya affects a person like the pure waters of a mikva, which can purify any water. Chaya infuses a person with a sense of serenity, knowledge that he or she is secure, whatever happens.

Yechida, meaning "single one," is the fifth level of the soul. It functions as if it were independent of the others, by itself, in a completely unique way. It manifests the spark of God and, as such, can overcome anything that stands in the way on any of the lower levels.

When the body dies, each component of the soul goes its separate way for a time. The lower levels of the soul, which must be purified, stick fairly close to their familiar surroundings. According to the Zohar, nefesh can stay with the body for as long as a year, during which time it guards the grave of the deceased. It may also roam the earth, especially when "… the children of men are in sorrow or troubled, and repair to the graves of the departed." (Zohar II 141b)

Ruach, which must be purged of the sins the person committed in life, travels to purgatory, or gehinnom. Neshama goes to heaven, or Gan Eden "to be united with the Throne," which appears to mean complete bliss in the presence of God. (Zohar II 141b) Chayyah and Yehida, in reflected of their exalted standing, go to an even higher level of heaven.

Talmud Tidbits

Gehinnom, Gan Eden means "the garden of Eden." The Jewish people when referring to heaven commonly use the term.

The soul will not be complete until its lower levels are purified and can be at rest in their realms. But even then, the soul is not completely divorced from the world.

Writings like these also speak to the Jewish belief that the soul is never completely detached from our worldly life, even after death. Some traditional Jewish observances, such as the Kaddish prayer, (we'll get into this more later), also demonstrate a close connection between the soul of the deceased and the living.

Let's Get Talmudic

Tractate Brachot 18b debates whether the disembodied soul is aware of what is going on down on earth. One such debate tells the story of the sons of Rabbi Hiyya, who went out to cultivate their property, and then began to forget their learning. They tried very hard to recall it.

Said one to the other: "Does our (dead) father know of our trouble?"

"How should he know," replied the other, "Seeing that it is written, 'His sons come to honor and he doesn't know it?'"

Said the other to him: "But does he not know? Is it not written: 'But his flesh grieves for him, and his soul mourns over him?'"

And R. Isaac said [commenting on this]: "'The worm is as painful to the dead as a needle in the flesh of the living?'

[He replied]: "It is explained that they know their own pain, they do not know the pain of others."

The Soul's Travel

As mentioned, everything that we go through in life helps to refine and perfect both our own "vessel"—our body, emotions, and mind—as well as the world around us. But a soul's journey doesn't end at death. What happens during and after death continues the purification process.

Jewish belief holds that the soul is severed from the body immediately after death. For a righteous person, this separation is painless, or as the Talmud puts it, "like removing a hair from milk." (Moed Katan, Chapter 3)

Talmud Trivia

Kabbalists teach that one who is buried on Friday, the eve of the Sabbath, will not go through this process, nor will the truly righteous.

But some souls, especially those of people who were less spiritually oriented in life and were more attached to material pleasures on Earth, have a difficult time detaching from the physical body. These souls bounce around a bit before they travel onward.

Rabbinic teachings describe several different scenarios for what happens to the soul during this period. All of them rectify serious flaws in the soul's matrix.

The Purgatory of the Grave, or the Suffering of the Grave (hibbut ha-kever)

Souls that go through this stage basically suffer from separation anxiety—they can't bear to detach from the body. But such anxiety doesn't serve the soul well. Its refusal to make a clean break means that it is subjected to the torturous sight of watching the body decay.

During this time, the soul suffers extreme mental anguish. As the Zohar puts it, "For seven days the soul goes to and fro from his house to his grave, and from his grave to his house, mourning for the body, as it is written: 'His flesh shall suffer pain for him, and his soul shall mourn for it.'" (Job 14:22) (Zohar I, 218b)

As painful as this stage can be, it does serve a purpose in that it forces the soul to face facts and give up its identification and attachment to the body.

Angelic Intervention

Jewish belief holds that at some point after death, people are summoned to heaven by angels who call their names. But some souls are so shocked by the death experience that they forget their names. They instead wander aimlessly about, and eventually decay into nothingness.

To keep souls on the right track, Dumah, the angel of silence, intercedes. He makes regular rounds of graves. As he does, he helps the dead retain their memories by asking them their names.

Talmud Tidbits _____

To prevent the destiny of the amnesiac soul, each Jew is taught to memorize a biblical verse that begins with the first initial of his name and ends with the last letter of the name. This verse is kept fresh in one's memory by saying it after the conclusion of the Amidah, which is the central prayer in the Jewish prayer service. When Dumah comes around, even if one has forgotten his name, he will remember the biblical verse, as the Torah is eternal and can't decay.

The Hollow of the Slingshot (Kaf Ha-Kelah)

The late Talmud scholar Rabbi Dessler described kaf ha-kelah as a situation where "a neshama is thrown by angels from one end of the 'world' to the other." He explains that the desires that a person attaches to in this world become part of that person. So much a part that even upon death, one still has those desires. Those angels that do the "tossing" are the ones created by those sins. They are there with the person after death as he, in the most frustrating situation imaginable, still pursues the physical desires that don't exist in the spiritual world. He is "tossed" by these angels that he created from one end of the world to the other, searching for that which can never be found.

Purgatory (Gehinnom)

In Judaism, gehinnom or purgatory differs greatly from the concept of hell as described in other major religious faiths. Gehinnom is seen as an intermediary stage where the soul is purified before attaining its next level of existence or eternal reward.

Talmud Tidbits _____

Belief in gehinnom plays an important and very practical role in everyday Jewish life. Not only does this belief arouse the conscience, challenging a person to reflect constantly on his spiritual state of affairs and to strive toward refinement of his deeds. In addition, it suggests what can be done for the soul in gehinnom, namely helping that soul to achieve the perfection for which it is destined, as we saw above.

Knowing that the grave will not serve as a refuge for the consequences of one's greedy or vainglorious lifestyle is, the kabbalists believed, one of humanity's best motivators for keeping one from "going south."

The righteous skip this period entirely as do martyrs. The Jewish concept of hell actually affords an opportunity for elevation of the soul. Of course, this does not mean that hell is a cup of tea. The metaphor of hell being a "consuming fire" is common to both Judaism and Christianity.

Talmud Trivia

Curiously, the word hell does not appear anywhere in Hebrew Scriptures. In fact, very few references are made to the concept of a fearful afterlife at all. When the Bible does refer to the state beyond life, it uses the word sheol, literally a "pit."

The Talmud uses seven different terms to describe hell. Gehenna and gehinnom, the best known of them, refers to the desolate Valley of Hinnom located south of Jerusalem. Talmudic sources tell us that trash fires burned there incessantly. During earlier biblical times it most likely served as a shrine where human sacrifices were offered to Canaanite gods.

In the Talmud, gehinnom is interpreted as a compound word meaning "one who falls into the valley (guy) for matters of inconsequence (hinnom)." (Eruvin 19a) In other words, in order to avoid the pains of gehinnom, one should avoid sin or matters leading to nothingness and frivolity.

Gehinnom is not entirely a negative concept—it is better than some other possible fates of the soul. However, a few of the processes can be rather agonizing.

Indeed, all but the very wicked will complete their term in gehinnom in 12 months, and most people in less time than that. The Midrash (Tanchuma, Re'eh 13) and Talmud (Rosh Hoshanah 17a) are the addresses for the 12 month concept: Chizkiyah said: There are 12 months of judgment for the wicked in purgatory (Gehinnom). Six months are suffered in heat, and the other six months in cold. God first places them in the heat, and then puts them in the snow.

The nineteenth-century Torah commentator Aitz Yosef suggests that there are two distinct places of purgatory. "Gehenom of Fire" is a punishment for all sins that were done with passion and energy against God. "Gehinnom of Snow" is designed for all sins that are due to laziness and lack of energy. In addition, the punishment of snow is given for all good actions done without zeal and excitement. At any rate, partially because the prophet Isaiah identifies the Jewish people as being intrinsically worthy, "Your people will all be righteous; they will inherit the land (world to come) forever, a shoot of My planting, My handiwork in which to glory." (60:21), this purgatory does not endure longer than 12 months.

Rather than physical torture, the torment in gehinnom is more a mental one, caused by the soul's sadness over the sins that were committed in life. It's also said that the distance and separation from God causes this sadness, which doesn't abate until purification is achieved.

Every Sabbath, the souls in Gehinnom are given a break from the pains they're going through. On this day, souls are permitted full access to God's splendor and glory.

Annihilation of the Soul (kiluy neshama)

The sages also describe a severe fate for one who completely ridicules and mocks any concept of performance of mitzvot, or divine instruction. This is reserved for an individual who ideologically assails or harbors heretical sentiments against God and his Torah. (Rosh Hoshanah 17a)

These souls don't even get to go to gehinnom, for their sins were too grievous. About these poor souls, the Talmud says, "The bodies of those liable to [the penalty of] being 'cut off' cease to exist. That is, the body's strength or animal power ceases, and 'their souls are burnt up,' that is, they are made incandescent, like iron in the forge; and 'the spirit,' that is the spirit of God, 'sprinkles' their ashes under the feet of the righteous in the [heavenly] garden of Eden." (Rosh Hashanah 17a)

Helping the Soul Along

Judaism holds that there is a one-year maximum period of refinement before the soul goes into its next phase. To help it along, a prayer called the Mourner's Kaddish is often said.

Although no reference to death or the afterlife appears in this brief prayer, it has become the focal point of tribute to the deceased and centerpiece of communal prayer This is arguably the best-known prayer in the synagogue liturgy. In most cases, the Kaddish is recited communally, with the congregation led by a leader, called a shaliach tzibbur, who represents the congregation in their collective supplications to God. It goes like this:

May His great Name grow exalted and sanctified in the world that He created as He willed. May He give reign to His kingship, and cause His salvation to sprout, and bring near His Messiah in your lifetimes and in your days, and in the lifetimes of the entire Household of Israel, speedily and soon. And let us say, "Amen."

May His great Name be blessed forever and ever. Blessed, praised, glorified, exalted, extolled, mighty, upraised, and lauded be the Name of the Holy-One-Blessed-be-He beyond any blessing and song, praise and consolation that are uttered in the world. And let us say, "Amen."

May there be abundant peace from heaven and good life upon us and upon all Israel. And let us say, "Amen."

He who makes peace in His heights, may He make peace upon us, and upon all Israel. And let us say, "Amen."

As the Kaddish is recited, the congregation responds Amen to affirm what the reciter is saying. This is considered to be both agreement and affirmation, but also as a substitute for them reciting the blessing or prayer themselves.

As much a prayer exalting the Divine Being, the Mourners' Kaddish epitomizes a vital gesture of kindness that a son (traditionally only sons recite the prayer, although in many religious circles a daughter [under 12, the age of Bat Mitzvah] may recite the Mourner's Kaddish during services) can perform on behalf of a deceased parent during the first year following his/her demise.

According to Kabbalistic sources, this seemingly ordinary ritual can redeem one's parent from the judgments of gehinnom. The Zohar Chadash, a well-known Kabbalistic text, contains a version according to which the deceased afterward came to Rabbi Akiva in a dream and told him: "When my son read the Haftarah (Sabbath selection from prophetic scriptures), they alleviated my punishment in Gehinnom; and when my son led the public prayer-service and recited Kaddish, they completely tore up my sentence. (Hence the custom of a son to recited these portions on the Sabbath coinciding with the anniversary of the death of parent.) And when he became wise and acquired Torah, they gave me a portion in Gan Eden."

The Torah concept derived from this homily is called "bera mezakeh abba," which is the Aramaic expression for "A son brings merit to his father." (Talmud Sanhedrin 104a) In this case the son, with Rabbi Akiva's assistance, was able to affect a complete rectification for his father. The dynamic relationship between the son and father was such that the son's actions were able to bail out the father's soul from suffering, posthumously and literally. The point is that even after bodily life ceases; we are connected to our ancestors and descendants, at the level of our souls. The biblical expression sometimes used for death, "He was gathered to his fathers" hints to this concept. Moreover, the practice of honoring ancestors after death is also known worldwide.

In Judaism, the ancient observance of reciting Kaddish, lighting a memorial candle which symbolizes the soul, and giving charity on the deceased's behalf are ways of acknowledging this important concept and fulfilling obligations to those who have gone before us. This custom is performed on the Yahrzeit (anniversary of the parent's death) for on this day the neshama is granted a furlough of sorts from Gan Eden, and has permission to travel about the lower worlds. It is also being judged at this time to prepare for a further elevation. The various activities performed by the surviving children bring great benefit to the soul, for they testify to the fact that the deceased is remembered on Earth and thus his or her mitzvot are still having an impact.

Moving Up: The Talmudic Concept of Heaven

For the Jewish people, the ultimate goal is entry to Heaven, or Gan Eden.

The Talmud, in Sanhedrin 90a, states that all Jewish people are intrinsically worthy of entering, quoting Isaiah 60:21—"Your people will all be righteous; they will inherit the land (world to come) forever, a shoot of My planting, My handiwork in which to glory."

Thus, after whatever purification sentence is completed by that soul, it receives its portion in Heaven or the World to Come. Some people, as mentioned, won't be able to pass go, but will go directly to Jail. Others might achieve their portion immediately, either through living a virtuous life of proper conduct, through some amazingly altruistic act, or through martyrdom.

The Zohar refers to a lower Gan Eden and an upper Gan Eden, suggesting that there are levels here as well, as the soul sheds its earthly ties and finds itself more and more able to experience heavenly bliss. The neshama, the highest level of the soul, says the Zohar "ascends at once to her place, the region from which she emanated, and for her sake a light is kindled to shine above." This passage suggests that the next higher level of the soul (and presumably the two higher levels as well) never experience punishment. This means to suggest, that according to the Zohar, the Neshama component is so lofty, that nothing a person can do down here can tarnish it to the point that it would need to go through the purging process we describe above. Only the nefesh and ruach parts need purification.

Soul Recycling or Reincarnation

Researchers have presented many possible cases of reincarnation over the years, but actual evidence if reincarnation is, understandably, quite scarce. Nevertheless, the incidence of beliefs in reincarnation in many cultures, together with this piecemeal evidence, makes it at least a good possibility that a soul might live in human form more than once.

Many people are surprised to hear that the idea of reincarnation is part of Jewish tradition. There is a scriptural hint to the idea in the book of Deuteronomy, in the law that states that a woman whose husband dies childless should marry his brother.

On the most obvious level, the law preserves the dead brother's property, keeping it within the family. The mystics suggested that the reason was to provide an opportunity for the soul to reincarnate.

However, the teaching about reincarnation, strictly speaking, is part of the Oral rather than the Written Torah. Though direct mention of this phenomenon is not found in the Talmud, the medieval mystics took it for granted that our souls are "sent back" into bodies to continue their work.

Let's Get Talmudic

The great scholar Rabbi Moshe Chaim Luzzatto, summarizing centuries of mystical thought on the subject, stated the principle of reincarnation in his book *Derech Hashem*, or *The Way of God*. He wrote that "A single soul can be reincarnated a number of times in different bodies, and in this manner, it can rectify the damage done in previous incarnations. Similarly, it can also achieve perfection that was not attained in its previous incarnations."

Each person's soul is on a journey, and the present life is one of the opportunities it has to achieve perfection. Rabbi Eliyahu Kramer (the Vilna Gaon), the outstanding Torah scholar of his era, explained that one's deeds in previous incarnations influence the kind of body, and its closely related animating soul, that one has in one's present lifetime. Rabbi Isaac Luria, who shaped modern Jewish mysticism, taught that the various generations of people described in the Bible (the generation of the Flood, the generation that built the Tower of Babel, and so on) were each reincarnations of blemished souls that went back to the years after Adam's expulsion from the Garden of Eden. Eventually, these souls were reincarnated again at the time of the Egyptian slavery and they had the opportunity to be redeemed.

Among mystical teachings one finds the account that some of the great rabbis promised themselves that, after their souls departed Earth, they would "refuse" to enter Gan Eden until they had persuaded God to bring the Messiah on Earth. What a fascinating concept!

Talmud Tutor

Dybbuk comes from the Hebrew word *dabbek*, which means to cling.

The dead can come back to Earth in a couple of different ways. One is by temporarily entering the body of a living human being. This sort of temporary reincarnation, called an *ibbur neshama*, is often undertaken to help the living person in some way, or to perform some additional good deeds. Another type of reincarnation isn't as positive. A *dybbuk* is an unhappy or vengeful soul that takes up residence in a living person to try to rectify some part of its past. Typically, it won't leave until a rabbi or similar holy person performs an exorcism, which is done to persuade the tortured soul to move along and find peace in some other way.

The Big Reunion: Resurrection of the Body and Soul

One of the great enigmas of the Jewish faith is the belief in the eventual resurrection, or techiya ("enlivening"), of the human body at the time decreed by God. As we know, resurrecting a lifeless body is an exception to all known physical laws. Yet, this belief can't be ignored.

Resurrection and the World to Come so intrigued the sages of Israel that they devoted an entire chapter of the Babylonian Talmudic tractate Sanhedrin to the subject. There, they cite numerous Scriptural references to this phenomenon:

In the Book of Deuteronomy the passage alludes to the divine power to resurrect: "I kill and bring back to life." (32:39) The Prophet Isaiah proclaims "Your dead shall live, dead bodies shall arise, awake and sing, you who dwell in the dust." (Isaiah 26:19) One of the most explicit sources identified by the Talmudic sages comes from the Book of Daniel: "Many who sleep in the dust shall awake, some to everlasting life, and some to reproach and everlasting abhorrence." (12:2)

> **Let's Get Talmudic**
>
> Even Maimonides insisted on including the belief in resurrection as the last of his Thirteen Principles of Jewish Faith: "I believe with perfect faith that there will be a resurrection of the dead at a time it will please the Creator."

According to traditional Torah thought, there is no clear consensus as to exactly how or when resurrection will come about. However, most classical authorities on Jewish Law, and all the leading Kabbalists of the last millennium, state that resurrection is the first step leading to the world of perfection and completion, a world where the Messiah, or God's anointed one, will lead the world to a "new heaven and a new earth," and the dead will be resurrected. In this world, the body and soul are reunited as one, and the resurrected dead will live forever. All our spiritual forces will then be gathered to transform the physical world.

The Talmud provides a provocative rationale for the phenomenon of resurrection …

Antoninus Marcus Aurelius said to Rabbi Yehudah the Prince, "The body and soul can both escape God's Judgment. The body can defend itself by saying 'It was the soul who sinned. For look, since the day the soul left me, I have lain still like an idle stone in the grave [and have not committed any wrong]." The soul can likewise say, "It was the body who sinned. Since I left the body, I have flown free like a bird."

Rabbi Yehudah replied, "I will offer you a parable in response. A human king once possessed a beautiful garden, full of young delicious figs. He assigned two guards to watch it, one crippled and one blind. The crippled guard said to the blind one, 'I see luscious fruit in this garden. Carry me on you shoulders and we will share them.' They did so, the blind man carrying the lame one, until they had consumed the choicest fruit in the garden.

"When the king returned he accosted his watchmen, asking, 'Where are my luscious fruit?' The crippled guard replied, 'Do I have feet that I could retrieve the fruit?' The blind man answered, 'Do I have eyes that I could locate the fruit?' The wise king, however, was not fooled. What did he do? He placed the crippled man on the blind man's shoulders, and judged them like one.

So, too, will God summon the soul and restore it to its body, and then judge the two together. It is thus written, "He will call to the Heaven above, and to the earth below to judge his people." (Psalms 50:4) "He will call Heaven above"—this is the soul, "and to the earth below"—this is the body." (Sanhedrin 91a–b)

The Least You Need To Know

- While the concept of the afterlife is not directly mentioned in Scripture, the Talmud teaches it.

- An entire chapter of the Talmud is devoted to demonstrating where the afterlife is alluded to in scripture.

- Gehinnom, or the concept of perdition, differs greatly from the concept of hell as described in other major religious faiths. Gehinnom is seen as an intermediary stage where the soul is purified before attaining its next level of existence or eternal reward.

- Though not mentioned in the Talmud directly, the notion that a soul may reincarnate, or be recycled, is discussed in traditional mystical literature. How and when this occurs is a mystery.

- The last of Maimonides' 13 Principles of Faith recounts the belief in the resurrection or reunification of body and soul. Many Talmudic passages, as well as kabbalistic sources, indicate this fundamental Jewish belief.

Part 5

Living the Talmud Way

The Talmud has been Judaism's ethical and moral compass for more than 3,000 years, but its influence has ranged far beyond this. Just as the Torah is considered to be a blueprint for the life of all humankind, the Talmud provides insights and guidance to all who choose to explore its wisdom and knowledge.

In this part, we'll take a closer look at what it's like to study the Talmud, what the Talmud has to say on some of today's hottest topics, and how the precepts of the Talmud apply—and can be applied—to modern living.

Chapter 23

Studying the Talmud

In This Chapter

- ◆ Getting the "inside scoop"
- ◆ Study methods
- ◆ Deciphering a Talmud page
- ◆ Study aids

By now you've gotten a good idea, hopefully, of what the Talmud is all about, and what can be found in it. Along the way, I've also given you an idea of what it's like to study the Talmud.

In Chapter 11, you were introduced to some of the methodology and logical approach of Talmud study. Now, it's time to really "get Talmudic" and see how it works.

Talmud Study as a Way of Life

The process of Talmud study is not only an intellectual exercise, but also a way of life. The Jewish people are frequently called the "people of the book." Most assume that phrase refers to the Bible, which indeed is regularly studied, cited, and read by many on a daily basis. But, by now, you probably know that bible study isn't the entire picture. If Jews are indeed the people of the book, it is more accurate to identify the Talmud as that book.

If you want an outline of the history and origins of the Jewish people, scripture works fine. However, it is only through the Talmud that you can get the "inside scoop" on who the Jewish people really are and their unique, divine calling.

> **Talmud Trivia**
>
> In many Jewish circles the constant study of the Talmud far surpasses the study of scripture alone.

Jewish people are not preoccupied with studying the Oral Tradition to see how clever they are, but to examine how closely they come in fulfilling the Lord's wishes and demands. This is what the sages had in mind when they extolled the virtue of "Learning that leads to (appropriate) action."

With its comprehensive recording of the sayings of the sages, biographies of its main characters, its outlook on life, moral and medical advice, rich parables and witticisms, all woven together into the fabric of Jewish life, the Talmud offers a picture of the love affair the Jewish people have with learning Torah and its observance.

The concept of constant learning is far-reaching and central to Jewish thought, as illustrated by this Talmudic parable:

Once the Roman government issued a decree forbidding Torah study. Papus ben Yehudah saw Rabbi Akiba conducting Torah classes and asked him, "Do you not fear punishment by the law?" Rabbi Akiva answered with a parable: A fox was strolling along the riverbank and noticed fish swimming swiftly from place to place. He asked, "Why are you running?" They replied, "We are afraid of the net that people set up to catch us." The fox slyly said, "Perhaps it would be wise to ascend to the shore and live together with me as my parents lived with your parents." The fish responded, "You speak foolishly. If we are afraid in our native habitat, our fear will be even greater on land, where death will be certain." Similarly, Torah is our source of life and may save us. Without it we will definitely perish. (Talmud Brochot 61b)

Like fish in their natural habitat, so are the Jewish people with the Talmud. But merely "existing" in water is not sufficient for us; we must swim efficiently to survive the dangers that lurk in the depths as well. Often, this means swimming against the tide, like salmon making their 1,000-mile run upstream to return to their spawning ground.

Studying the Talmud takes a supreme commitment to doing it right, to study in a deliberate fashion, and carefully analyze what is before you, even when that analysis might clash with conventional thinking or personal bias.

Teaching Your Children (and Others) Well

The system of study to induce proper action and further transmission of the Torah can be paraphrased in the words of the Mishna in the Ethics of the Fathers; "Rabbi Yishmael the son of Rabbi Yochanon said, "He who learns to in order to teach, will be granted (from Above) the means to learn and to teach. But he who learns in order to practice, will be given the means to learn, to teach, and to observe and to practice." (Chapter 4:5)

The Talmudic sages understood that linking the generations to the Revelation at Sinai was predicated on a system of students becoming teachers. In teaching the next generation, Torah scholars had to internalize the information, knowledge, and faith to impart the message to their charges. Therefore, the ultimate litmus test of comprehension of a lesson taught in the Academy was the ability to say it over accurately to someone else. This did not mean that every Talmud student would work in the teaching profession. But it did mean that every student should look for opportunities to share wisdom with others.

On the arranged table of Talmudic living, education clearly forms the centerpiece. The Talmud itself richly describes this reality:

> Remember for good the man Joshua ben Gamla, because were it not for him the Torah would have been forgotten from Israel. At first, one's father taught him, and as a result orphans were left uneducated. It was then resolved that teachers of children should be appointed in Jerusalem, and a father (who lived outside the city) would bring his child there and have him taught. However, the orphan was still left without tuition. Then it was resolved to appoint teachers in each province, town and village, and boys of the age of sixteen and seventeen were placed in their charge; but when a teacher got angry with a pupil, the student would rebel and leave. Finally Joshua ben Gamla came and instituted that teachers be appointed in every province and every city, and children from the age of six or seven were placed under their charge. (Baba Batra 21a)

Let's Get Talmudic

It seems that since time immemorial the Jewish people have been searching for the silver lining in the disproportionate misfortunes that have beset them. For example, in the wake of the destruction of the Second Temple, the Jews constructed the world's first system of universal compulsory education, paid for by public funds.

The Talmud made the importance of education very clear.

If a city has made no provision for the education of the young, its inhabitants are placed under a ban, until teachers have been hired. If they chronically neglect this duty, the city is excommunicated, for the world only survives by the merit of the pure utterances of the schoolchildren. (Maimonides, Mishna Torah, Laws of Talmud Torah 2:1)

The Rabbinical Academy and Ordination

Yeshivot, or rabbinical academies, were the systems established hundreds of years ago to allow young Jewish men to master the Talmud. It was not only considered a great honor for parents to raise a "Talmid chacham," or brilliant Talmud scholar, it was an honor for a family to house a yeshiva bochur (boy) in those predormitory days. Many of them left home at the tender age of 13 or 14 to study under the greatest masters. The host families often extended propositions for marriage for these "prized" pupils. To feed these budding Torah scholars, a system of "eating days" was set up in the community by these families.

These academies dotted the landscape of Europe before World War II. Popular folk writers such as Isaac Bashevis Singer (the author of Yentl) romanticized about the elite stature of the Talmudic sage. Scholars flourished in Eastern European cities such as Ponovezh, Telz, Radun, Mir, Vilna, Lodz, Kovno, Kamenetz, Warsaw, Prague and scores more. The Holocaust brought this 700-year-old way of life to a tragic, grinding halt.

Methods of Learning

Much of pre-World War II Talmudic study was facilitated through one-on-one partner study, or "chavruta" style learning, a highly animated learning process that was an educational innovation of the yeshiva academy. Although most popular during that time, it still exists to this day.

If you were to step into the world of the Beit Medrash (House of Learning) to witness this style of education, you might be taken aback. Exchanges between learning partners can, and often do escalate into 100 or more pairs of scholars shouting at each with great passion. It's all part of a most vibrant system of instruction.

Another style of Talmud study is the "shiur" or unit of study covered by a seasoned Talmudic scholar. Here, anywhere from 10 to 200 students might gather in a study hall to absorb a scholar's brilliant erudition on the section of Talmud the academy happens to be studying. Here, too, the interchange among students, and between students and teacher, can be very lively.

What might such a class be like? Here's an example of what one might look and sound like. This might not be an absolute facsimile of a typical yeshiva-type class, but you should get the idea of how the first 10 to 15 minutes of a contemporary Talmud class might sound: This community is an academic one. There are 15 students, ages 20 to 30. Some have taken leave of college. Others are recent college graduates. Around the table we will find professors of chemistry, economics, physics; a copy editor for a newspaper; a business manager; and even a rabbinical student. They have a few things in common; they are novices to Talmud study, they love the stimulating logic and moral teachings, and they love the wit or wisdom of their teacher, Rabbi Klein. As he opens the lesson, some are following with a photocopy of intricately arranged Hebrew characters, some have the actual Talmud text with an English translation, and there is a blackboard ready for an additional study aid.

In the spirit of the Talmudic sages who were wont to launch their lessons with a bit of clever wit or riddle to stimulate the thought process, Rabbi Klein begins his lesson by emphasizing the need for objective reasoning.

"Man's problem" he says, "is that he does not apply objective thought to even the most elemental of topics. Let me give you an illustration. Consider the scenario of three wagons laden with hay being drawn by three horses, one moving directly in front of the other. While they plod along the road in single file, two of the horses are feasting on the hay sitting in the wagon just in front of them. Now, please tell me, which of these horses is getting the better deal? Which is more fortunate than the other and why?"

"Well," starts the chemistry professor. "Surely not the first horse, he has no hay which to eat from, he is only pulling some."

Another student chimes in, "Since the first horse cannot eat, then the remaining two must be equally fortunate because they are both eating hay."

"That's exactly what I meant about man not thinking things out thoroughly," the rabbi sighs. "If you give it some thought you will conclude that the middle horse is deriving the most benefit for she is the only one eating and, at the same time, having her load lightened."

"Now let's learn!" the Rabbi exclaims.

He reads aloud from the original text of the Talmud and ad-libs a translation. The passage under discussion concerns the question of the minimum number of people needed for a minyan (a religious quorum), found in Brachot (47b). Rav Huna says nine and the Torah Ark (Aron haKodesh). Rabbi Nachman said to Rav Huna "But is the ark a person?" Rav Huna then amends his statement and says, "Nine men who appear as ten combine to complete the Minyan."

Only ten men over the age of 13 qualify. The challenge in front of these budding scholars is to explain the initial objection with Rav Huna's statement.

Rabbi Klein asks his students, "What do you suppose the fundamental issue of the debate is over?" The physicist remembers something he heard a few years back, and replies, "Rabbi, doesn't the Baal Shem Tov explain that every person is like a Torah scroll? Hence with the ark we have nine Torah scrolls and their ark, which gives a total of ten."

Rabbi Klein, impressed by the citation, comments "Ah, nice insight. And Rabbi Nachman in the Talmud jumped on that notion because each person needs to be a physical mentsch (person), in addition to being like a Torah scroll, so the ark doesn't qualify."

The business manager takes exception. "With all due respect, the Baal Shem Tov's approach to interpret Rav Huna's position is forced. How can everyone be at the level to be like a Torah Scroll? What did Rabbi Huna really wish to say? What did he mean? Maybe it all depends on how you vowelize the word "aron" for ark. Maybe it means something else altogether! The consummate skeptic, the businessman feels that this answer is too simplistic and perhaps foreign to the actual text.

The rabbi, encouraging the free exchange of ideas in his classroom, asks if anyone knows the origin for the requirement of 10 men to make a minyan. David, the newspaper editor weighs in:

"Rabbi, isn't it found in the Talmud Megillah 23b, where the reason for 10 men being required is drawn by analogy from the use of the word *edah* (congregation) to describe the 10 spies who returned from the Promised Land with evil reports?"

"Excellent David, that is the exact source." The rabbi continues the discussion by asking, "Now, does anyone else have an alternative solution to Rabbi Huna's perplexing statement?"

The rabbinic student accommodates. "I learned that ten people for a minyan have no significance by themselves. What ten accomplish is that they become a representative for all of Israel. Rav Huna feels that this connection is through the Torah and so the ark can be used as one of the ten. But Rabbi Nachman objects because we would still need ten people to represent the community and the ark simply can't help."

"Brilliant explanation!" the rabbi exclaims with enthusiasm. "Where did you hear that explanation, or is it your own?"

In essence, the future rabbi's remark was right on the money, so there was no need to exaggerate praise. But this is Rabbi Klein's method for encouraging people to not just learn the Talmud but to philosophize over it and strive to achieve a more insightful understanding of its mystique, and it's what makes him so beloved to his students. Not only for his wit and wisdom, but if someone asks a simple question on the Talmud passage, or makes an incorrect attempt at resolving an issue within the Talmud, he makes the person feel as if his comments were radiating with brilliance.

Where One Might Study

By this point, you might be wondering if you can join in such as class, or if it's possible to study Talmud on your own. If you're not Jewish, you might wonder if it's even permissible for you to study the Talmud. If you're a secular Jew, will you be welcomed? How can you find places in your community where Talmud instruction or discussion is offered? What should one expect? Is it okay to study on line? Do you need to know Hebrew? If so, should you study Hebrew first?"

These are all great questions. Let's answer them one by one before we study a piece of Talmud together.

First, there are generally three places where formal Talmud study takes place. The majority of serious Talmud enthusiasts study in a bona fide Talmudic academy or yeshiva, which cater to students ranging from green novices to advanced rabbinic scholars. Some yeshivot have only a handful of students, others number in the hundreds and even thousands. Generally, only cities with major Jewish populations (75,000 or more) have such academies. You'll also find some information on study listed in Appendix B.

The second option is the community synagogue or Torah center. Here, many rabbis of all streams of Judaism offer adult education classes in various subjects, including the Talmud. Looking at your local yellow pages directory under "Synagogues" or "Houses of Worship" will provide sufficient leads. Sometimes these classes are advertised in Jewish community newspapers or magazines.

Depending on the religious affiliation (e.g. Conservative, Orthodox, Reconstruction, or Reform), acceptance of nonconverting non-Jews will vary. All streams of Judaism

---

Let's Get Talmudic

"Study a page of Talmud everyday," was the advice given by Professor Erwin Radkowski, chief scientist of the U.S Atomic Energy Commission in the 1960s, when asked for his recommendation for enhancing one's ability to think.

mentioned are accepting of secular Jews seeking enlightenment through Torah study. Most, if not all, don't require synagogue membership or affiliation to participate in these classes.

Talmud Classes for the Masses

It is true, by and large, that Talmudic wisdom is available for all. There is a wide range of rabbinic opinion on being taught formally by a religious leader at an official venue. The sages are all concerned about one main passage in the Talmud itself, which reads, "Rav Ami said, 'Do not give over words of the Torah to an outsider, as it is written (Psalms): He did not do so to any other nation and His laws they were not informed about.'" (Chagiga 13a)

One school of thought holds that studying parts of the Talmud relative to the Seven Noachide laws that are incumbent upon non-Jews to uphold is permissible (and even desirable in most cases). Many legal authorities consider it obligatory to assist non-Jews in studying these laws. In this vein, Rabbi Meir goes so far as to say "A Noachide who studies the Torah is equal to the High Priest! (Baba Kamma 38a) Furthermore, where a person is seriously considering conversion to Judaism, there are no restrictions on any area of Torah and Talmud study.

Another position on the matter, held by Maimonides and the Meiri (Rabbi Menachem ben Solomon 1249–1316), a Provincial scholar and commentator of the Talmud, seems to hold that the only restriction for a non-Jew is to learn Torah or Talmud as if doing so is a divine commandment. But to access the knowledge and wisdom therein is fair game. The Meiri goes even further than that and states that only sharing the hidden secrets or deepest reasons of the Torah are restricted.

Traditional reluctance to share in-depth Talmud learning with "nonmembers" of the Jewish people is based primarily on Rabbi Ami's teaching cited above. There are a number of rationales behind this "ban." Perhaps the simplest way to understand this sentiment is to consider the Talmud a code of state secrets of Nation X. For those who serve in its military, protect its borders, pay taxes, and share in its good times as well as its tribulations, certain benefits are reserved (e.g., right to vote, pensions, free health care, etc.) Accordingly, those who are prepared to bear the yoke of Torah observance and survival, and place their lot with the Jewish people, are entitled to the full range of rights and privileges, the Talmud being one of them.

The third option for live Talmudic learning is a university or local community college. In many communities where there is a sizable Jewish population, one will find a decent Jewish studies department at institutions like these. Generally, the professor or instructor body will include someone fluent enough in Talmud to offer a course in the subject. Be prepared, they most likely will not include actual Hebrew or Aramaic instruction of the text, and may be very fact-oriented. However, some may prove to be an excellent tool for experiencing the stimulating give and take, thrust and parry, of actual Talmudic logic and discourse. It all depends on the quality level of program and personnel.

It is not absolutely necessary to know Hebrew or Aramaic to pick up the flow of the Talmud. However, a serious student will eventually have to master basic reading skills to excel. One can also gain quite a bit of Talmudic knowledge from reputable online resources or through reading appropriate texts, but Talmudic wisdom is something ideally to be gleaned from living examples and mentors.

Let's Really Get Talmudic! Sample Study

Now we're ready to learn. The objective here will not only be to demonstrate just how much information is needed to decipher a page of Talmud, but to give you a chance to participate in the process. It's a bit different than Rabbi Klein's hypothetical "lesson in progress" script mentioned above. This is but one exercise in tapping the content and understanding the structure of a page of Talmud.

If you were taking an actual beginner's Talmud class, a teacher might guide you through a similar exercise with the real thing—a Hebrew/Aramaic text. We won't attempt that here, but you'll find some resources for doing so in Appendix B should you wish to pursue that option. For this exercise, get out some colored pencils, pens, or highlighters. Even crayons will work. Don't consider it sacrilegious to write on the pages of this book—in fact, you'll need to in order to keep track of the various discussions and points made.

It all might be somewhat confusing at first, but don't fret. There are no grades! Just follow your own sense of where to place question marks, exclamation points, commas, quotation marks, etc. A good part of Talmud study for most novices is to figure out where the stops and starts belong, identify when a question is asked, a refutation made, or a reconciliation offered. Hopefully, even with an English translation, you will get a glimpse at what it is like.

For your convenience a few "/" slashes were inserted at strategic points to cut you a little slack and not totally overwhelm you. Remember, this is a nonjudgmental zone, so be creative!

The following example is from page 42a of the tractate Baba Metzia. It is the third chapter of that tractate and deals with monetary issues. Let's jump right in:

Mishnah: If one has deposited money for safe-keeping and the watchman tied it up and threw it over his shoulder or he gave it to his son or daughter who were not as yet of age or he did not lock it safely he is responsible for negligence if however he was careful with it as it is required of a watchman (and nevertheless an accident happened) he is exempt Gemara: It is correct in all cases mentioned in the Mishna that he is responsible for carelessness but in the case that he tied it and carried it over his shoulder why is this considered careless what more could he have done said Rava in the name of R. Isaac it is written/ [Deuteronomy 14: 25] and bind up the money in thy hand that means although it is "bound up" it shall nevertheless be in his hands R. Isaac said again/ that the verse intimates that one shall manage so that his money shall always be in his hands and he said again/it is advisable for one that he shall divide his money in three parts one of which he shall invest in real estate one of which in business and the third part to remain always in his hands the same said again Usually blessing does not occur but in things which hidden from the eyes, as it is said The Lord will command upon thee the blessing in thy storehouses [Deuteronomy 28: 8]/ similar to this it was taught by the disciples of R. Ismael the rabbis taught he who is going to measure the grain in his barn he may say/ It shall be thy will O Lord our God Thou shalt send blessing to the labor of our hands when he begins to measure he may say Blessed may be He Who sends blessings upon this heap if however he prayed after measuring his praying was in vain because blessing does not occur on things which are weighed measured or counted but on things which are hidden from the eyes as it is written The Lord will command upon thee the blessing in thy storehouses.

Samuel said/ nothing is considered safety with money unless it is hidden in the ground said Rabba/ Samuel admits that if it was in the twilight of the eve of Sabbath that the rabbis would not trouble him to do so if however after the Sabbath departed and he had time to hide it and he did not do so and in the meantime something occurred he is responsible unless he was a budding scholar who thought probably I will need money for the benediction of the Havdalah it happened that someone deposited money with his neighbor who hid it in a hut made of branches and it was stolen/ when the case came before R. Joseph he said although concerning fire it is a willful negligence concerning thieves it is considered safe and there is a rule that if in the end it was an accident although it was started in neglect there is no responsibility the Halakha however prevails that in such a case there is liability (like the sage Samuel).

If you strained your eyes in an attempt to follow the flow and felt a bit frustrated, that is natural. Also, do not be concerned that your punctuation and quotation marks were, well—off the mark. No one truly learns unless they first stumble a bit, no? In "real life," as the Daf (folio) begins to take shape, it feels like the end result of a master sculpture's art. The finished product has its own beauty and resonance like a Monarch butterfly emerging from its cocoon.

Go through this piece again. Spell out any previously abbreviated words. Keep in mind that ancient texts did not use quotation marks, however words like "As it is written," "As it is said," etc. were scripture's way of introducing dialogue.

Next, underscore or highlight important words and phrases that fit into the seven principles, or elements, of Talmudic reasoning that were discussed in Chapter 11. Here they are again as a refresher:

1. Statement—the speaker states a single statement of fact.

2. Question—a sage asks another, often the original speaker, for information.

3. Answer—the sage asked responds to the question.

4. Contradiction—the speaker disproves a statement and totally refutes it.

5. Proof—The speaker presents evidence from which the truth of a statement or idea is made obvious.

6. Difficulty—A sage points out something untrue or unsavory in a statement or idea.

7. Resolution—a sage reconciles the difficulty raised against a statement or idea.

Here's the same page, with these principles applied. I've also added some information to clarify and amplify some of the points being made.

MISHNA: If one has deposited money for safe-keeping, and the watchman tied it up and threw it over his shoulder, or he gave it to his son or daughter, who were not as yet of age, or he did not lock it safely, he is responsible for negligence. If however, he was careful with it, as required of a watchman*, (and nevertheless an accident happened), he is exempt.

GEMARA: It is correct in all cases mentioned in the Mishna, that he is responsible for carelessness, but in the case that he tied it and threw it over his shoulder, why is this considered careless? What more could he have done?

Said Rava in the name of R. Isaac: It is written, [Deuteronomy 14: 25] "and bind up the money in thy hand." that means although it is "bound up," it shall nevertheless be in his hands. R. Isaac said again, That the verse intimates that one shall manage so that his money shall always be in his hands.*

And he said again, It is advisable for one that he shall divide his money in three parts, one of which he shall invest in real estate, one of which in business, and the third part to remain always in his hands. The same said again, Usually blessing does not occur but in things which are hidden from the eyes, as it is said, "The Lord will command upon thee the blessing in thy storehouses" [Deuteronomy 28: 8] [Similar to this] it was taught by the disciples* of R. Ismael, The rabbis taught, "He who is going to measure the grain in his barn he may say, "It shall be thy will O Lord

Mishna: Starting point for virtually all Talmudic discussions. Beginning of Talmudic discussion always indicated by the Hebrew letters "Gimmel Mem." Rava was a fourth-century Babylonian sage. R' Isaac was a third-century sage from the Land of Israel. Samuel was a primary second-century Babylonian authority. R' Joseph was a fourth-century Babylonian sage who served as a judge on the Beit Din (Rabbinic Court).

This mishna is speaking of a Shomer Chinam, or one who watches without compensation. Talmudic Discussion begins here in Aramaic, indicating the later sages called Amoraim. The proof provided here, transitioning back into Hebrew, indicates its origins are from the Land of Israel." Talmud brings authoritative support to this advice from and earlier source, the Academy of Rabbi Ishmael who was an early second-century sage from the Land of Israel. Rava's statement is said in Aramaic indicating that this the Talmud speaking and that he was from Babylonia. Havadalah, literally means "Separation." It was a ritual ceremony utilizing wine, to delineate the end of the Sabbath and beginning of the mundane week. "Halacha," means legal practice.

our God Thou shalt send blessing to the labor of our hands." When he begins to measure he may say, "Blessed may be He Who sends blessings upon this heap." If, however, he prayed after measuring, his praying was in vain, because blessing does not occur on things which are (already) weighed, measured, or counted, but on things which are hidden from the eyes, as it is written, "The Lord will command upon thee the blessing in thy storehouses."

Samuel said: "Nothing is considered safety with money unless it is hidden in the ground." Said Rava,* "Samuel admits that if it was in the twilight of the eve of Sabbath that the rabbis would not trouble him to do so." If, however, after the Sabbath departed, and he had time to hide it and he did not do so, and in the meantime something occurred, he is responsible, unless he was a budding scholar who thought, "Probably I will need money for the benediction of the Havdalah." *

It happened that someone deposited money with his neighbor, who hid it in a hut made of branches, and it was stolen. When the case came before R. Joseph*, he said, "Although concerning fire it is a willful negligence; concerning thieves it is considered safe; and there is a rule that if, in the end, it was an accident although it was started in neglect, there is no liability. The Halacha, however, prevails that in such a case there is liability (like the sage Samuel).

Because of the technical details necessary to understand the actual text and its minutiae, most teachers who offer classes for adult beginners do not go into such detail. They are more interested in conveying the lesson and what is being taught. But this will give you a taste for what actual Talmud study is all about. As mentioned, you'll find additional resources for it, if you decide to pursue it, in Appendix D.

As you've probably noticed by now, this isn't easy stuff. As the historian and Talmud scholar Rabbi Berel Wein cautions, "The Babylonian Talmud can be deceiving to those who approach it with a superficial, even if scholarly based, method of study. For without concentrated effort and rigid methods of traditional analysis and study, the Talmud will not easily give up its secrets. It is finely organized; yet will, at any given moment, apparently stray far away from the original topic under discussion, only to return to it eventually with a fresh approach and a new vision."

To the rabbi's assessment, we say can say amen. Just from the brief segment we looked at earlier, we see how on the ball one must be to follow the flow of thought. To correctly access the well structured and organized subject matter, one is advised by the Talmudic sages to first seek to learn a wide range of information, be-fore delving deeply into the logical infrastructure. (Succah 28b–29a) This is the reason why concentration on mastering the Mishna was so important. Once a person became familiar with the general outline of the Oral Law, probing deeper into the specific arguments and debates is made easier.

As for the, "concentrated effort," mentioned by Rabbi Wein, that is exactly what the Talmud itself articulates in the following passage …

Rebbe Eliezer learned: "A person is obligated to teach his student each lesson four times. This is deduced by the following inference: Aaron—who learned from Moses who learned it from God—had to learn his lesson four times; how much more so an ordinary student who learns from an ordinary teacher."

Rebbe Akiva said: Where do we know that a teacher must continue to repeat the material until the student has mastered it? Because the Torah says, (Deuteronomy 31:19) "And you shall teach it to the children of Israel." And where do we know that it must be taught until the students know it fluently? Because the Torah says, (Ibid.) "Put it in their mouths." And where do we know that the teacher must also explain the reasons? Because the Torah says, (Exodus 21:1) "Now these are the ordinances which you shall put before them." (Eruvin 54b)

> ### Let's Get Talmudic
>
> One cannot compare learning something 100 times, to one who reviewed 101 times; but both are completely righteous people." Talmud Chagigah 9b

One of the main secrets to success with the Talmudic method of learning are the "three R's"—repetition, repetition, and repetition! Or as the sages put it, "If one reviews his learning, he will retain it; otherwise, he will lose it." (Talmud Eruvin 53a; Succah 46b) The Talmud adds, "One will be more successful if he learns small sections and reviews them, rather than learn large sections and then review." (Eruvin 54b)

Study Aids

As with any new endeavor, you will want to find reliable aids to assist in your learning. Among the fine tools published today are dictionaries such as the English version of the *Jastrow Aramaic*. There are smaller pocket guides that serve as a companion to the Talmud text, such as *Aid To Talmud Study* by Rabbi Aryeh Carmell. Many fine translations in English with linear Hebrew text abound as well. Finally, excellent websites and CD's are available to facilitate Talmud study. You'll find a list of these study aids in Appendix D.

Talmud Tutor

Use of mnemonics is seen as a very important tool of the trade for memorization of details in learning. (Talmud Shabbat 104a) For instance, one who wishes to remember the five varieties of flour one can use to bake matzoh for Passover, might use the mnemonic BROWS. This alludes to, barley, rye, oats, wheat, and spelt.

The Least You Need to Know

◆ Talmud study is more than intellectual gymnastics; it is a way of life.

◆ Study with the intention of teaching others is not only a virtue, it actually helps one retain his or her knowledge.

◆ Many opportunities abound in contemporary settings to engage in Talmud study, some of them are available through community synagogues, others through online resources and excellent published English language texts.

◆ Study of the Talmud takes the 3Rs—repetition, repetition, and repetition to master a subject.

Chapter 24

The Talmud's Take on Contemporary Issues

In This Chapter

◆ Making human carbon copies

◆ Death with dignity?

◆ Extraterrestrial life

◆ Abortion: Is Talmud Pro-Life or Pro-Choice?

As you now know, the Talmud has quite a bit to say on some of the most diverse subjects. The sages check in on everything from immunization to astronomy, and from artificial insemination to dream interpretation. In many cases the proclamations of the Talmud are perfectly in sync with modern science, and they occasionally even foretell discoveries of the future.

It stands to reason that the sages even have something to offer on some of the most controversial issues of our day. In this chapter, we'll take a look at some of the hottest of the hot topics.

Cloning

Perhaps no area of medical science creates more controversy today than cloning. We're not going into great detail about the process, but here's what's involved, very briefly, on the technical end.

Basically cloning technology involves taking genetic material (DNA) from a person's cells and introducing it into the nucleus of an egg, or ovum, whose own genetic material has been destroyed. The result is an egg that contains a complete set of genetic coding identical to the donor's DNA.

Talmud Tidbits

The author Erich von Daniken, in the 1961 book *Return to the Stars*, said he believed that Eve was actually the first "test tube baby," and was basically cloned from Adam.

The egg is then stimulated to behave like a naturally fertilized egg, which causes it to start the process of cellular division, just like any newly fertilized egg would. This continues until the egg—now referred to as a zygote—is ready to be implanted into the uterus of the gestational mother.

The child born from this gestational mother would be genetically identical to the donor of the genetic material, and bears no genetic relationship to the gestational mother.

The Ethics of Cloning

Does cloning present a moral problem? For a great many people, it does. Some feel that killing the nuclear material in the unfertilized egg constitutes a type of abortion. (This notion is erroneous, as the egg/ovum is removed from the egg donor prior to fertilization.) Others are concerned about eggs that are discarded after they are fertilized, such as what sometimes happens during in-vitro fertilization procedures when too many eggs are fertilized at once.

Most Jewish legal authorities insist that the laws of abortion apply only to procedures in the womb. There are no prohibitions whatsoever when conception happens in vitro, or outside of the body. Using donated sperm to aid conception, as long as it is done with the husband's permission, also gets the go-ahead, a point which will become important as we progress further into this discussion.

Does this then mean that Jewish law permits, or supports cloning? In theory, perhaps, some authorities might permit cloned children if a husband can't produce sperm. But many authorities believe that the danger of abusing the science is too great to allow its use.

Creating a "Super Race"

One of many moral issues related to cloning is natural diversity within species. In other words, letting nature take its course and refraining from manipulating it to create a "super race," comprised only of attractive, intelligent, and physically well-endowed individuals. Two places in the Talmud—Sanhedrin 38a and Berachot 58a—hint to the concept that genetic diversity is part of the divine plan. Based on this, if an unscrupulous "mad scientist" were ever planning to develop such a race, a Talmudic-minded person would join forces with any coalition to thwart such efforts.

There's no denying that in some cases cloning presents a fascinating approach to curing a number of diseases that challenge humankind. But what's important is that the technology be used, not abused. Cloning embryos, for example, is one way to produce stem cells, which researchers now believe might cure a number of chronic debilitating diseases, such as cancer, leukemia, multiple sclerosis and a host of others, as well as paralysis and damage to the heart.

So with these many benefits, and the potential to improve people's lives, and assuming we can control this "good technology," what is the general outlook of traditional Jewish law on the issue of cloning? The words of the great Maharal of Prague shed some light on the subject:

The creativity of people is greater than nature. When God created in the six days of creation the laws of nature, the simple and complex, and finished creating the world, there remained additional power to create anew, just like people can create new animal species through inter-species breeding .... People bring to fruition things that are not found in nature; nonetheless, since these are activities that occur through nature, it is as if it entered the world to be created ...."

Talmud Tidbits

Human creativity is part of the creation of the world. To fulfill the Biblical mandate to "conquer the earth," it is understood, and expected, that there will be some modifications made along the line. In fact, the Jewish tradition permits such modifications—conquests—to nature, which in turn makes it more agreeable and inhabitable. In this context, cloning is an example of these modifications. When used appropriately—that is, used to advance humanity—it doesn't pose a theological problem in Jewish law.

Ending Life with Dignity

Euthanasia is a situation where one kills another, allegedly for his or her own good. Let's say a person is lying in a hospital bed in a "locked-in," persistent vegetative state. To keep such an individual in the hospital and treat him or her is a tremendous expense, and not just financially. It's a burden to the medical staff that has to look after such a patient. And it's an even bigger burden to the patient's family.

All factors taken into account, euthanasia, or "death with dignity," seems not such a bad thing, at least on the face of it. Let's see what the Talmud and Jewish tradition have to say about this.

The most famous and probably the earliest account of euthanasia is found in the Talmud, in Avoda Zara 18a. One of the Ten Martyrs of Rome, Rabbi Chanina ben Teradyon, was sentenced to death for teaching Torah publicly, and was burned alive at the stake wrapped in the very Torah scroll he used for instruction. As he suffered his very slow death (the barbaric Romans decided to prolong his agony by putting wet wool over his chest), his students asked him what vision he was having. He said that while the flames were consuming the Torah parchment, he saw its letters "floating in the air." His students stood around and implored him, "Rabbi, open your mouth. Let the flames enter your body. Let the smoke enter your body and choke you so that you will die quicker and not prolong this terrible torture."

Rabbi Chanina answered his students with one of the greatest lines in martyrdom history, "No," he said. "He who gave me my soul, He and only He will take it from me."

The vision of the Torah's letters "floating in the air," beautifully symbolizes that while suffering and persecution can wreak havoc on our physical shells, our essence, or our soul, can never be destroyed. We must not interfere while God determines the "expiration date" for the shell.

Let's Get Talmudic

In the beginning of Genesis, God says, "Only the blood which belongs to your souls shall I demand." (9:5) The Talmud explains that this refers to the act of taking one's own life. Taking a human life is forbidden regardless whether it is ours or someone else's. The general attitude of the sages against suicide, and the need to relinquish control over one's own life and death to the Creator, is epitomized with this sentiment, "Against your will you were born, against your will you die, and against your will you are destined to give an account before the supreme King of kings, the Holy One, blessed be He." (Ethics of our Fathers 4:22)

Death with Dignity?

From the Jewish point of view, the phrase "death with dignity" is actually somewhat of an oxymoron. Judaism teaches that human life is inherently dignified, something the state of death has never been. True, death is a culmination and part of the human life cycle. When it occurs naturally, it is often a blessing from above to relieve the misery of an individual who is in unremitting pain. Conversely, to deliberately choose to die and fail to embrace every moment of the blessing of life is in itself denigrating. Other cultures accept this notion as well. One of the core teachings of Buddhism, for instance, is that on one hand, life is suffering. On the other hand, one should enjoy life's every moment.

"Active" vs. "Passive" Euthanasia

Hastening one's demise in any way is forbidden according to Jewish law. That is how precious a moment of life is viewed in the Torah tradition. Nonetheless, there are certain conditions where it may be permitted to withhold certain medical treatments, a form of "passive euthanasia" so to speak, which would otherwise prolong life. Traditional Jews are required to consult expert rabbinical authorities if such a situation arises.

The following is the relevant passage from the Shulchan Aruch, or Code of Jewish Law:

> "And similarly it is forbidden to cause a dying person to die quickly; for example, a person who is in the throes of death for a long time and is unable to separate [from the world of the living]—it is forbidden to remove the cushion or the pillow from underneath him, on the grounds that people say that there are feathers from certain birds which are causing this, and similarly one should not move him from his place; similarly, it is forbidden to place the keys of the synagogue underneath his head in order that he should depart [from the world of the living].
>
> However, if there is something which is preventing the soul from departing, for example if there is a knocking sound near the house, such as a woodchopper, or if there is salt on his tongue, and these are preventing the departure of the soul—it is permitted to remove these from there, since this is not an act at all, but merely removing the preventing agent."

Although the distinction is subtle, this passage in Jewish law precisely draws the line between that which is considered active euthanasia and passive euthanasia. In this case, passive euthanasia is nothing more than holding back a substance that is impeding the natural process of dying.

Finally, once again we turn to the Maharal of Prague for his wisdom concerning the phenomenon called aging and dying. The subject at hand is the Torah precept to rise in deference to an older person who is drawing near:

> "The loosening of the bonds of the body, leaving behind the transcendent soul, is cause for giving honor. We provide this honor when the body leaves entirely, as in delivering eulogies upon death. But we honor even the partial liberation of the soul in old age. This forms one rationale behind the Torah's commandment that we should rise in the presence of the elderly."

In conclusion, let me share the words of Job, who knew of suffering perhaps like no one else in history, and refrained from asking God to put him out of his misery, "The spirit of God hath made me, and the breath of the Almighty gives me life." (Job 33:4)

Human life, coming as a gift directly from God, is holy, and should be cherished with great care. On a mystical level, while it's a virtue to alleviate as much discomfort as possible, a person who is physically suffering may be rectifying tremendous issues with his/her soul in this fashion. Therefore, all human beings, since they are endowed with such unique and hidden purpose must be allowed to live the fullness of their years and days.

Extraterrestrial Life

Do a search on the Internet under UFO and you will find myriads of links directing you to websites that are entirely devoted to the subject of UFO's and extraterrestrial phenomena. You might even come across statements that support the existence of extraterrestrial life from some pretty reliable sources. Astronaut Gordon Cooper has been quoted as saying that he believed UFOs do exist, and that the "truly unexplained ones are from some technologically advanced civilization." Former President Jimmy Carter has even gone on record as saying that he can't laugh at people who say they've seen them as he's seen one himself.

Talmud Tidbits

A Russian physicist in 1960 claimed the sinful cities of Sodom and Gemorrah were bombarded by an apocalyptic alien atomic blast.

Are we truly not so alone on this earth? Have we already been visited by aliens from other planets? Does scripture or the Talmud provide fresh "Biblical Manna" to support these life-in-outer-space speculators? Let's take a look.

Historically, legends about alien intelligence, mostly enshrined in myth, extend from the Far East to the lands of the Mayans, and from North America to the Dead Sea. A UFO-like object even appears on an ancient Roman coin.

Some people, most notably author Erich von Daniken, have even reinterpreted certain Biblical occurrences as indications of extraterrestrial life. In his 1961 book, *Return to the Stars*, von Daniken postulated that the Prophet Ezekiel's vision of the Divine Chariot, found in Chapter 1 of the Book of Ezekiel, was perhaps a spaceship, maybe even a "scout" vehicle. (Maybe someone was spying on the ancient Israelites going out to battle.) Although mainstream scientists have discredited much of von Daniken's theories, there's no denying that there's a preponderance of evidence pointing to the possibility that we're not alone in the universe, and some of the most brilliant minds have dedicated years of their lives in research to discover if there's fire behind all that smoke.

What do the sages of the Talmud have to say about all this? The fourteenth-century Spanish Rabbi Chasdai Crescas was one of the first Talmud scholars to discuss the possibility of extraterrestrial life. In his magnum opus Or Hashem, or "Light of God," he concluded that there is nothing in Jewish religious writings or theology to deny the existence of extraterrestrials.

As support, Crescas cites a well-known Talmudic passage where a sage, in answer to question as to what God "does" during the night responds, "He flies through 18,000 worlds on His chariot …" (Avodah Zarah 3a) Assuming that these worlds also require God's supervision, it stands to reason that there is intelligent life inhabiting them.

The late Talmudic scholar and physicist Rabbi Aryeh Kaplan, quoting the teachings of the Arizal, suggested that this is not an absolute proof, as the sages could easily be speaking about 18,000 spiritual worlds. He even discards the notion that King David alluded to this in his Psalms "Your kingdom is a kingdom of all universes," (145:13) for this scripture too, may be speaking about spiritual worlds.

> **Let's Get Talmudic**
>
> The Tikunei Zohar writes that every righteous person will rule over a star, and therefore, have a "world unto himself."

The earliest Jewish source, however, to give us some indisputable proof that the sages of Israel believed there was life in the cosmos comes from the Zohar. In the Talmud, there is a teaching on the significance of the number seven that states that there are seven earths. These seven, according to the Zohar, are all separated by a firmament and contain inhabitants. Some Talmud experts suggest that, based on Kabbalistic teachings, these "earths" are not inhabited by humans, but that some form of intelligent life can be found on them.

The sole Talmudic source suggesting intelligent life on other planets besides Earth is found in tractate Moed Katan 16a. The sage Ulla, basing his words on the Song of

Deborah in the Book of Judges (5:23)—"Cursed is Meroz … cursed are its inhabitants," posited that Meroz is a star (or planet) and its inhabitants are intelligent beings. Thus, Deborah, speaking on behalf of her husband/general Barak, is essentially cursing these beings for not assisting him in his war against the Assyrian leader Sisera.

> **Talmud Trivia**
>
> The three Hebrew letters comprising the name Meroz: Mem, Reish, Zayin, without their vowels, can be pronounced as "Mars."

There is a mystical teaching that while the earthy armies of Israel and Syria were having it out, their corresponding celestial hosts were engaged in battle as well. This is a very strong indication that the Talmudic sages believed there is extraterrestrial life out there.

Is the Talmud Pro-Life or Pro-Choice?

The traditional Jewish view of abortion, based on Talmudic law, doesn't conveniently fit into the pro-life/pro-choice debate. Judaism neither bans abortion outright, nor does it tolerate indiscriminate abortion. For this reason, the view that abortion should be available on demand or performed as a form of birth control, is out of sync with Jewish tradition and values.

However, "pro-choice" is a poor choice of words from a Jewish standpoint. Nobody denies a woman "free choice" over her body. She can do pretty much what she wants to her body—pierce herself, have a lift and a tuck, erase some wrinkles with Botox, even shave her head anytime she pleases. However, there are limits to "free choice." Like everyone else, a woman must abide by the law.

Does Abortion Constitute Murder?

So, the entire question boils down to this: Does abortion constitute murder? In other words, does a developing fetus have the status of human life?

> **Let's Get Talmudic**
>
> The source of the Talmud's stance for Noahides on abortion is the verse spoken by God to Noah, "One who spills the blood of a person, by a person (B'Adom) shall his blood be spilled." (Genesis 9:6) The second time "a person" is mentioned is superfluous for it simply implies that a third person (or judge) shall pass a death sentence on the murderer. Accordingly, the sages interpreted the phrase "B'Adom" as saying, "within a person," thus giving an entirely new meaning; "One who spills the blood of a person, within a person (e.g. a fetus). A "person within a person" aptly describes a fetus.

In Jewish law, a fetus transitions into a full-fledged "independent" human being when the head emerges from the womb. Before then, the embryo/fetus is considered a "potential life." Before the 40th day of gestation, the Talmud even considers it "maya B'alma" or "mere water." (Yevamoth 69b) Even so, is it permitted to destroy this potential life for any reason?"

In practice, feticide, or destroying a fetus, is not regarded as murder. Based on Talmudic tradition, one is only held liable for killing a complete and viable human being. Nonetheless, the sanctity placed on even an unborn child is such that one is forbidden to injure a gestating woman in anyway to harm or kill the fetus.

> ### Talmud Trivia
>
> Although the Jewish faith holds that one's basic soul is imparted at conception or formation (around 40 days), according to Jewish law a fetus isn't considered a "person" until birth.

How does this law apply practically? As mentioned, once the head is born, or if breech, the majority of the body, the baby is viewed as an independent life. Therefore, even if the mother's life is being threatened at the end of delivery, the Talmud clearly instructs that one life may not be set aside to ensure another life. In other words, our hands are tied at this point. Since we cannot determine "whose blood is redder," (in other words, who deserves to be "saved" at the expense of whom), no harm may be done to the child to save the mother. The implication is that up until the point of "partial birth," everything can and should be done to save the life of the mother. Which circumstances constitute "life threatening" is also subject to controversy, but it is clear, as you will see later, the mother comes first.

> ### Let's Get Talmudic
>
> The concept of "Whose blood is redder?" is one taken up by the Talmud in a number of places. Rabbi Akiva, for instance, rules that if two men are lost in a desert with one flask of water, the owner of the flask may drink it at the expense of his friend's life. No one is required to give up his or her life to save another. One's own life, in this scenario, takes priority, Talmud Bava Metzia. (62a)

Set Aside One Life to Ensure Another Life

In the spirit of Talmudic discourse, I want to take a detour. But it is a detour with relevance, as you will see. Let me share with you a true story involving application of the reverse principle, where we do set aside one life to ensure another life. It has a direct bearing on the issue of abortion as well.

In 1977, newborn Siamese twins were brought to Children's Hospital in Philadelphia, where Dr. C. Everett Koop (subsequently the Surgeon General of the United States) was the hospital's chief of surgery. Physicians had clearly indicated that since the twins were sharing vital internal organs, both would die if remained conjoined. The only option was to operate, thereby killing one and saving the other.

The moral dilemma was set in motion when doctors on the case asked themselves if this procedure constituted murder. A heated debate ensued. Koop is reported to have taken the initiative and suggested that the issue be referred to a rabbi who was known to be a great scholar and a pious individual. Whatever he said was proper, Koop said, would be the approach taken with the children.

The rabbi was Moshe Feinstein, recognized as the greatest Talmudic and legal authorities ever to live in the United States. Rabbi Feinstein asked the doctors how they intended to do the surgery. They replied, "We will save Baby A, and kill Baby B."

> **Talmud Tutor**
>
> A **rodef** is one who is threatening the life of another and may therefore be killed in an act akin to self defense. But the law of a rodef, as found in Sanhedrin 74a, states that killing a rodef is only permissible where less draconian measures are not possible.

Rabbi Feinstein then asked, "Could you reverse the procedure and achieve the same results? In other words, could you use the available organs to sustain Baby B and allow Baby A to die?"

The doctors answered no, that Baby A was the only one they could save.

Rabbi Feinstein advised them to proceed with the surgery. His decision was based on the Jewish law that if one person is directly threatening to kill another, then it is morally appropriate to thwart the pursuer, even by means of killing him. The law of the pursuer, a *rodef*, in Hebrew, applies even in the case where the threat to life is unintentional.

The Rodef Principle

Returning to our discussion, the "rodef" principle relevant here is where a fetus is threatening the life of its mother. Such a fetus that threatens the life of its mother may be aborted. The law permitting abortion is found in a Mishnah, "If a woman in labor has a [life-threatening] difficulty, one dismembers the embryo within her, removing it limb by limb, for her life takes precedence over its life." (Ohalot 7:6) Thus, it is clearly established that saving the mother's life is top priority; but the Mishnah does not rule out the use of alternative methods to save her life. Indeed, Maimonides ruled that abortion is permitted (as opposed to required) in the case of a fetus that threatens its mother's life. (Mishneh Torah, Laws of Murder and Preserving Life 1:9)

However, in a labor where the baby's head has exited the birth canal, as mentioned previously, making it a full fledged human and the process of labor is endangering the lives of mother and child, the child cannot be reckoned a rodef. The Talmud gives a reason for this, because "from heaven she is being pursued." (Sanhedrin 72b) The Jerusalem Talmud offers a slightly different rationale why the baby and mother are left alone during such childbirth. They are viewed as mutual antagonists, like two people who are both pursuing each other, and thus neither has the status of a rodef. The threat is mutual; the mother and child are unwittingly jeopardizing each other's lives, hence we have a stalemate.

Talmud Tidbits

Judaism recognizes psychiatric as well as physical factors in evaluating the potential threat that the fetus poses to the mother. However, determining the danger posed by the fetus, whether physical or emotional, must be substantial and substantiated, e.g. professionally evaluated. Cases of rape, incest, and adultery are not cut and dry justifications for abortion and are dealt with on an individual basis. Such determination requires close consultation between a mental health professional and rabbinic expert. The degree of existing mental illness of mother that must be present to justify termination of a pregnancy is also a gray area in Jewish law and not well established. Concerning abortion where a deformity has been diagnosed that would cause the newborn child to suffer, or termination of a fetus with a lethal fetal defect such as Tay Sachs, at least one major authority permits the former within the first trimester and up to the end of the second trimester, for the latter. However, the majority of authorities disagree.

We can now answer the question asked earlier, "Is the life of an embryo, from the viewpoint of Jewish law, of equal value relative to a mature person?" The answer from Talmudic sources is clearly 'no' based on the Mishna in Ohalot cited above. That said, the value of fetal life is hardly insignificant. Indeed, the Talmud rules that one may desecrate the Sabbath in order to save the life of a fetus of a woman who has died in childbirth. (Talmud Arachin 7b) Furthermore, recent Jewish legal authorities have agreed that abortion to save a mother's life is not mandatory. One such ruling permits a pregnant woman with a terminal disease to carry to term, though the pregnancy might very well shorten her own life.

In review, Judaism strongly believes in allowing nature to "take its course." The easiest way to conceptualize a fetus in Jewish law is to imagine it as a full-fledged human being—almost. In most circumstances, the fetus is treated like any other "person."

However, when its life comes into direct conflict with an already viable person, the "independent" life takes precedence. It is also clear that a healthy woman may not abort a viable pregnancy merely because pregnancy and childbirth per se are potentially life-threatening experiences. Since these experiences are normal and the risk of danger is relatively low, the life of the fetus must be respected.

The Talmud and the Land of Israel

The Land of Israel is central to the Jewish people and a major theme in traditional Jewish daily prayer. Jews the world over intone the words, "And to Jerusalem, Your city, may You return with compassion," and "Show favor O Lord toward Your people Israel and their prayer and restore the service of the Holy of Holies of Your Temple," three times a day. King David wrote about the Jewish connection to the Land of Israel, "For the Lord selected Zion, He desired it for His dwelling place. For God selected Jacob as His own, Israel as His treasure." (Psalms 132:13, 135:4)

Considering what has transpired over the last two millennia to the Jewish people—being exiled from their land, and dispersed to the four winds—this relationship with the Almighty and His love for them has certainly been a rocky one. As far as we know, no other group of people or national entity has ever had its land rendered desolate, banished into exile, and returned after nearly 2,000 years to establish a new country. Scriptural passages actually allude to this phenomenon:

"As for you, O mountains of Israel, you shall shoot forth your branches and bear your fruit for My people Israel, when their return is close at hand … I shall cause you to be inhabited as in former times and I will make you even more bountiful than you were in your beginnings." (Ezekiel 36:8–11)

Let's Get Talmudic

Rami bar Ezekiel traveled to Bnei Brak. There he saw goats eating under the fig trees. Honey was dripping from the figs and milk flowing from the goats and they were mixing together on the ground. He exclaimed "This is what is meant 'A land flowing with milk and honey.'" (Ketubot 111b)

In a chapter of the Talmud discussing scriptural prophecies indicating messianic times and the return of the Jewish people to their land, Rabbi Abba commented, "There can be no more manifest sign of redemption than this, for it is written "As for you, O mountains of Israel … and bear fruit for My people." (Sanhedrin 98a)

Rashi comments that when the Land of Israel yields its fruits again in a cornucopia-like abundance this will signal the end of the exile—for there is no clearer sign than that. Rabbi Shmuel Eliezer Aidels, the Renaissance-era Talmud scholar also known as the Maharsha, also comments on this Talmudic passage adding, "As long the Jewish people do not dwell on their land, it does not give of its produce."

The Bible itself, in a very unusual way, predicts a time when the land will become desolate because of Israel's transgressions:

> "So devastated will I leave the land that your enemies who shall dwell therein will become desolate on it." (Leviticus 26:32)

Yet, even here, the love of God for the Land of Israel and its rightful owners, the Jewish people, is manifest. Nachmanides, writing in the thirteenth century, makes a profound observation when commenting on this strange passage. He wrote, "'Your enemies who shall dwell therein will be desolate on it,' is actually a 'blessing in disguise,' proclaiming that during their exile, the Jewish land will not accept their enemies either. The proof is that in the entire inhabited parts of the world one cannot find such a good and fertile land which has always been lived on, and yet is as ruined as it is."

Talmud Trivia

The Mongols invaded Israel around the same period Nachmanides wrote about, which in addition to the ravages of the Crusades left the land in total ruin.

How long did this "inhabitation with desolation" last? Mark Twain visited a good portion of Israel in 1867. In The Innocents Abroad or The New Pilgrim's Progress, he wrote, "We traversed some miles of desolate country whose soil is rich enough but is given wholly to weeds—a silent mournful expanse—a desolation is here that not even the imagination can grace with the pomp of life and action ... the further we went the hotter the sun got ... and the more repulsive and dreary the landscape became ... there was hardly a tree or shrub anywhere ... even the olive and the cactus those fast friends of worthless soil, had almost deserted the country ... Palestine sits in sackcloth and ashes ... And why should it be otherwise? Can the curse of the Deity beautify this land?"

Mark Twain did not live long enough to experience the absolutely miraculous response to his somewhat rhetorical question. For during the last century of intense Jewish immigration to the land, Today, Israel is one of the most agriculturally productive and technologically advanced nations in the world. Its $100 billion a year economy is larger than all of its immediate neighbors combined. Its exports of military equipment and diamonds make it one of the biggest players per capita in these industries. So why all the fuss? Why has the last century of gradual resettlement of this land been wrought with such blood, tears, and suffering? Why does it seem that every other United Nations resolution (66 since 1967) is against Israel?

Conflict in the Middle East and the Zohar

Many political pundits, academicians, and historians have offered theories as to why this part of the world continues to be the center of such intense territorial struggles, factional hatred, religious fanaticism, and so on. Granted, some of them offer interesting insights. However, their attempts to understand this conflict in wholly rational terms is an exercise in futility, for no rational explanation exists. One must transcend the ordinary into the metaphysical to get a glimpse at what is really happening behind the scenes. And that's where we will go to examine what the Talmudic sages have to say.

In the Zohar, Rabbi Chiya said, "In the merit of Israel being circumcised, their enemies are subdued before them and they inherit their land." Where does he derive this teaching? It is found in the placing of two Biblical verses side by side. First, it says "Three times each year (allusion to the festivals) all your males shall appear before God the Master." (Exodus 34:23) Males, in this passage are understood through Oral tradition, to include only circumcised males. This verse is immediately followed by the verse "For I will dispossess nations from before you and enlarge your boundaries …" (Ibid. 34:24)

From this juxtaposition the Zohar teaches that the Almighty reckons the merit of circumcision and uproots one group of inhabitants and restores another. Historically, this first occurred to the Canaanites in favor of the Israelites.

Let's Get Talmudic

The Kuzari, written by the great Spanish sage Rabbi Yehuda HaLevi in 1140, contains one of clearest presentations on the philosophy of Judaism. Halevi writes about the Jewish people's attachment to the land, "The Jewish people may be compared to grape seeds that will only flourish in certain soil, for it is known that Italian grape seeds will not produce the same quality of wine, if they are planted in the soil of Spain."

We still do not understand why that should propel Israel's neighbors into frenzy over Jewish resettlement. However, we do see that despite Israel's collective neglect in upholding some of the Torah commandments over the centuries, one that has been universally observed all these ages is the Covenant of Abraham and ritual circumcision called Brit Milah. The reason? Rabban Shimon Gamliel says "Every commandment which Israel accepted upon themselves with rejoicing, they continue to perform with great rejoicing." (Talmud Shabbat 130a) And that is precisely the case with Brit Milah until this day. The Prophet Zechariah, in fact, made the liberation of the

Israelites from the bondage of exile dependent solely on the performance of this precept, "As for you (Zion) for the sake of the blood of your covenant shall I send forth your prisoners out of the pit (exile) ... return to the stronghold, you captives who have yearned for deliverance." (Zechariah 9:11–12)

Now enter the connection to Israel's hostile neighbors. We know from the Book of Genesis that Abraham had another son, named Ishmael. We also learn that he was circumcised as well. (Genesis 17:23) In the Zohar, Rabbi Chiya cites a "conversation" between the guardian angel of the nation of Ishmael who pleaded with the Almighty that inasmuch as Ishmael was circumcised (at age 13) he, too, is deserving of a portion in the land. God's answer, as it were, was that Isaac was attached to God through a circumcision that was a complete act, involving both cutting and pulling back of the foreskin, unlike Ishmael's, and performed at the age of eight days.

Yet the angel of Ishmael continued to argue that his people still deserve some type of reward. God acquiesced and gave them a portion below in the Holy Land. The Zohar comments that the children of Ishmael will rule the Holy Land for a long period of time, so long as the Land is empty—just as their circumcision is "empty" and incomplete. They will also try to prevent the children of Israel from returning to their place until the merit in the land has expired.

A Centuries-Old Conflict

So, we now know that this conflict began a long time ago. In fact, it began centuries before the Zohar was written. During Alexander the Great's conquest of the Holy Land we find the children of Ishmael and Egypt making a claim on the property and the land of the Jews. The Talmud, in Sanhedrin 91a, relates: "On one occasion the Egyptians came in a lawsuit against the Jews before Alexander of Macedonia. They pleaded thus: 'Is it not written, And the Lord gave the people favor in the sight of the Egyptians, and they lent them gold and precious stones, etc." (Exodus 12:36) Then return us the gold and silver which you took!'

"Thereupon a commoner, Geviah ben Pesisa, said to the sages, 'Give me permission to go and plead against them before Alexander of Macedonia: should they defeat me, then say, "You have merely defeated an ignorant man amongst us;" whilst if I defeat them then say, "The Law of Moses has defeated you."'

"So they gave him permission, and he went and pleaded against them. 'From where do you adduce your proof?' he asked.

"'From the Torah,' they replied.

"'Then I too,' said Geviah, 'will bring you proof only from the Torah, for it is written, 'Now the sojourning of the children of Israel, who dwelt in Egypt, was four hundred and thirty years.' (Ibid 12:40) Pay us for the toil of six hundred thousand men whom ye enslaved for four hundred thirty years!'

"Then King Alexander said to them, 'Answer him!'

"'Give us three days' time,' they begged. So he gave them a respite; they sought but found no answer. Immediately they fled, leaving behind their sown fields and planted vineyards."

The next suit was filed by "the children of Ishmael and Keturah [Abraham's second wife, identified by the Midrash as Hagar]." The plaintiffs in this suit claim that Canaan, or the Land of Israel, is partially theirs, as the Torah identifies their ancestors, no less than Isaac, to be progeny of Abraham. (Based on Genesis 25:12)

Once again, Geviah responded on behalf of the Jews. "What is your source?" he asked. "The Torah," they responded. "If so," he continued, "I too will invoke only the Torah, which says that Abraham gave 'all that was his to Isaac; and to the children of his concubines [other wives], he gave [only] gifts, and he sent them away from Isaac his son ... eastward.'" [Genesis, 25:5,6] A father who assigns distribution of his estate during his lifetime and sends his sons away from each other, does one have a claim on the other?" Curiously, the Talmud records no Ishmaelite reaction in Alexander's court—not even a request for time to formulate a response. Evidently, Ishmael's descendents are silent, which is a form of tacit admittance to the limitation of their claim.

The Israel of the Future

According to the Jewish religious tradition, though, the entire world, including Ishmael's descendants, will one day come not only to countenance the idea of Israel's sovereignty over the entire Biblical land, but also to fully embrace it. The world longs for that day and it will not come about through contemporary military or political proceedings; it will be achieved by the restoration of the messianic Davidic reign. What will that look like?

Picture this imaginary event—a moment in the future—when a benevolent and holy teacher, a direct descendent of King David, will teach children of all faiths. Maybe a small group will gather around a fire on a Judean hillside. The sage in the middle begins by picking up a chunk of granite. "At one time, in the beginning of creation, the planet was a boiling sea of molten rock. All energy was unified in this primordial stew. We revere rocks because everything comes from them, the trees and mountains—even your bodies—as it says, 'for you are Earth and to Earth you shall return.' These rocks are your grandfather and grandmother. When you remember all those who have inspired and helped you in this life, you begin with the rocks."

Then the sage will finish his lesson by raising the stone to his ear in silence and show each child in turn. "Do you hear the rock singing? In the last era some people abused rocks and thought there was no music in them. But now we know it's not true. Some of these rocks became King David who composed beautiful lyrics and played the harp. One of the lyrics he sang has something to do with that beautiful new edifice on the next hill (Third Temple). It goes like this, "(God), you will arise and show Zion mercy, for there will come a time to favor her … for your servants have cherished her stones." (Psalms 102:14,15) And perhaps some of these rocks even became the great prophet Isaiah who proclaimed, "For My House shall be a house of prayer for all people." May it happen in our time.

The Least You Need to Know

♦ Jewish law does not forbid cloning. However, creating "monsters" or a "monster race" is a liability that all people of conscience must be cautious of.

♦ Judaism respects life as a precious gift from above. Alleviating the pain of a terminally ill patient is a blessed virtue, however, actively facilitating one's death can be tantamount to murder.

♦ Intelligent, extraterrestrial life is a subject that intrigued the Talmudic sages. While no communication with alien beings was documented, theoretically there is nothing in Talmudic teachings to deny their existence.

♦ Judaism neither bans abortion outright, nor does it tolerate indiscriminate abortion.

♦ Determining "life-threatening" conditions, or serious other considerations that would permit abortion, is a decision to be placed in the hands of medical and rabbinic experts.

♦ The Land of Israel figures prominently in Talmudic literature and Jewish liturgy. Understanding the contemporary conflict in the Middle East is predicated on a deeper awareness of the spiritual underpinnings of players involved.

Chapter 25

Living a Talmudic Life

In This Chapter

- ◆ Being on good behavior
- ◆ Serving others
- ◆ The value of teachers and friends
- ◆ Learning for life

The Jewish people take their Talmud very seriously. In fact, they live by it. The Talmud has shaped Jewish thinking for centuries and continues to do so to this day. But you don't have to be Jewish to follow some of the precepts of the Talmud, or to use the principles embodied in the Talmud to order your life.

Although separated by thousands of years, there continues to be a deep and inextricable link between the teachings of the sages and modern practice. The original shapers of the Talmud succeeded in their goal of preserving the oral teachings that were divinely conveyed to Moses at Mt. Sinai for the generations that would follow them. It continues to be a living, breathing document to this day.

Just about everyone who has ever opened the Talmud has wondered about the real life applications of the wisdom it contains. Though much of what the Talmud teaches is applicable on a daily basis, some of it is quite theoretical. But there are things to be learned and applied from the more theoretical teachings of the Talmud, by coming to a fuller understanding of the principles behind them and the values that they teach.

In this chapter, we will examine how the teachings of the Talmud are indeed timeless, and can be applied by everyone. The goal here is not to walk in the shoes of the sages (in most cases, they would have been sandals, anyway), but to look at how some of the basic tenets of the Talmud can be used to order one's everyday life, no matter who you are or where you're going.

Being Good

As mentioned, one does not have to be Jewish to benefit from the wisdom of the Talmud. Humankind in general can gain from the sages's proclamations and teachings on how to live a good life according to divine will. The Talmud even provides a template for doing so with the Seven Noachide Laws, the seven universal principles that form the basis of God's moral expectations of all humankind.

As a review, the Seven Noachide Laws prohibit the following:

- Idolatry (worshipping other gods)
- Blasphemy
- Murder
- Robbery and grand theft
- Immorality and forbidden sexual relations
- Removing and eating a limb from a live animal

They also encourage the establishment of a judicial system, including courts of law, to ensure the enforcement of the other six.

For the most part, these laws govern what is considered "good" behavior, which encompasses three very important relationships: to God, to others, and to oneself. Doing good works—mitzvahs—reflect one's adherence to these laws.

Being of Service

Doing good works calls for having a good heart, and for doing them for the right reasons. This speaks to one's motivation, and the concept of selfless acts, about which the sages had quite a bit to say. In Baba Kamma 92a, it is written, "He who prays for his fellowman, while he himself has the same need, will be answered first." This almost clashes with the concept found in the Ethics of the Fathers, "Antigonus of Socho received [the oral tradition] from Simeon the Righteous. He used to say: "Don't be like those servants who serve their master in the expectation of receiving a reward; rather, be like those servants who serve their master without the expectation of receiving a reward." (1:3)

The purest service, of course, is to help others and to seek the welfare of others without the expectation of reward. Is there not a pitfall in the Talmudic statement about praying for someone else's welfare, that it might be motivated by a person feeling he/she will be answered first?

God fashioned the world to be a place where people naturally feel inclined to reach out and serve others, even if there is an expectation that someone else will reciprocate. The expression "what goes around, comes around," is a powerful goad or motivation to inspire people to help others.

Talmud Tidbits

Altruistically speaking, the only form of loving kindness one can perform for another, is participating in their burial. That is why the Talmud exclusively refers to burying the dead as a *"mitzvah shel emet,"* which loosely translates as "a completely selfless deed." The recipient is obviously not in a position to reciprocate. However, every other kind act we perform for another can hypothetically be "rewarded" or recompensed.

On this issue, the sages state that true character growth is possible despite a limitation of pure motives. They said "One should always learn Torah and perform good deeds, for even though one is doing them not for their own sake, he will eventually come to do them for their own sake." (Talmud Pesachim 50b) One great sage commented that this doesn't mean a person will live 90 years doing virtuous deeds with ulterior motives and in his ninety-first finally get it right. Rather, in each action we perform there is that potential, that one moment of pure lucidity where our souls are being driven solely to do right thing, without recompense—for it's what God wants us to do!

Granted, it is hard to capture those selfless moments on a regular basis. At times, those who give of themselves in a seemingly selfless manner may even seem a bit suspect. There is a Yiddish expression "tzadik b'peltz" which translates as "a pious one in fur." Perhaps the Jews of Eastern Europe, who first coined this phrase, were a bit weary of individuals who externally gave the air of piety, but in essence, were far from it. The Talmudic sages weighed in on this one as well, "A Torah scholar whose inner self does not match his outer veneer, should not enter the house of study !" (Brachot 28a)

The sages insisted that a Torah scholar's public behavior must be a true reflection of his inner character. In other words, he could not profess one set of beliefs in his relationship with God while acting in a manner unbecoming a person of his spiritual stature in his interaction with people. Proper character should be expressed in his total demeanor, even in his motivations when extending kindness to others. These pure motives are especially important when it comes to a man's relationship with his wife, since she is the best judge to sense whether he is being sincere or not. If she senses that he is not being sincere, then she will be terribly hurt, since he is taking lightly something that is so precious to her—her feelings.

> **Let's Get Talmudic**
>
> Building character has always been a top priority of Jewish and Talmud education. However, it is not merely book knowledge that accomplishes this. According to the great scholar and teacher Rabbi Joseph Ber Soloveitchik, "good character is like an illness, it cannot be taught it must be caught."

It is obvious that one must be careful to be honest in all one's actions. But, what does one do to develop this purity of character?

While it is important to assist in the welfare of others, developing one's own character is equally important. One must arrange individual priorities in order to accomplish this. As the sages put it, "Perfect yourself and afterwards, perfect others!" (Talmud Baba Batra 60b) Nothing is so incongruous to growth however, when the individual needs so much improvement him/herself and fails to take action. This should be one's focus first.

With political correctness the way it is today, learning, studying, even teaching for oneself almost seems a little selfish. But as we progress through our life, it's important to never think of life as some great sacrifice, requiring you to deny yourself so you can give to others, or even denying from yourself so you can live spiritually.

God has many messengers to take care of His world and bring it to perfection. When the time is ripe, we will all get into the act. Sometimes, the best thing you can do for others is to take care of yourself. But, the time comes in a person's life when one will grow most by giving over to others—whether to students or to a spouse and children.

The following story is a wonderful illustration of this point …

A father, just returning from a hard day at work, is met at the door with his enthusiastic young son, who can't wait to play a game of catch with his dad. The father pats his son on the head, and wearily makes his way into the living room, where he slumps into his easy chair, and requests the daily paper and a cold drink. His son eagerly accommodates him, hoping that a few minutes of rest and libation will revive his poppa.

The father, on the other hand, hits on an idea that will buy him a little more time at ease. He notices a map of the world on a page in the newspaper. He tears it out, rips it into 50 or so pieces, and challenges his son to piece the map together with some tape. When he's done, they'll go play.

Much to the father's surprise, his son returns in less than five minutes with a completed patchwork of the globe in his hands. "Look, Dad, I'm done," the boy exclaimed. "I can see that," his father replied. "How did you do it so quickly?"

"Simple," the boy replied. "when I spread out the pieces I noticed that on the backside of the map was a picture of a man. All I had to do was put the man together and the world fit into place."

The Value of Mentors and Friends

One of the most important parts of studying Torah or Talmud in religious circles is seeing its values in action and embodied in a living Torah scholar. In a world that is increasingly moving toward online interactions to replace interpersonal relationships, it's important to find a live, breathing, sensitive, and seasoned teacher to learn from, regardless of what you're studying, Talmud or not.

The conventional way that keeps the Talmud vibrant and ensures its survival is first studying with a teacher, then reviewing with fellow students, and finally passing along what one learns to one's own students. However, this progression is not fixed nor a merely linear one. Ideally, as one progresses from one level to the next, he/she reaches higher levels of wisdom and understanding.

In the Talmud, Rabbi Judah, the Prince stated that he learned much from his teachers, more from his colleagues, and the most from his students. (Makkot 10a) Explaining and giving over to others is a symbiotic process that is the "culmination" of hard work and ensures the message gets passed on to the next generation. Having said that, it is as much a growing experience for the teacher as it is for the nascent student. As the Talmud puts it, more than the calf wants to suckle, the cow wants to nurse. (Pesachim 112a)

There is no greater aid to acquiring wisdom in this area than a reliable partner, someone who will truly stand by you and "watch your back."

Let's Get Talmudic

The first century C.E. sage Choni, also called Choni, the Circle-Maker, was about the best friend anyone could have. A very colorful figure (some say he was the inspiration for the Rip Van Winkle story), he literally stood in the gap for the children of Israel.

It once happened that the land of Israel was suffering from a drought. The sages sent a message to Choni to pray so that rain would fall. He prayed, but no rain fell. So Choni drew a circle and stood within it, in the same fashion that the prophet Habbakuk had done centuries earlier.

"I (Habbakuk) will stand at my post and I will set myself for a siege until I get an explanation from God as to why the wicked often succeed and the righteous often suffer." (Habbakuk 2:1) He declared his intention to stand in a circular pit that he had dug until he got an answer.

[Choni] said before the Lord, "Master of the Universe! Your children have turned their faces to me because I am like a member of the household before You [but I am not really worthy]. I swear by Your great Name that I will not budge from here until You take pity on Your children!" (Talmud Taanit 23a) In response to Choni's words rain began to sprinkle.

Choni is also famous for another statement "Give me friendship or give me death." (Seems as if Patrick Henry studied Talmud as well!)

Work with a Purpose

Among the Jewish people, dedicating one's life to Talmud study is an exalted calling, one of the best things you can do. But you don't have to opt for a career in rabbinics to do worthy and valuable work.

The Talmud spends considerable time discussing the subject of work, for the profession one chooses affects everything—what you earn, of course, but also the amount of time you'll have available for spiritual aspirations and duties, and honoring family obligations.

Working Hard

The Talmudic sages put a high value on hard work. Many of them were laborers themselves. Some were farmers, shepherds, and even cowboys. Others were businessmen or artisans.

Talmud Tidbits

The Talmud teaches, by example, a great deal of respect for labor. The sages disdained idleness and felt it led to mental illness and sexual immorality. (Kethuboth 59b) Rabbi Yossi felt that a person does not die except through idleness (Avot D'Rabbi Noson 11:1), "A person should love work and not hate it; for just as the Torah was given with a covenant, so too was work given with a covenant." Finally, "One who does not teach his son an occupation, it is as though he taught him to become a robber." (Talmud Kiddushin 29a)

It's Not Just About Money

It is also clear from the teachings of the sages of that being absorbed with making money is not the ideal for most individuals (unless major support of the community depended upon them). Hillel stated "Nor can one who engages too much in business become wise." (Ethics of the Fathers 2:5) Rabbi Meir advised "Rather limit your business activities and occupy yourself with the Torah instead." (Ibid. 4:10)

Finding the Right Job

Rabbi Yochanan imparts one tidbit of guidance on how to find a job one is likely to succeed at. He advises that one should consider the profession of his father and ancestors in choosing a vocation since one is most likely to find success in the same occupation as his father. (Talmud Arachin 16b)

The Talmud stress that a person should even hire himself out to do work that is foreign to him and beneath his dignity than be dependent on people for charity. (Bava Bathra 110a) On this notion, the sage Rav told his disciple Rabbi Kahana (remember the precocious student found under his master's bed), "Skin a carcass in the street and receive wages and do not say I am an important person and this type of work is beneath my dignity." (Ibid.)

Work That's "Clean and Light"

The Talmud uses the expression "clean and light" to describe work that aligned itself with one's right livelihood. Where does this expression come from? Bar Kappara, the sage who gave Rabbi Yehudah the Prince so much grief at his daughter's wedding, stated: "A person should always teach his son a light and clean occupation. What is it? Rabbi Chisda said, "stitching in doublets." (A short coat that was customary to embroider with stitches that appeared like rows of a plowed field.) (Talmud Berachot 63a)

The commentators felt that "light" implied it did not involve risky investments. It was also not too taxing on the mind and left time for spiritual pursuits. "Clean" connotes that wages earned were clean of theft.

Let's Get Talmudic

A most simple, yet profound proclamation comes from Rabbi Meir. He said, "One should make sure to teach his son a trade which is clean and easy; then pray to He who controls all wealth and property. For there is poverty and wealth in every occupation. One's occupation does not cause poverty, nor does it bring wealth. All is determined on the basis of one's merit. (Babylonian Talmud, Kiddushin 82a)

The same tractate also taught, in the name of Rabbi Yehudah, that a father who fails to teach his son a trade is reckoned as if he taught him to steal. (Ibid. 29a)

In summary, an ideal occupation that encourages a Talmudic lifestyle has these characteristics:

- It is clean, pleasant, and dignified work.

- It provides an individual with time to pursue more spiritual pursuits like study of Torah.

- It functions as a benefit to society.

- It is profitable and enables one to become wealthy.

- It is not overly taxing or strenuous mentally or physically

- It does not tempt one to become dishonest or sexually immoral

The Value of Lifelong Learning

As mentioned in Chapter 23, many who study the Talmud choose to do so every day, guiding their efforts by learning a folio, or daf, of Talmud a day. This approach teaches the discipline and commitment that's necessary to keep up with the daily quota. If this commitment isn't met, one risks being wiped out by the relentless undulating waves of the "sea of Talmud."

It's hard to put a price on the value of remaining a lifelong learner. Beyond the obvious gain in knowledge, just keeping your mind busy keeps you fresh and makes you someone who people want to have something to do with, regardless of how old you are. The curiosity of the sages was a virtue that not only gave immortality to their words and deeds—but allowed them to remain vibrant, and in demand, well into their nineties and beyond!

Always looking for ways to investigate, to explore, and to improve gives ultimate excitement and meaning to life. Rabbi Tarphon, in Pirke Avot, or Sayings of the Fathers, wrote: "The day is short, the work is plenty, yet the laborers are lazy, (even though) the wages are great, and the House owner (God) is insistent." Then he continues, "It is not necessary for you to complete the work, but neither are you free to desist from it." (2:21) Thus, one is always capable of doing more, growing wiser, and learning new things.

In every generation seekers of wisdom from all walks of life have followed the advice of the Talmudic sage Ben Bag Bag, who said, "Delve into it (the Torah), delve into it, for it contains everything." (Pirke Avot, 5:22) Doing so will reveal principles and truths that illuminate each unique and fascinating dimension of life's challenges and experience.

In closing, Rabbi Yehoshua Leib Diskin, the great rabbi of late nineteenth century Jerusalem, once explained, "There are two ways that a person's time can come. Some complete their life's work while still young and move on to the next world, while other people die of old age without having completed their missions. In Moses' case, the Torah testifies, (Deuteronomy 34:7) "His eye had not dimmed and his vigor had not diminished."

Clearly, Moses did not die of old age; rather, his mission was complete—the time during which he was meant to lead the Jewish people had ended. However, had his mission continued, his vim and vigor were readily available, and poised to continue his life's work.

As the consummate teacher, Moses had sharply honed his faculties from the sublime pleasure he received in constantly delving into God's Word. May we all be a little like Moses, and find pleasure and excitement in our pursuit of divine wisdom.

The Least You Need to Know

- ◆ Though much of what the Talmud teaches is applicable on a daily basis, some of it is quite theoretical.

- ◆ By coming to a fuller understanding of the principles behind more theoretical Talmud teachings, one can also learn from them.

- ◆ Building character has always been a top priority of Jewish and Talmud education. But good character can't simply be taught. It is learned by being discriminating in choosing who one associates with.

♦ The Talmud teaches that sometimes the best thing you can do for others is to take care of yourself. But, the time comes in a person's life when one will grow most by giving over to others—whether to students or to a spouse and children.

Glossary

aggadata   Sections of the Talmud and other rabbinic literature that deal with biblical narrative, stories and legends on biblical themes.

Amora (pl. Amora'im)   The rabbis of the fourth to fifth centuries.

Amidah   Hebrew for "silent prayer" or "stand."

apocrypha   A group of books that are included in some versions of the Bible, but not all.

Apocryphal   Information or stories that are widely believed to be true, but may not be.

ayin harah   Hebrew for "the evil eye."

ayin tovah   Hebrew for "a good eye."

bal tashchit   Hebrew for "don't destroy."

bar   Aramaic for "son of."

Beit Din   A religious court of three rabbis specifically trained to rule on issues related to divorce, conversion, monetary disputes and the like.

beraita (pl. beraitot)   A legal teaching or saying by one of the sages of the Mishnaic age that was placed outside the actual Mishna.

chok   Hebrew for ordinance or decree.

chomer   Hebrew for physicality. The word for donkey, is related and pronounced "chamor."

daf   A page of Talmud.

exegesis   An explanation or critical interpretation of a text.

Gan Eden   Hebrew for the Garden of Eden. Commonly used by the Jewish people when referring to heaven.

Gemara   Means "to finish." Used to describe the rabbinical discussions on Jewish law that comprise one part of the Talmud.

gematria   An ancient system, based on the numerical value of Hebrew letters, for discovering hidden truths and meanings in words.

get   A legal document, based on Jewish law, drawn up to establish the terms of a marital dissolution, and used to actually affect the divorce.

halacha   Hebrew for "law." Derived from a Hebrew word that means "to walk," "to travel," or "to go."

hyperbole   The deliberate and obvious exaggeration used for effect; i.e. "She cried buckets of tears."

intercalation   Inserting an extra day or month into a calendar year to keep it consistent with the solar or lunar year.

Kabbalah   The Hebrew word for "receiving." Also the term used to describe Jewish mystical teachings.

kashrut   The Hebrew word for kosher.

kiddush   The Hebrew word for special or unique. The name of the special blessing said to consecrate a Sabbath or holiday meal. Also refers to a reception for congregants of a synagogue, at which drinks and snacks are served after the kiddush blessing is said.

kosher   Means sanctioned and ritually fit for use according to Jewish law.

lashon harah   Hebrew for "evil tongue." The term is often used to describe gossiping or tale bearing.

Levi, tribe of   One of the 12 tribes of Israel that descended from the twelve sons of Jacob.

matzah   Specially prepared, unleavened flatbreads eaten in observance of Passover.

melachah   Hebrew for "creative work."

mezzuzah (pl. mezzuzot)   A scroll with biblical passages on one side and a name of God on the other, inserted in a small case attached by Jews to doorposts of their homes entries.

midrash (pl. midrashim)   Hebrew for "to search" or "to seek." It describes a main technique used to interpret or comment on Hebrew scripture.

mikvah   Hebrew for "gathering." *Also* refers to the ritual bath used for cleansing and purification.

mishpot   Hebrew for judgment or justice.

Mishna   Hebrew for study, gift, or repetition. Also the term used to describe the primary body of Jewish law that, along with the Gemara, comprises the Talmud.

mitzvah   A duty, obligation, or act of kindness carried out in keeping with the commandments of Jewish religious law.

nasi   Hebrew for patriarch, ruler, prince or president.

nefesh   Hebrew for "soul."

nevailah   Hebrew for "corpse." It refers to an animal that was improperly slaughtered or died by natural causes, rendering its meat nonkosher.

Noachides   Individuals who choose to live by the principles of the Seven Noachide Laws.

Tikkun olam   A Hebrew phrase meaning "rectification of the world."

pardes   An orchard of grapevines or other fruit-bearing trees. *Also* a kabbalistic term describing a very high state of meditation where the person enters into the highest level of God's "orchard" of profound spiritual secrets and delights.

Pareve   The Hebrew word used to describe food made without animal or dairy ingredients. No literal English translation, but commonly accepted as meaning "neutral." *Also* spelled parve.

Pentateuch   The first five books of the Bible—Genesis, Exodus, Leviticus, Numbers, and Deuteronomy.

Pesach   Hebrew for "to pass over."

Pharisees   Members of an ancient Jewish religious group who followed the Oral Law of the Torah.

predetermination   The belief that nothing happens in the world, or to the individual, except through divine providence or guidance.

rodef   One who threatens the life of another.

Sanhedrin   The ancient Jewish "Supreme Court." Its name is based on the Greek word *sunedrion*, or council, or from *sunedros*, which means sitting in council.

seder   Hebrew for "order."

Seven Noachide Laws   Seven universal principles that form the basis of God's moral expectations of all humankind. Also called the Seven Universal Laws, or the Seven Laws of the Children of Noah.

Siddur   The name for the Jewish prayer book. Derived from the word seder.

taiku   Hebrew for "sealed" or "let it stand," taken to mean a tie. In Talmudic debate, taiku happens when it's impossible to decide who is correct, based on the information presented.

Tanna (pl. Tanna'im)   The Jewish sages whose teachings are recorded in the Mishna and its contemporary works, from the middle of the first century until about 220 C.E.

tefillin   The small leather boxes containing Hebrew scriptural texts ritually worn by orthodox Jewish men.

tikkun   A Hebrew word meaning "rectification" or "setting in order."

tithing   The payment of one tenth of one's income or produce to support a religious house and its officials.

Torah   The body of Jewish teaching—the Written Law—contained in the first five books of the Bible.

World to Come   A term sometimes used by the Jewish people to refer to an afterlife following death. Can also mean the world of perfection and completion where the Messiah will lead the world to a "new heaven and a new earth."

Zohar   Hebrew for "splendor" or "radiance." *Also* the primary text of Kabbalistic writings.

Appendix B

The Order of the Talmud

The Talmud is organized by topic, and divides the traditions of Jewish oral law into six main areas, as described below. Each area, in turn, is divided into separate topics, or tractates. There are 63 tractates in all.

Order Zeraim

Berachot—Blessings and prayers (liturgical rules)

Peah—Corners of fields and gleanings left for the poor

Demai—Produce bought from a person whose tithing is suspect

Kilayim—Forbidden mixtures of plants, animals, and clothing

Sheviit—The Sabbatical year

Terumot—Produce set aside as gifts for the Kohanim (the priests)

Ma'aserot—Tithes given to the Levites

Ma'aser Sheni—Tithes eaten in Jerusalem

Challah—The portion of dough given to the Kohanim

Orlah—Forbidden fruits of trees during the first four years after planting

Bikkurim—First fruits brought to the Holy Temple in Jerusalem

Order Moed (Festivals)

Sabbath—Sabbath observance, the 39 forbidden labors of the Sabbath

Eruvin—Rabbinical decrees regarding the Sabbath (extension of Sabbath boundaries)

Pesachim—Observance of the Pesach (Passover festival)

Shekalim—The annual half-shekel head tax paid to the Holy Temple

Yoma—Observance of Yom Kippur

Succah—Observance of Sukkot

Beitzah—The Rabbinical decrees regarding the Festivals

Rosh Hashanah—Observance of Rosh Hashanah, the Jewish New Year

Taanit—Public fast days

Megillah—Reading Megillat Esther on Purim

Moed Katan—The intermediate days of Passover and Sukkot

Chagigah—Sacrificial offerings during the three Pilgrimage Festivals

Order Nashim

Yevamot—Levirate marriage, Challitzah, Agunot (women unable to remarry)

Ketubot—Marriage contracts and financial obligations, the mutual rights and duties of husband and wife

Nedarim—The making and annulment of vows and oaths

Nazir—The Nazirite vows

Sotah—The suspected adulteress

Gittin—Laws of divorce and the annulment of marriage

Kiddushin—Laws of marriage (betrothals)

Order Nezikin

Baba Kamma—Damage to person and property, loans and interest, stolen goods

Baba Metzia—Lost and found property, embezzlement, fraud, usury, sales, rentals, rights of hired laborers

Baba Batra—Real estate, possessions, inheritance, partnership, evidence, testimony.

Sanhedrin—The judiciary, judicial procedure, capital punishment

Makkot—False witnesses, exile (cities of refuge), corporal punishment

Shevuot—Oaths, private or court administered

Eduyyot—Testimonies primarily of the High Court

Avodah Zarah—Idolatry and superstitions

Avot—Ethics of the Fathers

Horayot—Erroneous judicial rulings

Order Kodashim

Zevachim—Animal and bird sacrifices in the Holy Temple

Menachot—Flour offerings, wine libations

Chullin—Laws of nonsacred animal slaughter and dietary laws

Bechorot—Firstborns (human and animal)

Arachin—Valuation and consecration of personal worth to the Holy Temple

Temurah—Exchange of sanctified things

Keritot—Spiritual excision and sin offerings

Me'ila—Trespass, misappropriation or (sacrilegious treatment) of Holy Temple property

Tamid—Daily morning and evening sacrifice

Middot—Holy Temple architecture

Kinnim—Birds (nests) offerings

Order Tohorot

Kelim—Ritual uncleanness of utensils and garments

Oholot—The defilement of houses caused by a corpse

Negaim—The complex laws of Tzaraat (similar to leprosy)

Parah—Regulations concerning the red heifer (used to purify one who has become defiled from contact with a corpse)

Tohorot—Lesser degrees of uncleanliness lasting until sunset

Mikvaot—Ritual baths and immersion

Niddah—The laws of family purity

Machshirin—Liquids and foods that are susceptible to ritual uncleanness

Zavim—Secretions that render a person unclean

Tevul Yom—Cleanness acquired at sunset after daytime immersion

Yadayim—The defilement of the hands and their purification

Uktzin—Fruits and plants susceptible to uncleanness

Rabbinic Leaders from Moses to the Completion of the Talmud

The transmission of the Jewish law from Moses until today comprises an unbroken chain of 120 generations. The following list is taken from the introduction to Maimonides' Mishneh Torah. (Prophets who appear in the Bible are asterisked.)

- Moses*
- Joshua*
- The Elders (1260–860 B.C.E.)
- Pinchas and the 70 Elders
- Eli the Kohen
- Samuel the Prophet*
- King David*
- The Prophets (860–360 B.C.E.)
- Achiyah

- Elijah the Prophet^
- Elisha*
- Yehoyada the Priest
- Zechariah ben Yehoyada*
- Hosea*
- Amos*
- Isaiah*
- Micah*
- Joel*

- Nachum*

- Habakuk*

- Zephaniah*

- Jeremiah*

- Baruch ben Neriah

- The Members of the Great Assembly (360–260 B.C.E.)

- The Members of the Great Assembly consisted of 120 elders, including Ezra*, Zechariah*, Daniel*, Mordechai, and Shimon the Tzaddik.

- Tana'im—Mishnaic Era (260 B.C.E.–200 C.E.)

- Antigonos of Socho

- Yose ben Yoezer, Yose ben Yochanan

- Yehoshua ben Perachiah, Nittai of Arbel

- Yehuda ben Tabbai, Shimon ben Shatach

- Shemayah and Avtalyon

- Hillel and Shamai

- R'Shimon ben Hillel, R'Yochanan ben Zakkai

- Rabban Gamliel the Elder, R'Eliezer ben Hyrcanus, R'Yehoshua ben Chananiah, R'Shimon ben Netanel, R'Elazar ben Arakh

- Rabban Shimon ben Gamliel I, Rebbe Akiva, Rebbe Tarfon, R'Shimon ben Elazar, R'Yochanan ben Nuri

- Rabban Gamliel II, Rebbe Meir, Rebbe Yishmael, Rebbe Yehudah, Rebbe Yose, R'Shimon bar Yochai

- Rabbi Shimon ben Gamliel II

- Rabbi Yehudah the Prince (codifier of the Mishnah in 190 C.E.)

- Amora'im-Talmudic Era (200–500 C.E.)

- Rav Shmuel, Rabbi Yochanan (compiler of the Jerusalem Talmud)

- Rav Huna, Rav Yehudah, Rav Nachman, Rav Kahana, Rabba bar Channa, Rav Ami, Rav Asi

- Rabbah, Rav Yosef, Rav Chisda, Rabba bar Rav Huna

- Abaya, Rava

- Rav Ashi, Ravina (compilers of the Babylonian Talmud in 500 C.E.)

Appendix **D**

Resources

Books

Now that you have graduated to the next level of Talmudic expertise, it's time to expand that knowledge. The following books provide a general perspective on the Talmud and the Jewish people:

Cohen, Abraham. *Everyman's Talmud: The Major Teachings of the Rabbinic Sages*. New York: E.P. Dutton & Co., Inc., 1949.
One of the earliest American publications to describe all the basic doctrines of Judaism in a scholarly fashion.

Donin, Hayim Halevy. *To Be a Jew: A Guide to Jewish Observance in Contemporary Life*. New York: Basic Books, 1991.
A basic text describing Jewish practice that has become a modern classic for the novice as well as potential convert.

Frankiel, Tamar. *The Gift of Kabbalah: Discovering the Secrets of Heaven, Renewing Your Life on Earth*. Vermont: Jewish Lights Pub., 2003.
A practical guide for reclaiming Kabbalah's religious meaning, beginning with its origins in Talmudic times.

Glatt, Rabbi Aaron. *Women in the Talmud*. New York: Orthodox Union, 2003.
  An anthology of the Talmud's stories about women, from Seder Zeraim and
  Moed, as explained by the classic commentators.

Goldin, Judah. *Living Talmud*. New American Library, 1984.
  The late University of Pennsylvania professor portrays many fascinating passages of midrashic literature in colorful fashion.

Hoenig, Samuel N. *The Essence of Talmudic Law and Thought*. Jason Aronson, 1993.
  Professor Hoenig captures the essence of Talmudic reasoning and understanding in many areas of Jewish practice and philosophy. A very readable text.

Kaplan, Rabbi Aryeh. *The Handbook of Jewish Thought*. New York: Moznaim
  Publishers, 1979.
  From a "once in a century" Talmudic genius and physicist, Rabbi Kaplan's comprehensive work on Judaism, the Written and Oral Law is a must read for
  everyone.

Kolatch, Alfred J. *Masters of the Talmud: Their Lives and Views*. Jonathan David
  Publishers, Inc., 2002.
  The author discusses each sages' contribution and cites the precise talmudic pas-
  sages where they are quoted—a very useful aid to any student of the Talmud.

Pruess, Julius, and Rosner, Fred, M.D. (translator). *Biblical and Talmudic Medicine*.
  Jason Aronson Publishers, 1994 (reprint edition).
  The late nineteenth-century physician/scholar Dr. Julius Preuss wrote the defin-
  itive text on Biblical and Talmudic medicine in German. A fascinating read.

Steinsaltz, Rabbi Adin. *The Essential Talmud*. New York: Basic Books, 1984.
  Rabbi Steinsaltz is one of the most respected Talmudists of his generation, and
  has devoted significant effort to introducing the Talmud to a wider audience.

———. *The Talmud: The Steinsaltz Edition: A Reference Guide*. New York: Random
  House, 1989.
  Rabbi Steinsaltz, who resides in the Old City of Jerusalem, continues his quest
  to complete his English translation of the entire Talmud. This volume is a reference guide that describes the many facets of the Talmud and its various components. A particularly good source toward better understanding of Talmudic
  exegesis of scripture.

Study Guides

Bergman, Rabbi Meir Tzvi (Rabbi Nesanel Kasnett, trans.). *Gateway to the Talmud*. New York: Artscroll/Mesorah Publications, 1990.
A leading rabbinic figure in Israel traces the origin and development of the Mishnah and Talmud. Includes translations of Talmudic terms and the guideline for deciding Jewish Law in Talmudic disputes.

Carmell, Rabbi Aryeh. *Aids to Talmud Study*. New York: Feldheim Publishers, 1975.
Technical and useful aid to understanding Aramaic language and terminology in the Talmud.

Encyclopedia Judaica, Israel. Keter Publishing House, 1972.
A profoundly useful resource. Students taking Talmud learning seriously might want to refer to its entries on the Mishnah and Talmud subject matter. In addition, many important sages of the Talmud and later commentators are covered. It is available in many University and Synagogue libraries, and of course, on the Internet.

Frank, Yitzhak. *The Practical Talmud Dictionary*. New York: Feldheim Publishers, 1991.
Good definitions of the words that form a "basic vocabulary" of Talmud. This book includes the structures, concepts, and sages most likely to be encountered in casual study, but omits rare words. Also includes charts of weights and measures.

Jastrow, Marcus. *Dictionary of the Talmud*. Philadelphia: Horev Publishing, 1903.
The definitive Aramaic/English dictionary includes virtually every word in the Talmud (Babylonian and Jerusalem) and some Midrashic Literature. Students at intermediate and advanced levels will benefit most. A later version is also available, published as *A Dictionary of the Targumim, the Talmud Babli and Yerushalmi, and the Midrashic Literature*, by Hendrickson Publishers, Inc. (Massachusetts, 2003).

Talmud Translations

The Schottenstein Edition. New York: Artscroll/Mesorah Publishers, 1990.
This translation and commentary is published by Artscroll/Mesorah; the entire Talmud is meticulously covered. Several world-class Talmudic scholars have

been engaged to render the esoteric nature of the Talmud readily accessible to the English speaking public. It includes a treasure trove of traditional commentaries. There are copious notes to give background and explanation of unfamiliar ideas. The notes also often contain diagrams to help understand the difficult concepts presented. It is the easiest version, to date, for following the debates and discussions of the Talmud.

The Steinsaltz Edition. New York: Random House, 1989.

Rabbi Adin Steinsaltz's edition of the Talmud includes a translation and running commentary in Hebrew, along with traditional commentaries, biographies of sages, references to the classical legal codes, and sidebars with descriptions and illustrations of Talmudic *regalia*. Volumes are available for more than half of the Talmud, with new ones appearing regularly. An English edition is appearing even more slowly.

Websites

The following websites offer more information on Talmud study and on Judaism in general:

♦ www.613.org
An audio crash course in Talmud and other subjects

♦ www.jewishstudies.org/index.asp
Interactive course based in Israel

♦ www.peshitta.org/initial/peshitta.html
Ancient Aramaic texts

♦ www.aishdas.org/webshas
The most comprehensive subject index of Talmud on the Internet

♦ www.davka.com/cig-bin/product.cgi?product=37
Interactive multimedia tools for Talmud study. Narrates and explains word by word in concise English.

♦ www.vbm-torah.org
Virtual Beit Midrash (House of Learning)

♦ www.partnersintorah.org
Learn to read Hebrew or analyze Biblical texts with a personal trainer

- http://dafyomishiur.com/videl.html
  Video version of the Daf Yomi

- www.dafyomi.org
  Daf Yomi study on the Internet

- www.jewfaq.org
  Judaism 101—an online encyclopedia of Judaism

- www.torah.org
  Project Genesis—Jewish outreach program

- www.jewsforjudaism.org
  Jews for Judaism—an online encyclopedia of Judaism

- www.virtualjerusalem.com
  Virtual Jerusalem—news and information resource

- www.aish.org
  Aish HaTorah (The Flame of Torah)—resource for Jews with lots of questions

- www.shamash.org
  Shamash (To Serve)—huge link database

- www.Jlaw.com
  Examines Jewish law, Jewish issues, and secular law

- www.us-israel.org/jsource/index.html
  Jewish virtual library

- www.chabad.org
  Chabad and AskMoses.com

- www.tfdixie.com
  Torah from Dixie—Jewish resources from Atlanta

- www.angelfire.com/mt/Talmud
  The Real Truth About the Talmud—debunks many of the canards against the Talmud

- www.sacred-texts.com/jud/index.htm
  Sacred texts of Judaism

- www.ucalgary.ca/~elsegal
  Online course in Talmud, offered by Eliezer Segal, a professor at the University of Calgary

- www.library.yale.edu/cataloging/hebraicateam/index.htm
  Yale University Judaic Library

- www.torahscience.org/index.html
  Torah and Science Foundation

- www.ohr.org.il
  Ohr Somayach—College student friendly site for Talmud study opportunities
  and special Israel trips

Index

Other Judaism and Jewish culture books
from *The Complete Idiot's Guide®* series

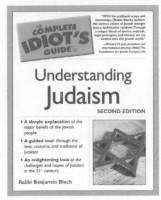
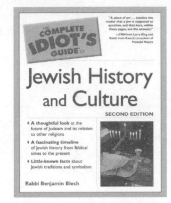